FICTIONAL DECEPTIONS

FICTIONAL DECEPTIONS

USING DECEPTION TO BAFFLE, SURPRISE AND ENTERTAIN YOUR AUDIENCE

BY

K. SCOT MACDONALD

Kerrera House Press

Macdonald, K. Scot
Fictional Deceptions/K. Scot Macdonald—1st Edition
p.   cm.
ISBN: 978-0-9916653-7-2
Kerrera House Press
Culver City, CA
www.KerreraHousePress.com

First Printing: 2017
Printed in the United States of America

10 9 8 7 6 5 4 3 2 1

To Dad,
Neil William Macdonald,
Who loved a good mystery, real or imagined,
as long as it was deceptive.
Thanks for all the long talks;
they were never long enough.

And to Kira,
Thanks for the title.

Mundas Vult Decipi
"The world wishes to be deceived."

Spoiler Warning

To analyze the use of deception in fiction, this book describes how writers use deception to surprise and entertain their audiences. The analysis gives away key plot points in the movies, novels, plays and television shows mentioned in this book. While this may decrease the enjoyment you will derive from reading the novels or watching the plays, television and movies, it will allow you to learn how you can use the principles and techniques of deception in your own stories to mislead, surprise and entertain your readers and audience.

Table of Contents

Chapter 1

Deception in All Fiction

Deception is the act of trying to make someone believe that something that is false is true, or that something that is true is false. Few things are 100 percent true or false, so the deceiver often tries to convince the target that something that is partially true is completely true or that something that is completely false contains a kernel of truth.

Of all genres, mysteries rely the most on deception. To write a mystery, you must deceive the reader. As mystery author Sue Grafton wrote, "Mystery writers are the magicians of fiction. We're the illusionists, working with sleight of hand in the performance of our art." The goal of a mystery story is to deceive readers and surprise the audience at the end; *She* was the murderer? A mystery without deception is not a mystery. It is just the recitation of a crime with no plot twists, no surprises and, probably, no readers. To succeed, a mystery author must learn how to deceive readers. Therefore, this book focuses on the use of deception in mysteries, although with examples from every genre.

In one sense, since the goal of all fiction is to make the reader or audience believe that something imagined is real, deception is at the heart of all fiction, regardless of the genre or medium. Readers and audiences want to believe that the fictional world in the novel or on the screen is real. When London newspapers published obituaries for Sherlock Holmes and thousands write Holmes every year at 221b Baker Street, it shows that Sir Arthur Conan Doyle's deception succeeded in making readers believe the fictional Holmes was real. When Hercule Poirot's obituary appeared on the front page of the *New York Times* on August 6, 1975, it showed that Agatha Christie had succeeded in making the world believe her fictional detective really existed. When audiences anguish over the fates of David Copperfield, Scarlett O'Hara, Bilbo Baggins, Jon Snow (*Game of Thrones*), Bridget Jones, or Glenn Rhee (*The Walking Dead*), they show how the writers of those novels and shows have created real characters in real worlds for their audiences.

Since deception is used in all fiction, the lessons from this book are applicable to all fiction whatever the genre or medium. Mysteries, action-adventure, crime, horror, conspiracy, and thriller novels and movies are predominantly based on deception, while dramas, love stories, comedies, and literary works must include some deception to surprise and thereby entertain the audience. Without deception, all novels, plays and movies fall flat, lacking suspense and the twists and turns that transform a pedestrian story into a tale that engages readers and makes them believe a fictional world is real. Life is full of surprises, so your fictional worlds must also be full of surprises, and deception is crucial to creating surprises. Deception has been called "the midwife of surprise." In 68 major battles between 1914 and 1967, without deception, surprise was only achieved about half the time. Just as military commanders seek to surprise their enemies on the battlefield, writers try to surprise their audience, since a surprised audience is an entertained audience.

Every artist must know the principles and techniques of their craft in order to create great art. Even though Picasso created abstract cubist masterpieces, as Alfred Hitchcock said, Picasso "knows every muscle in the human body. If you ask him to draw the figure of a man or woman, there wouldn't be a muscle out of place. You've got to know your craft in order to express the art." Fiction is based on deception, so you must know the craft of deception embodied in its principles and techniques to create compelling art in the form of fictional stories. Learning a deceptive trick or two will allow you to craft a workmanlike mystery or thriller, but learning the principles of deception will allow you to understand how to use different deceptive techniques in particular situations, as well as the effect of each technique on an audience. Such knowledge will help you write a series of mystery novels applying the principles and techniques of deception in surprisingly different ways in each novel to build an audience of millions or to write a blockbuster movie franchise to deceive and entertain a global audience of moviegoers.

Few writers truly understand or even consciously know how they achieve surprise based on deception in their stories, let alone to the extent required to explain their machinations simply and clearly to other writers. As with the finest athletes, often the finest writers make the worst teachers. What comes naturally and almost without thinking to the gifted author requires extensive thought and practice for everyone else.

Books on writing detective fiction or mysteries offer general guidelines for building suspense and hiding clues, but no book on writing focuses on the techniques, let alone the principles, authors use to deceive readers. Some books mention a gimmick or two, but none thoroughly discuss the techniques authors use to create mysteries, let alone how deception is used in other genres or mediums.

Where's a law abiding, morally upstanding writer to turn for lessons on the principles of deception, the fine art of misdirection, and the ins and outs of obfuscation? From these very pages. Let me show you how the masters of deception in the worlds of spies, warfare, con games, magic, and fiction use the principles and techniques of deception to deceive, surprise and entertain their adversaries, marks, and audiences—and how you can, too.

Chapter 2

Spies, Generals, Conmen, Magicians, and You: Masters of Deception

When most people hear the term deception, their mind is instantly filled with images of nefarious double agents, spies in disguises and clever ruses devised by never-photographed spymasters. Deception is at the core of espionage work. Double agents deceive their colleagues for years while working for their country's enemy. Intelligence services stage fake attacks on their own troops to lend credibility to fake anti-government guerrillas. Spies misrepresent themselves as serving one nation to convince individuals to work for them, such as when East German agents during the Cold War posed as anti-nuclear activists to woo West German women and convince them to steal government secrets. "Trust no one" is an axiom from the world of spies that epitomizes the central role of deception in the life of a spy.

While deception is at the core of the cloak and dagger world of spies, most people don't realize that deception is also crucial in warfare. As Sun Tzu, a 6th century BC Chinese general, wrote, "All warfare is based on deception." Deceiving your adversary about where, when and how you will attack is the key to victory on the battlefield. The Trojan Horse may be one of history's most famous battlefield deceptions, but deception has played a prominent role throughout military history. In 1066 at Hastings, William's troops feigned a retreat to lure King Harold's men out of their strong and as yet unbroken shield wall. Believing the Normans had broken, Harold's men charged after the Normans, who turned and hacked them to pieces, turning William into The Conqueror and England into a Norman kingdom. The British in World War II were masters of deception, creating a "bodyguard of lies" to deceive the Germans about the timing and location of the D-Day landings. In 1973 the Egyptians deceived the Israelis into believing that the movement of Egyptian troops up to the Suez Canal was another in a long series of exercises. The Israelis decided not to mobilize until it was almost too late and the Egyptians crossed the canal, seized part of the Sinai Peninsula and almost won the Yom Kippur War.

Conmen are masters of deception. You receive a letter in the mail. The sender predicts that the Chicago Bears will defeat the Green Bay Packers this Sunday. On Sunday, the Bears win. Wednesday a second letter arrives, predicting that the Seahawks will defeat the Colts next Sunday. You decide to take a flutter as the British say. You bet $10 in the office pool on the Seahawks. Again, the letter writer is right and you win a tidy sum. A third letter arrives Wednesday predicting victory for the underdog Giants against the Patriots. Deciding to trust the apparently perfect predictive abilities of the letter writer, you put $50 on the Giants. Again, they win. Amazing. A fourth letter arrives Wednesday, but with no prediction. Just wire him $1,000 and the writer will send you his infallible system. Riches are within your grasp and the system is proven. It is three for three. You write the $1,000. You never hear from the letter writer again. What happened? A conman sent 60 letters to 60 different homes; 30 predicting victory for the Bears and 30 victory for the Packers. The second week, the conman sent letters to the 30 Bears-victory recipients, 15 predicting victory for the Seahawks, 15 for the Colts. Liking the Giants more than the Patriots, a week later the conman sends 8 letters predicting a Giants' victory and 7 a Patriots' win to the winners of the previous week. Then the 8 "lucky" three-time winners receive the offer to buy the system. Three wire the money. The conman just made $3,000 tax free for printing just over 100 letters and the price of some postage, unless he's a modern conman and uses email. A criminal deception operation has successfully been conducted. All con games rely on deception in one form or another, from turning odometers back on used cars to making the basketball hoops slightly smaller on the midway when you attempt to win your girlfriend that adorable stuffed bear.

Like spies, generals and conmen, magicians are masters of deception. They make rabbits appear from empty hats, saw assistants in half and, as David Copperfield did in 1983, make the Statue of Liberty disappear. The empty hat has a hidden compartment, the assistant's legs are nowhere near the saw, and the Statue of Liberty is still there and has been continuously since 1886. "Magic" always involves surprise and magicians always base surprise on deception.

You might think as a law-abiding, morally upstanding individual who has never run an espionage operation, attempted to deceive a rival general, or obtain cash in a con game from a mark that you are ill suited to employ deception in your stories. You underrate your abilities. You probably already use deception in your everyday life without realizing it. As Leonardo Da Vinci concluded in his *Notebook*, "Man has great power of speech, but the greater part thereof is empty and deceitful." Do you tell your spouse they look great even when they're having the hair day from hell? Do you agree that the boss's proposal is brilliant, even when you think it is moronic? Do you dress up for a date or job interview? Are you on your best behavior during the date or job interview? In fact, we are almost always attempting to manage the impressions we make on others, whether at home, work or play, which are all forms of deception.

You probably even attempt to deceive adversaries. Do you leave lights on in your house when you go out to convince burglars to burgle elsewhere? If you do, then you have practiced deception based on the principle of using the truth to deceive an adversary (See Chapter 6). The information—that the lights are on—is true. The conclusion the burglar draws is false: that you are home. As long as your house is not burglarized, you have conducted a successful deception operation.

At work, you may deceive your boss by working at your computer every minute of every workday. If your boss believes you're a hard worker, then you have deceived your target by using facts. You do work hard. The conclusion he draws that you're hard at work on the next mind-numbing yearly report is false. You're really working hard on your next deceptively gripping novel.

Applying deception to your writing involves recognizing the principles and techniques of deception, and applying that knowledge, which you already use every day, to your novel, play or script. Once you learn how, using deception effectively is relatively easy in the real world and in your fictional stories. Why? Because there is no defense against deception.

Part I

The 7 Principles of Deception

Chapter 3

Principle 1: No Defense

Once you understand the principles and techniques, deception is remarkably effective in the real world and in the fictional worlds you create. The available evidence (spies are a secretive lot) strongly suggests that in the real world all forms of deception are extremely, even extraordinarily, effective, even when the stakes are the fate of nations. Barton Whaley in *Stratagem: Deception and Surprise in War* composed a 600-page appendix listing all of the known twentieth century military deceptions. How many succeeded? Almost all.

The key to the success of deception is the fact that humans cannot learn not to be deceived. As one deception expert, J. Barton Bowyer, concluded, "There is no apparent defense against trickery, any more than the human eye can turn a movie into frozen frames or make the stick in the water look straight....There seems to be little hope of detecting deception. The trained and innocent are duped." A magician can still deceive their audience when the audience knows the magician is trying to deceive them and even when the audience are themselves magicians and experts at deception. In the 1920s, the American master magician Dr. Harlan Tarbell and 11 colleagues attended a play, *The Charlatan*, starring Frederick Tilden as Count Cagliostro, an 18th century alchemist. The magicians were amused by the many simple tricks Tilden used in the play. Then the villain, a lawyer, forces Cagliostro to either back down in disgrace or accept a challenge to test his skills as a magician publicly. Cagliostro accepts and in full view of the villain and several skeptics displays a handful of sand, a clear glass flowerpot, a tall paper cone, and a seed. The lawyer inspects each prop, showing them to the audience to verify they are as they seem to be and are otherwise empty. Cagliostro pours the sand into the pot, plants the seed in it, covers it with the cone and steps back. The lawyer rudely intervenes by checking under the cone to verify he has not been tricked. Then Cagliostro steps forward and confounds his enemy and the audience by raising the magic cone to reveal a full-grown rose bush. The audience applauded, but the magicians in the audience were amazed. They knew the trick, an old one called the Indian Mango Tree, yet none of them could figure out how the trick had been done. Usually a confederate covertly passes the rose bush to the conjurer or the container is rigged to allow the rose bush to be hidden in it. The magicians thought Tilden had devised a new way to perform the trick. After the show, Tilden explained he was just an actor and knew of no new way of performing the trick. Tilden simply had the lawyer, when he checked that the cone was empty, add the rose bush. The magicians failed to catch on that Cagliostro's archenemy had been his confederate. By buying into the play's story, the magicians had failed to detect the deception, a hopeful story for those attempting to deceive an audience or readers.

Your task as an author or screenwriter is made infinitely easier because it is extremely difficult to perceive reality accurately. Looked at in a certain way, almost all of psychology deals with deception. Studies of perception analyze how we perceive the world, yet almost all such studies find that humans rarely perceive reality accurately with any of our five senses. We see that a stick bends as it enters a pool of water even when we know it is not really bent. CDs sample music, leaving out bits, yet our brains fill in the missing parts to make the music sound better than an LP. Eyewitness accounts and descriptions of criminals are almost universally inaccurate. We even err in perceiving ourselves, leading the great Scottish poet Robbie Burns to plead for the gift to "see ourselves as others see us."

An old saw states "fool me once, shame on you; fool me twice, shame on me." But it is a comforting myth to believe that you can't deceive someone repeatedly with the same deceptive principle or technique even in the real world where the stakes are men's lives. All that is required is to offer a choice. The military call it the principle of alternative goals. Union General William Tecumseh Sherman's 1864 drive to Atlanta during the US Civil War is a classic example of a serial deception. Sherman's supplies were tied to a single railway and he had to attack along that railway. The Confederates knew this fact, yet in every attack, save one at Kennesaw Mountain, where there was little room to attack on either side of the railway and Sherman had to frontally assault the Confederates, Sherman surprised the Southerners. Sherman had the left/right option and he used it to repeatedly deceive the Confederates about which side of the railway he would attack along.

The same principle applies to fiction: offer the audience at least two alternatives and there is an excellent chance they will repeatedly choose the wrong alternative or at the least be far from certain which option is the "truth." In *Gone with the Wind*, Margaret Mitchell repeatedly deceives the reader about whether Scarlett O'Hara and Rhett Butler are going to be together, as Scarlett pursue Ashley Wilkes, marries Charles Hamilton and then Frank Kennedy, until finally marrying Rhett, before he leaves her. Repeated choice leads to repeated deception and repeated surprises for readers.

Even using the same techniques, authors can repeatedly deceive readers. Agatha Christie sometimes used the same deceptive techniques to surprise and entertain readers. In *The Mysterious Affair at Styles*, Belgian sleuth Hercule Poirot's (and Christie's) first mystery, everyone suspects Alfred Inglethorp of murdering his older, wealthy wife, but early in the story Poirot clears him. At the end of the story, however, Poirot unmasks Inglethorp as the murderer. Inglethorp framed himself at first with weak evidence in order to be cleared as a suspect. Christie used the same deceptive technique in her first Miss Marple novel, *Murder at the Vicarage*. When Colonel

Protheroe is murdered, his wife and her lover are the first to be suspected. Miss Marple clears them, only at the end to deduce that they framed themselves and are indeed the murderers. Both novels were well received and sold well.

One exception to the rule that deception invariably succeeds is when the target is very young children, who are difficult and even sometimes impossible to deceive. This fact explains why true mystery stories are never written for the very young. Young children will not follow a fake or feint because they perceive the world literally and only react to reality. For deception to be effective, the target must be smart enough to fashion the desired false reality. If an individual is too inattentive, naïve or literal, they fail to create the false reality and are not deceived. As the American comedian Joe Penner said, "You can't fool me; I'm too ignorant." Some authors recognize this fact. Harry Kemelman in *Thursday the Rabbi Walked Out* has a simple young man, Billy realize that the apparently random shots the murderer fired around the room in which the murder occurred are not random. Billy doesn't "see" the deception and realizes that each shot is purposefully placed: in the center of a clock, the finial on a lamp, a pill bottle, and the mouth on a picture. The key shot amongst the dazzle (Chapter 11) or "noise" of many shots was the one that stopped the clock, thereby establishing the killer's alibi. The murderer set the clock back before shooting it. Rabbi Small, who at first is deceived, concludes, "I suppose it shows that it takes age and experience and the wisdom of maturity to be fooled."

In one respect, the more intelligent the target, the easier they are to deceive, in that they will quickly follow the feint or misdirection. Even so, the intelligent target is not the best target for deception. Ironically, the best targets are those who are deceitful, since the individuals most likely to be deceived need to have at least a sliver of the belief or idea the deceiver wants to reinforce already present in their minds. As the seventeenth century Cardinal de Retz said, "The most distrustful persons are often the biggest dupes." As the deception expert Bowyer wrote, "Con artists feast on those with larceny in their hearts and devious counterspies prey on cheating spies." Shakespeare's Iago is only able to deceive Othello because the Moor harbors some suspicion and jealousy already. If he didn't, then Iago's subtle hints about Desdemona's alleged infidelity would have found a distinct lack of fertile ground in which to fester and grow in Othello's mind. Luckily for authors and scriptwriters, almost everyone reading a mystery has a sliver of deceit in them, everyone who reads a romance wants to find true love, and everyone who reads a conspiracy story has a sliver of the conspirator in them; if they didn't, they wouldn't like that type of story.

Given the difficulty of perceiving reality accurately, the effectiveness of deception in the real world, and an audience primed for deception, the odds are heavily in your favor to write an entertainingly deceptive novel or film, especially since you create the world of your story and control all the characters. In order to create such a story, however, you will need help—you need a bodyguard.

Chapter 4

Principle 2: Protect the Truth with a Bodyguard of Lies

The overarching principle for using deception in real life or in fiction is to use cover stories to mask the real story; show the false and hide the real. Although a novel is fiction, the story of what really happened in a mystery to the (usually) murdered victim, which is revealed at the end of the novel, can be thought of as the true (or real) story. The cover stories that mask the real story and deceive the reader can be thought of as false. The same is true of the cover stories concealing a conspiracy in a thriller or rival suitors masking Mr. Right in a romance.

Protecting the truth with a bodyguard of lies applies in the real world just as much as it does in the fictional worlds you create. In 1943 the Allies used cover stories to conceal their plan to invade Nazi-occupied Sicily. The British used a submarine to release off the neutral Spanish coast a corpse disguised as a British Royal

Marine officer carrying bogus invasion plans for Corsica, Sardinia and Greece. The Spanish passed the plans to their German friends, who moved military forces to Corsica, Sardinia and Greece, leaving Sicily less well defended when the Allies later invaded. When it was time for the D Day landings in 1944, the Allies created cover stories about planned invasions at different times in Norway, southern France, and the Pas de Calais, among many others to distract the Germans from the real landing sites in Normandy and the key date of June 6, 1944. The British successfully created a "bodyguard of lies" to protect the truth and in so doing surprised the Germans on D Day.

Conmen use the same principle. Charles Ponzi used international postal coupons as his cover story to explain his tremendous returns and hide the real story that he was using new investors' money to pay dividends to earlier investors. Bernie Madoff used a cover story about various complicated investments to hide the real story of how he back-dated trades to produce his astronomical returns.

Magicians have a different terminology for their deceptions, but the principle is the same. Magicians call what the audience sees the front view, which is the cover story, and what is really happening the back view, which is the real story. When the magician shows the audience their empty top hat, it is the front view or cover story. The rabbit is hidden in a fold in the black lining of the hat, which is the back view or real story. The magician says, "Abracadabra," reaches into the "empty" hat and pulls out the rabbit, revealing the real story to the audience.

Just as the Allies used bogus plans to distract the Germans, Ponzi used international reply coupons to explain his amazing returns, and magicians use "magic" to deceive audiences, your goal as a mystery writer is to distract the reader's attention from the real culprit and their motive, means and opportunity to commit the crime by focusing your readers' attention on cover stories that revolve around:

- Other characters' motives to commit the crime
- Other characters' opportunities to commit the crime
- Other possible methods of perpetrating the crime
- Other crimes, affairs or immoral and suspicious acts
- Misrepresenting the villain's motive

- Misrepresenting the villain's whereabouts when the crime was committed (opportunity)
- Misrepresenting the villain's ability to commit the crime (means)
- Adding information or entire subplots unrelated to the real crime, such as a seemingly significant love story, another crime, or focusing on an exotic location or on an intriguing historical setting

Authors have devised a multitude of ways to write a mystery (or any other type of story that uses deception effectively), but all rest on the author first devising either beforehand or while writing the manuscript the real story of the crime (almost always a murder or series of murders). To develop the real story of the crime, it is best first to think from the villain's point of view. What did he or she do? How? Why? The real story of the crime usually can be summarized in a sentence or two.

In his bestseller *Presumed Innocent* (and later excellent movie), Scott Turow used a relatively simple real story about the wife of Chief Deputy Prosecuting Attorney Rozat "Rusty" K. Sabich. Rusty had an affair with Carolyn Polhemus, who was an attorney in his office. In the real story, Rusty's wife, Barbara, murders Carolyn, leaving evidence at the scene to frame her husband so he will know it was her, but with enough holes in the evidence to ensure he will not be convicted.

Turow then layers deceptive cover stories onto the real story to mislead his readers. The main cover story is that Rusty committed the murder. Turow adds evidence against Rusty, including:

- A glass found with his fingerprints on it at Carolyn's apartment the night of the murder
- Fibers from carpeting that matches carpet fibers from his house found in her apartment
- A semen sample from her that matches his type
- He was home alone the night of the murder with his young son, who was asleep
- Carolyn used spermicidal jelly, so she engaged in consensual sex with someone she knew before she was murdered
- The murderer knew police procedures and tried to make the murder look like a rape-murder by a stranger

Turow gives Rusty a logical and believable motive; Rusty murdered Carolyn because she ended their affair to start seeing Rusty's boss, the District Attorney.

Turow adds a second cover story in the form of a corruption case Carolyn was investigating involving attorneys and judges. The judge in Rusty's murder trial is implicated, ensuring the cover story is entangled with the real story of Carolyn's murder. Turow adds the suggestion that a judge Carolyn had an affair with murdered her to prevent the corruption case from proceeding. The same motive is suggested for Rusty's boss, the current DA, who also might be implicated in the corruption case.

Turow adds yet another deceptive cover story based on the possibility that Rusty is being framed. Rusty's boss is in the midst of a bruising re-election campaign. His opponents, Nico Della Guardia and Tommy Molto, may have framed Rusty to help win the election. To strengthen their motive, Rusty fired Nico from the DA's office years before.

The evidence falls apart because Carolyn had her tubes tied. If so, why was she using spermicidal jelly? It looked like someone was trying to frame Rusty. The case is dismissed. Even so, Turow makes it look as if the defense investigation of the corruption case may have persuaded the judge to rule there was insufficient evidence to take the case to a jury. Is Rusty getting away with murder because a corrupt judge fears exposure?

It is only at the very end of the novel/film that Turow reveals the real story: Rusty's wife, Barbara logged onto the university mainframe to establish an alibi, then went to Carolyn's house and killed her. Barbara tied Carolyn up, left the glass with Rusty's fingerprints, injected into Carolyn his semen she has saved from an encounter with him for which she used spermicidal jelly, and tied Carolyn up. Turow layers the deceptive cover stories over the real story to create a masterfully deceptive mystery.

Just as the British used other fake invasion plans to mask their real intention to invade Normandy, it is often effective in a mystery to use cover stories about other crimes or immoral acts to mask the real crime. In *A Mind to Murder*, P. D. James uses another crime to mask the real story. Peter Nagle, a porter, is blackmailing a patient at a psychiatric clinic, which masks the murder of Administrative

Officer Enid Bolam. James skillfully sets out clues pointing to Nagle as the murderer. At first even Superintendent Adam Dalgliesh believes Nagle is the killer since he was the blackmailer and Nagle's chisel is the murder weapon.

In Felix Francis' *Front Runner*, Francis expertly uses another crime to divert attention from the crime in the real story. The novel deals with two crimes involving British Horseracing Authority investigator Jeff Hinkley. In one cover story, a jockey calls Hinkley to confess that he has been blackmailed into purposely losing races. Apparently having changed his mind about telling anyone about the lost races, the jockey appears to try to kill Jeff by locking him in an overheated sauna. Jeff survives to investigate the blackmail scheme, which he learns involves at least two other jockeys and large amounts of betting. The other crime involves Jeff's new girlfriend (a romantic cover story that distracts readers from the real story), who is the niece of a shipping magnate. The shipping company is headquartered in the tax-friendly Cayman Islands. The real story's crime involves a mistake by a board member related to residency status, which in Britain determines whether a company pays higher British or lower foreign taxes. The key clue to the real story's tax crime is given near the start of the novel amidst all the events and clues related to the horse-race fixing cover story and the beginning of the romance cover story. Unless a reader has great memory and knowledge of tax laws, the odds of figuring out the mystery is slight. Francis deceives readers into thinking that race-fixing is the real crime with tens of thousands of pounds at stake, when in fact the far more important tax crime with half a billion pounds at stake is the real story.

The same principle of devising a real story and then masking it with cover stories to mislead, surprise and entertain your audience applies to writing a novel or script in any other genre. The 2003 thriller *The Da Vinci Code* uses a cover story about the investigation of a bizarre murder at the Louvre in Paris. The real story is slowly revealed as a battle between the Priory of Sion and Opus Dei over the possibility that Jesus Christ was married to Mary Magdalene. In the 1988 thriller film *Die Hard*, the real story about a gang of international thieves intent on stealing $640 million in bearer bonds from a Japanese corporation's high-rise headquarters is masked by a cover story involving international "terrorists" intent on blowing up the building with dozens of hostages inside. In the real story, the "terrorists" plan to steal the bonds and then blow up the building to hide the theft.

In the 1987 thriller movie *No Way Out* based on Kenneth Fearing's 1946 novel, *The Big Clock*, the real story is about a Soviet sleeper agent in Washington, DC. In a romantic cover story, US Navy Lieutenant Commander Tom Farrell begins an affair with Susan Atwell, only to discover she is also seeing the US Secretary of Defense, David Brice. In a jealous rage Brice accidentally kills Susan. Farrell then attempts to avoid being implicated in the murder. In yet another cover story, which shows that you can use characters to spin cover stories, Brice blames Atwell's death on an unconfirmed KGB sleeper agent, code named Yuri, who, Brice argues, was seeing Atwell. The actual murderer, Brice, is spinning one cover story (about a sleeper KGB agent murdering his mistress), while the hero, Farrell, is spinning two others (about his wonderful affair with Atwell that ends tragically and about his innocent entrapment in Brice's cover up). Readers know that Brice is lying and that Farrell is telling the truth, at least in relation to Atwell, but the revelation of the real story at the end of the film reveals that Farrell is also lying: not about murdering Atwell, but about being a KGB sleeper agent. He is a KGB agent. Robert Garland's script is a masterful example of deceptive cover stories created by characters to deceive each other and the audience.

In romances, the real story about one relationship is usually masked by a cover story about another relationship. Billy Wilder's Sabrina tells the story of a chauffeur's daughter, *Sabrina,* who has been in love with the playboy son, David, of the family her father has worked for her whole life. Sabrina and David's relationship is a cover story that masks the real story. In the end, the real story reveals that David's workaholic brother, Linus, is in love with Sabrina and the pair run off to Paris together.

Young adult novels also use cover stories. In Suzanne Collins's *The Hunger Games*, the heroine Katniss Everdeen loves Gale Hawthorne, her hunting partner, but during a gladiator-style game, she must appear to fall in love with Peeta Mellark, a boy from her district. Is the story of her falling in love with Peeta a cover story or the real story? Only at the end of the trilogy do readers learn which is the real story and which the cover story.

In the 2008 superhero comedy/drama *Hancock,* Will Smith plays the eponymous hard-drinking, somewhat psychotic superhero who woke up 80 years ago with amnesia in a Miami ER. In one cover story, a PR expert whose life Hancock has saved seeks to fix Hancock's negative public image. A second cover story involves three convicts who escape intent on killing Hancock for having sent them to prison. The real story is only revealed late in the film when the PR man's wife turns out to be Hancock's wife from decades before. They are aliens of some sort, gods or angels, who do not age and have lived for 3,000 years. The problem is that when a pair of them is together they slowly lose their superpowers and the last time it happened Hancock almost died.

In a drama, the real story is also masked by cover stories. Ian McEwan's 2001 novel *Atonement* tells a story about lovers who are separated, but then reunited. In the final pages, the reunion story is revealed to have been a cover story and the true story is finally revealed: a young girl when the lovers first met has written a novel in which the lovers are reunited (which the reader has just read), but in reality the lovers may both have died in World War II. Even that ending, given the unreliable narrator, is suspect and may be yet another cover story.

Unreliable narrators are a common technique for creating a cover story to mask the real story. Chuck Palahniuk's 1996 novel *Fight Club* tells a cover story about the narrator's involvement with Tyler Durden, who introduces the unnamed narrator to the Fight Club, a secret society in which white-collar young men fight each other, no holds barred. The cover story reveals layers of deception, culminating in the final revelation of the real story: Durden is a figment of the narrator's imagination.

If you write horror stories, you can use cover stories to heighten suspense and surprise your audience with a twist ending when you reveal the real story. Dennis Lehane's 2003 horror-suspense novel (and movie) *Shutter Island* begins with two detectives arriving at a mental hospital to investigate the disappearance of a female patient. By the end of the book, it's revealed that the entire story up to then has been a cover story. In the real story, all of the events in the cover story have been an attempt by psychiatrists to break one of the patients of his conspiracy-laden insanity by allowing him to play the role of a detective.

Even science fiction relies on cover stories to surprise the audience. The first three films made in the space opera *Star Wars* saga used cover stories to baffle, surprise and entertain the audience. In one of the cover stories, Luke Skywalker is one of a trio of heroes battling Darth Vader's nefarious galactic plans. Luke learns part of the real story, that Vader is his father, only at the end of the second movie, *The Empire Strikes Back*. Deceptive cover stories continue and it is only in the next film, *The Return of the Jedi*, that Luke learns that Princess Leia is not his love interest (a cover story), but his sister (the real story).

Spy stories always use cover stories to mask the real story. Barry Unsworth's historical spy/conspiracy novel *Pascali's Island* at first appears to be about Basil Pascali, who lives on a Greek Island and fears for his life because he suspects the Greeks have discovered that he is a Turkish spy. The spy story is a cover story and sets a tone of distrust to mask the real story. A second cover story is about a con game run by an English archeologist, Anthony Bowles, who negotiates with the local pasha to rent a plot of land to survey for a possible archeological dig. In an example of using real information to deceive (Principle 4), Bowles plants the head of a real ancient Greek statue on the land he rented to prove to the Pasha that it might contain vast archeological riches. The cover story becomes centered on the confidence game: will Bowles con the Pasha? Unsworth adds another deceptive cover story about a German businessman, who, Pascali discovers, has maps referring to "red earth" in his room. With World War I on the horizon, is the German searching for valuable minerals? The cover story about the con game is made even more deceptive when Bowles really does find an ancient Greek kouris (a bronze statue) and, contrary to what Pascali and the audience expects given his shifty background, decides to do the right thing and take the kouris to a museum for safe-keeping, instead of conspiring with the Pasha to sell it to the highest bidder. Unsworth hides one crime with another (Pascali's spying masks the con game), which in turn masks Bowles's emerging honesty, all of which is also masked by the German businessman and by a love triangle involving Bowles, Pascali and an ex-pat female artist. The Pasha offers to buy back Bowles's lease. Bowles replies that he can't until he finishes digging. He claims it is not a question of money. He wants his name associated with any discoveries he unearths. He is also writing a book and wants to further his research. The reader, accustomed to thinking of Bowles as a con-artist, assumes the real story is about Bowles holding out for more money, but in the end, for Bowles, the real story is not about money at all.

Questions for Authors:

The Real Story:

What is the real story in your novel?

If your story is a mystery, who is the murderer? What is her motive? Means? Opportunity? Who is the victim?

For a thriller, what is the real story of the conspiracy? Who are the conspirators? What is their goal? How are they going to accomplish their goal? What is their motive?

For a romance, who are the real lovers? What obstacles are keeping the lovers apart?

For any other genre of story, what is the real story? Who is the principal character? What is their goal? What obstacles are keeping them from their goal? Who are their adversaries?

You should be able to state the real story in a sentence or two. Simple is best or the audience may be more confused by the real story than by your deceptive cover stories. The key is that the real story must logically and clearly explain everything that has happened before.

Cover Stories:

What are the cover stories for your real story?

For a murder mystery, how are the murderer's identity, motive, means, and opportunity masked by cover stories? Who else has a motive to murder the victim? Who else has an opportunity to commit the murder? How else could the victim have been murdered? Could the victim have been murdered at another location and moved, and/or murdered at another time, casting alibis in doubt and creating an alibi for the murderer? Which other characters are hiding other crimes, affairs and/or immoral acts?

For a thriller, how do those involved with the conspiracy hide their evil plans? Are there one or more cover stories that explain almost all of the facts in a logical and clear fashion?

For a romance, is the rival love interest likable enough to the heroine and the audience to appear to be the "real" love interest?

Just as the rival love interest in a romance must be a worthy rival for the real love interest, the murderer in a murder mystery must be a worthy adversary. She must use deceptive techniques actively to hide their crime. How has the villain masked her:

- Motive?
- Opportunity?
- Means?
- Relationships with other characters?

In a thriller, the same questions apply to the villain behind the conspiracy. The villain must hide his motive, opportunity and ability to carry out the conspiracy. In Fletcher Knebel and Charles W. Bailey II's 1962 thriller *Seven Days in May*, the Joint Chiefs of Staff conspire to overthrow the US government. They hide communications about the coming coup by creating a cover story about participating in a betting pool.

Can a love story be added as a cover story? Most thrillers and many mysteries have love stories as a sub-plot to divert attention from the main story and to provide lighter scenes in contrast to the more intense scenes related to the murder or conspiracy. In the thriller *Three Days of the Condor,* Condor (Robert Redford) falls in love with a woman he kidnaps in order to have a safe place to stay—and to supply a distracting romantic cover story.

Common Mistakes and How to Fix Them:

The two most common mistakes authors make are too many or too few cover stories. Regardless of the genre, one way to determine the balance between your cover stories and your real story is to go through a draft of your novel or script and use different colored pens to mark which stories (real or cover) are advanced in each scene. Use a different color to mark each cover story, and another color for your real story. If your real story disappears for several scenes beneath cover stories, then you should add clues about the real story to some of those scenes. In some cases, you may need to delete an entire cover story if cover stories dominate your real story for too long. Conversely, if your real story takes center stage for several scenes with few or no clues about your cover stories, then you should add information about cover stories to some of those scenes to mask the real story. In some cases, you may need to add an entire cover story to ensure that your real story remains effectively hidden from readers' prying eyes. In a story with a twist ending, clues must do double duty. The clues must relate to the main cover story and the real story throughout your novel or script.

You may need to reorder some of your scenes so your real story and at least some of your cover stories start at the beginning of your novel and continue through at a steady pace until the end. The more your draft looks like a rainbow of colors when you finish marking the stories advanced in each scene, the more effectively your cover stories will mask your real story, and the more effective, nuanced and deceptive your novel or script will be for the audience.

You should not have so many cover stories that your story becomes so complicated no reader can keep everything straight. Simple, clear stories are best. You should be able to state each story's main plot (cover and real stories) in a sentence or two. The plots of *Hamlet, Macbeth* and *Othello* can be explained in one sentence, as can *And Then There Were None, Murder on the Orient Express* and *Double Indemnity*. To plan a mystery or a thriller, you need to plot out the villain's actions (the real story), the cover stories, and then the clues that arise from the villain's actions (or others' actions) that will lead the hero to the truth. Break each story into scenes and try to determine if any scenes can be combined to advance several stories (the real story and a cover story) at once. Conversely, you should not have so few cover stories that the real story is apparent to all. Remember, your real story needs a bodyguard of lies composed of cover stories to hide it from the prying eyes of your audience.

Chapter 5

Principle 3: Cover Stories as Realistic, Interesting and Hidden as the Real Story

Whether in fiction or real life, cover stories must be realistic and interesting enough to be believed so that they effectively mask the real story. They must also be hidden so the target doesn't conclude that the deceptive cover story was too easy to discover and, there-fore, must be false. Although attempts at deception rarely fail in fiction or in the real world, when they do it is usually because the cover stories don't appear to be realistic or believable enough, or because they are offered too openly to the target audience.

Even professional deception experts sometimes fail to deceive their target. In World War II, the British devised Operation Star-key to convince the Germans that the Allies planned to invade France in 1943, when in fact they would not invade for another year. The Allies didn't want Hitler to transfer troops and aircraft to the Eastern front to fight against their ally, the Soviet Union, so the threat of invasion in the West had to be maintained. The Allies flew 18,000 fighter and bomber missions over the "planned" invasion area, moved troops to the English coast, and assembled landing craft to convince the Germans that an invasion was imminent. Even with so much effort, the Allied deception failed. A German general wrote, "The movements (the British) made, were rather too obvious—it was evident (they) were bluffing." Following a key principle of deception, the preparations for a real invasion would have been masked by deceptive cover stories. Lacking such deceptive cover, the Germans realized the preparations for an invasion in 1943 were fake and shifted their forces east to fight the Soviets.

By 1944 the British had learned and ensured that preparations for the invasion of Normandy were well masked by realistic, but hidden cover stories about invasions of the Pas de Calais, Norway, southern France, and Greece, among others. The main Allied cover story involved the creation of an entire fictitious army, led by US General George S. Patton, positioned to invade the Pas de Calais. The deception was realistic in part because the Germans believed the Allies would invade the Pas de Calais since it was at the narrowest part of the English Channel. Crucially, the fictitious army was well hidden with camouflage, communications security and forbidden security zones so the Germans had to work hard to discover its existence, making it appear that the Allies were attempting to hide from their enemy an army poised to invade France, just as they would a real invasion force. This time the deception worked.

Just as the British made their cover stories realistic, yet hidden, the confidence man in a three-card Monte game keeps up an entertaining patter while moving the cards with great speed. The patter and the moving cards are the cover story, even as he manipulates the queen (the real story) so the mark will never win, unless he wants to set the mark up to later lose big. The conman even shows the queen to the mark repeatedly (showing the real), before hiding it again, making the cover story as realistic, interesting and hidden as the real story. Magicians create a cover story with a sexy assistant, flashes of light and pulsating music to mask the real story of their illusion. The assistant, lights, and flashes are real and entertaining, as well as often seeming to come out of nowhere (hidden), such as when the magician causes a puff of smoke and a flash of light to appear.

Just as with the failed British Operation Starkey, if cover stories are too easy to discern or lack any deceptive cover, readers will easily spot the real story amidst the false stories and solve the mystery of what really happened or discern the conspiracy long before the hero. A romance is similar. You can think of the heroine in a romance as a detective, searching for clues to her future romantic happiness, which is hidden behind various cover stories. "Intelligence easily obtained is intelligence easily discounted," so make the reader via the detective character, the hero in a thriller, or the heroine in a romance work hard to gather clues about the cover stories; just as much as they work to discover the real story. Readers tend to think that having spent so much time and effort reaching the core of a cover story that they have discovered the identity of the murderer, source of the conspiracy or the identity of Mr. Right. The more time and effort they spend, the more certain the reader will become that the character they suspect is the villain is the real criminal or that Mr. Wrong is really Mr. Right. You want your hero or heroine to spend time and effort digging into each cover story so readers become certain that the cover story is the real story, making them certain, but wrong.

To mystify and satisfy the audience, both the real story and each cover story must offer an apparently logical and realistic explanation of the crime or conspiracy. In this respect, writing a mystery or thriller is like orchestrating a deception operation for a spy agency. As James Jesus Angleton, a CIA counterintelligence officer during the Cold War, advised, "Deception must mimic reality enough to be accepted." Even so, in fiction or in the real world, the real story and the cover stories need not be probable. They must be believable and realistic, but they do not need to have any significant chance of ever actually occurring. When the Allies used a corpse to carry bogus invasion plans to the Germans via their Spanish friends, such an occurrence seemed highly unlikely, but possible. The corpse appeared to have been a real Royal Marine officer down to the tiniest details. The British ensured the corpse carried identification, a love letter from his girl, her photograph, a bill from his tailor, and even ticket stubs from a recent London show. Stranger things had happened than vital plans falling into the hands of the enemy through unlikely events. The Germans believed the information the corpse carried and moved forces to defend Sardinia, Corsica and Greece.

Similarly, many mystery stories use plots that are logical and re-alistic, yet highly unlikely to ever occur in real life. W. Somerset Maugham wrote, "Unless a novelist makes you believe in him he is done, and yet if he is entirely believable he may very well be dull. That (complete verisimilitude) is at least one reason why people turn to detective fiction. It has suspense, it excites their curiosity, it gives them a thrill; and in return for so much they make no great demand that it should be probable. They want to know who done it, and they are willing to accept the most unlikely and inadequate motive for who done it having done it." (*A Writer's Notebook*, p.324)

Christie's plots for *Murder on the Orient Express* in which 13 char-acters conspire to murder one vile man, *And Then There Were None*, in which one character plots the murder of nine other characters, and the story of the murder of a boy related to the quest for a me-teorite in Peter Hoeg's novel *Miss Smilla's Feeling for Snow* (1997 film *Smilla's Sense of Snow*, also the title for the US edition) are all highly unlikely to have occurred in real life, yet succeeded wonderfully as fictional plots. Similarly, thriller and conspiracy plots have to be logical and realistic, but can be as outlandish and unlikely as a battle between secret societies over whether Jesus Christ married Mary Magdalene (*The Da Vinci Code*), cloned dinosaurs created for an island amusement park (*Jurassic Park*), the US Joint Chiefs of Staff planning a coup d'état (*Seven Days in May*) or a Soviet submarine captain who defects with a ballistic missile submarine (*The Hunt for Red October*). The low probability of such scenarios actually occur-ring is irrelevant. Alfred Hitchcock called all of his movies "fanta-sies" because he realized that for all their realism, they were highly unlikely to ever occur in real life. Don't confuse the "real" world of fiction with the everyday world you live in. In the real world, most murders in the United States are committed under the influence of alcohol during an argument by young males using a gun. Only in mysteries, as Agatha Christie once commented, can the murderer be the little old lady in the corner knitting in a rocking chair. As long as the little old lady could have done it, you can make her the murderer in your novel or screenplay. Readers expect to read about unique characters facing rare and unexpected events. Stories about everyday characters and common events are boring, although some events may not be as unlikely as you think. Tom Clancy based *The Hunt for Red October* on not one, but two similar events: a November 1975 mutiny aboard a Soviet frigate, the *Storozhevoy* (the ship's political commissar tried to sail the ship to Leningrad), and a Soviet submarine tender captain who in 1961 sailed his ship to Sweden to defect with his crew.

Even if cover stories don't have to be likely, you can't just randomly assign implausible or illogical motives to different characters to mask the villain's motive for committing the crime. Readers will not believe such illogical motives. Each character that is going to serve as a deceptive screen for the real criminal must have as plausible and realistic a motive as the real villain, as well as equally plausible and realistic opportunity and means to have murdered the victim. The same is true of the villains behind a conspiracy or, in a different sense, the heroine's suitors in a romance. Each suitor should appear to have an even better chance than Mr. Right to win the heroine's heart—at least at first.

No matter how improbable the solution to the mystery or conspiracy, your story should not violate any physical or natural laws, judicial proceedings or any other factual elements. If they are crucial to the solution, secret passages, twins, fictional poisons, arcane knowledge, and other uncommon phenomena must be mentioned in the narrative well before the solution of a crime or the audience will feel cheated, as if you just created something new to solve the mystery or conspiracy. The methodology of the crime should at least seem plausible even if unlikely to occur. The story itself can start with a highly unlikely coincidence, although it should never end with a coincidence or the audience will think you have cheated them by creating an ending that doesn't seem in retrospect inevitable from all that went before.

Not only should cover stories be as seemingly realistic—even if they are improbable—as the real story, the cover stories should be as interesting and exciting as the real story. Psychological research shows that vivid information is remembered more easily than information presented in a matter-of-fact manner, and vivid information is also given more weight, especially if it is presented in the form of an anecdote or scene. Therefore, if the real story involves an international playboy, a beautiful Parisian model and an ancient map leading to a golden horde hidden by Bonnie Prince Charlie after the Scottish Highlander's defeat at Culloden in 1745, while a cover story involves a plumber, his wife and a lost Scottish terrier, then readers will focus on the real story instantly, ignoring the cover story. You can use this tendency to your advantage to hide clues by providing key clues as dry facts in the middle of an entertaining and vividly told anecdote, since readers are far more likely to remember the vivid anecdote and not the dry fact. In the middle of a character telling the story of an exciting scuba-diving adventure, another character might mention that oysters are their favorite food, which later proves crucial to how they were poisoned.

Ross Macdonald, pen name for Kenneth Millar, was a master at creating cover stories that were just as realistic, believable and interesting as the real story, and just as well hidden. By revealing the real story at the end of the novel, Millar often cast the entire preceding story in a believable and logical, yet surprising new light. In *The Zebra-Striped Hearse*, a wealthy colonel, Mark Blackwell, hires Millar's hard-boiled sleuth, Lew Archer, to investigate his daughter's fiancé. After Archer has dug hard to discover clues, near the end of the novel Blackwell commits suicide, apparently to avoid the shame of having to stand trial for the jealousy driven murder of his ex-lover and her new husband. The novel could end there; all the loose ends are tied up, all the clues accounted for. Then in the final few pages, Millar provides his twist by peeling away the cover story and revealing the real story: the murderer is the daughter. Out of jealousy for the woman who had seemed to steal her father's love from her, the daughter murdered her father's ex-lover and the ex-lover's husband. The father committed suicide to cast suspicion on himself in an attempt to save his daughter from arrest. The key is that both the father and daughter had believable, realistic, logical, and interesting motives, opportunities and means to commit the murders. Crucially, Millar makes Archer spend most of the novel discovering the well-hidden cover story, thereby making it appear to be the real story until the dramatic final twist and revelation of the real story.

To create a twist ending worthy of Millar, create at least two valid stories of a crime. Throughout the novel or script, provide clues about both stories. Subtly emphasize the cover story while subtly hiding the real story until the end of the novel. The cover story masking the real story should have as much deception built into it as the real story. If the real story is far more obscured than the cover story, readers are likely to home in on the real story and ignore the cover story as irrelevant information too easily obtained. Questions for Authors:

How realistic are your cover stories? Are they as plausible, logical and realistic as your real story, and as well hidden? For each cover story write down:

- The main plot points
- Main characters
- Each character's motivations, goals and actions
- The deceptive techniques masking each cover story

If it is a murder mystery or a conspiracy, are your suspects too easily and quickly cleared of the crime? Does your hero have to work hard to see through the cover stories before she can focus on a single villain behind the murder or conspiracy?

Are each character's motives, goals and behaviors logical and believable? Do people you know behave like your characters, even if only in extreme circumstances? If you told your best friend the cover story or if it appeared on the news, would they believe that it might have happened, even if it is unlikely?

How interesting are your cover stories? Are they as fascinating, intriguing and full of detailed supporting information as your real story?

Common Mistakes and How to Fix Them:

In some mysteries, the real story is so entertaining and dramatic that it makes the cover stories appear bland and uninteresting. To deceive readers, the cover stories must appear as entertaining and dramatic as the real story. Go through each cover story and think of it as if it was the real story. For each cover story:

- Add fascinating details
- Add scenes between characters who have a conflict in the cover story to highlight their conflict
- Use deceptive techniques to mask, distract from, and hide clues related to the cover story
- Raise the stakes in the cover story: make a rocky marriage involve young children or control of a multi-billion dollar

family-owned corporation; set a cover story against the backdrop of a war, economic depression or natural disaster; make
an illness life-threatening instead of just a cold.

Make each cover story interesting enough to stand by itself, as
if it was the real story. If after you have polished all of your cover
stories, you find that one of your cover stories is more interesting
than your real story, consider making that cover story the real story
and your real story a cover story, such a switch may vastly improve
your novel or script. For a romance, is Mr. Right blander than Mr.
Wrong? If so, consider switching their roles.

When authors offer readers a suspect or a cover story, too often
the information is offered on a silver platter. In children's stories,
the real story is clear to adults from the start. If you are writing for
adults, make sure your real story is nowhere near as apparent as the
real story in children's stories such as *Cinderella, Dumbo* and *Snow
White and the Seven Dwarfs*. Make sure you use deceptive techniques
to mask the cover stories you want the audience to believe, as well
as use your villain to deceive the other characters about her plans.
Make your detective character (and readers) work hard to identify
the initial prime suspect in your story. A suspect too easily suspected is a suspect too easily dismissed.

Chapter 6

Principle 4: Base Deception on the Truth, Not Lies

Whether in fiction or in real life, cover stories must appear real because, counter-intuitively, effective deception is based on information that is true, yet is interpreted in such a way as to reach an inaccurate conclusion. Angleton, the Cold War counterintelligence officer, said, "The essence of disinformation is provocation, not lying."

In the late 1930s, the Germans deceived Soviet leader Josef Stalin into believing that his generals were conspiring with the Germans against him. Instead of creating an entirely fake conspiracy, the Germans used real meetings between German and Soviet officers in the 1920s when Germany and the Soviet Union were cooperating as the basis for the fake conspiracy in the 1930s. The Germans merely changed the dates of meetings between German and Soviet officers from the 1920s to the 1930s, thereby using real information as the basis for their successful deception operation. The German deception operation based on the truth led Stalin to brutally purge his officer corps, effectively decapitated the Soviet armed forces on the eve of the Second World War.

In 1943, as the Allies prepared to invade Normandy, they created the phantom First Army Group led by the real General George S. Patton to appear to be poised to invade the Pas de Calais. The British used as much real information as possible to create their phantom units. They made units larger than they were in reality, making brigades into divisions, divisions into corps and corps into armies. Many of the phantom units had been created years before during fighting in North Africa. Based on several years' worth of real radio communications traffic, press announcements about new commanding officers, movement orders, newspaper stories about locals complaining that the huge influx of US troops had caused many of their daughters to become pregnant out of wedlock, and even "soldiers'" requests for songs from local radio stations dedicated to their mates in their (phantom) unit, the deceptive units were so "real" that at one point General Dwight D. Eisenhower was furious to discover the units he had earmarked to reinforce the front in Italy did not in fact exist.

During the Cold War, the Soviets used telephone poles as targets on their missile ranges. The Americans concluded that Soviet missiles were extremely accurate because craters from missile impacts were always extremely close to the telephone-pole targets. Unknown to the Americans, after a test the Soviets moved the telephone poles closer to the missile impact points to make it appear their missiles were more accurate than they were in reality (Technique 5: Manipulating Time). The Soviets used real information—the use of telephone poles as aiming points—to deceive the Americans into an invalid conclusion about the accuracy of Soviet missiles.

The real and the false can reinforce each other. Early in World War II, the British in North Africa built plywood and canvas dummy aircraft to make the Germans and Italians believe they had far more aircraft than they possessed. The British soon discovered that the Germans could tell which aircraft were dummies because the dummy's wings sagged. The British placed wooden supports under the dummy's wings, which solved the sagging problem, but led to another problem: the British soon learned that the Germans could spot the supports. A brilliant deception officer in North Africa, Brigadier Dudley Clarke, devised the perfect solution: placing wooden supports under the wings of real aircraft. That way the Germans could never be sure which were dummies and which were real planes. Real information—the wooden supports—was used to make the real appear false and the false appear real.

Conmen also use facts to deceive their marks. When a mine owner salts a mine with gold, there is gold in the mine sample. The conclusion that the gold occurred naturally and predicts a mother lode is an invalid conclusion based on that fact. When a crooked garage mechanic shows you worn brake shoes and an empty box for a new pair of brakes he just installed, all of the props are real. The conclusion that the old brakes are from your car and that the new brakes are now in your car is an invalid conclusion based on those facts.

Magicians also use facts to deceive. Harry Houdini was famous for escaping while manacled from a sealed watertight cabinet full of water. The facts Houdini wanted the audience to see were real. The cabinet was full of water. The manacles were real. The conclusion the audience drew—that Houdini could drown—was incorrect. The facts he did not want the audience to see were carefully hidden. The manacles could easily detach from a board to which they were attached. The cabinet was far less full of water after he was dropped into it and water splashed out, giving him an air space at the top. Based on the facts, the audience concluded that he might drown, but there was almost no risk of that ever happening.

It is crucial to understand that it is only relatively easy to deceive in real life and in fiction because almost all information, whether true or false, looks alike. Was President George W. Bush the 42nd or 43rd US President? Is Toronto, Canada north or south of Portland, Oregon? Is Africa larger or smaller geographically than South America? The truth does not clearly present itself, especially if a choice is offered. The truth and the falsehood often appear the same. Keep this concept in the front of your mind when you write a mystery, thriller or any other type of novel or screenplay: the real story and the cover stories must all appear equally believable and true to deceive, surprise and entertain your audience.

In the same way as spies, generals, conmen, and magicians use real information to deceive their adversaries, marks or audiences, authors use facts in their fictional stories to mislead, surprise and entertain their readers. Earlier we saw how Scott Turow used facts (fingerprints on a glass, carpet fibers, semen, an affair, and lack of an alibi) to make it appear that Rusty Sabich murdered his ex-lover in *Presumed Innocent.* Agatha Christie also used facts to lead readers to invalid conclusions. In the classic *Witness for the Prosecution*, a man who has been seeing a wealthy older woman stands accused of her murder. The man's wife claims to love him, even though she appears devastated by his infidelity and agrees to testify against him. Her love is a fact. The conclusion the reader draws—that she is testifying to get back at him for his cheating—is incorrect. She has forgiven him and is testifying to help him, which leads to the classic twist when her testimony destroys the prosecution's case against him.

The key to remember as you craft your stories and develop your characters, as well as their motivations, is that the same motivation or emotion (a fact) can lead to different, even diametrically opposed behaviors. As Christie showed in *Witness for the Prosecution,* love can lead a character to help or harm the object of their love (upon learning that her husband has no more use for her after he is acquitted, the wife stabs her husband to death). Greed (a fact) can lead to the hoarding of wealth or to risky gambles in an attempt to get even more money. If your characters have motivations that can lead to opposite behaviors, it will be far easier for you to deceive readers. Readers will assume that the real motivation—love, hatred, jealousy, greed, pride, fear, or ambition—will lead to one action, such as lying to the police, blackmail or murder, while ignoring the fact that the same motivation can lead the character to do something entirely different than the reader expects, including a noble, courageous act.

Luckily for mystery authors, there are many causes of guilt (a real emotion) and each one offers an opportunity for you to deceive readers. In Candace Robb's Medieval mystery *The King's Bishop*, an Austin friar, Don Ambrose, is murdered, followed soon after by two men-at-arms. Soon after, Bardolph, a comrade of the murdered soldiers, bumps into the Archdeacon of York, Jehannes, on the street and, falling to his knees, asks for forgiveness. What was the act that drives Bardolph to ask for absolution: murder or something else? As Robb's hero, Owen Archer asks, "Are we simpletons…? Can there be only one cause of guilt?"

By focusing on one interpretation of the facts, authors can focus readers' attention on that one interpretation, setting them up for a surprising and deceptive twist. In John D. Macdonald's *The Quick Red Fox*, someone is trying to blackmail a movie starlet with compromising photos of an orgy on a sun deck in California. The blackmailer is later found murdered and suspicion falls on Vance M'Gruder, an aging playboy who is engaged to an 18-year-old Swedish actress, whose father is a professor. Macdonald uses facts to make Vance appear guilty. The photos do show Vance at the orgy. Vance is being blackmailed. Vance does fear that if the photos reach his future father-in-law, the professor will call off the wedding. Only in the final pages does Travis McGee, Macdonald's detective hero, learn that Vance was at a poker game the night of the murder. Vance has an alibi, but his fiancé does not. She wanted to marry Vance as much as he wanted to marry her, and murdered the blackmailer to ensure their marriage. Macdonald creates two characters with the same motive and means: one for the cover story and one for the real story, but only one of the characters has the opportunity to commit the murder.

Authors can tell a story in a deceptive way as Macdonald did, or you can have a character deceive other characters (and the audience) by using facts to lead them to an invalid conclusion. The English archeologist Bowles in *Pascali's Island* uses the head of a real ancient statue he brought with him to deceive the local pasha into believing that he has found an archeologically rich site at which to dig. In a similar fashion, Rusty's wife in *Presumed Innocent* used facts to frame her husband for the murder of his former mistress.

Romance stories also use facts to deceive. In *Gone with the Wind*, Scarlett O'Hara's main love interests are Rhett Butler and Ashley Wilkes. Rhett is a rogue who opposes the coming war of secession because he believes the South will lose, becomes a blockade runner/smuggler, and consorts with a madam who owns a house of ill repute—all facts. Ashley is an honorable man who seeks a quiet life with a wife and family on a plantation after fighting in the war to defend his way of life—all facts. It seems based on facts that Scarlett O'Hara should end up with the paragon, Ashley, not the rogue, Rhett, but Mitchell uses facts to deceive. Scarlett will never be happy with the Ashley and only realizes she loves Rhett when it is too late.

In fantasy novels authors can use facts to lead audiences to the wrong conclusion. In *A Song of Ice and Fire*, George R. R. Martin has Rob Stark, the King of the North, win every battle in a civil war between the aristocratic houses of the mythical land of Westeros. The victories are facts leading most readers to conclude Rob will win the war, but Rob breaks a marriage vow, angers the wrong lord, marries someone else, and ends up paying for his betrayal with his life, thereby losing the war for his family and house.

Comedies use facts to mislead audiences for comedic effect. *In Arsenic and Old Lace*, Mortimer Brewster (Cary Grant) has two eccentric aunts who feel deeply for the loneliness of elderly bachelors. The aunts' concern is real and leads to the conclusion that they help old bachelors. They do, but not in the way the audience expects. The aunts murder the lonely old bachelors with poisoned elderberry wine and bury them in the basement to put them out of their lonely misery. In the excellent *Yes, Minister* television series episode "The Compassionate Society," a British minister learns that a hospital has a perfect record: no one has died at the hospital. The minister wants to visit the hospital, since the facts suggest the staff is outstanding. The facts have led the minister (and the audience) to an invalid conclusion. The hospital has no deaths because it has no patients. Once the building was built and staffed with administrators there was no money left to hire doctors or nurses, so there are no patients. Every episode in the series is a case study by writers Sir Antony Jay and Jonathan Lynn in using facts to lead to completely invalid and hilarious conclusions.

Westerns also use facts to mislead. In *The Oxbow Incident*, Walter Van Tilburg Clark sets his story in 1885. News reaches a saloon that a local rancher has been shot. Since there has been cattle rustling in the area, everyone concludes that the murderer is a cattle rustler. A posse rides out in search of the murderer. Three men are found asleep in a canyon with a few head of cattle, which the posse believes have been rustled. The men claim to have bought the cattle from the man who was shot, but they don't have a bill of sale. All the clues are real and all point to the conclusion that the three men are rustlers and shot the rancher. The posse hangs the three men. Only in the final scenes does Van Tilburg Clark reveal the real story: the "murdered" man is alive and well, and he did sell the cattle to the three men.

Questions for Authors:

What facts support each of your cover stories? If a cover story is based on lies, readers will see through it too easily and too early in your novel or film.

What facts related to the crime or conspiracy in your story point to more than one suspect? Does more than one character have a clear and compelling motive to commit the murder or to be behind the conspiracy? Do multiple characters have the opportunity and means to commit the crime?

If you are writing a love story, do your heroine's suitors each have real, positive attributes that would make her love them, and make readers believe she could end up with each man?

Common Mistakes and How to Fix Them:

The most common error authors make is to believe that characters must lie to deceive. Characters, especially villains, can certainly lie, but the most effective mysteries, conspiracies and deceptive stories are based on characters telling the truth or parts of the truth that lead readers to invalid conclusions. *Witness for the Prosecution* is a masterpiece because the wife does not lie. She states that she still loves her husband, but feels betrayed, which is all true. What she does in response to that betrayal is the surprise. *Gone with the Wind* is powerful in part because Scarlett, Ashley and Rhett don't lie to each other. They just go through long and dramatic struggles to discover what their true feelings are and what they mean for their relationships with each other.

Chapter 7

Principle 5:
Give Readers a Choice

In the real world and in fiction choice is central to deception. In 1800, the chief of the Prussian General Staff, Helmuth von Moltke, the Elder, said, "Gentlemen, I notice that there are always three courses open to the enemy, and that he usually takes the fourth." In one sense, Moltke was talking about deception. The options that an audience believes are open to a character can be reinforced to deceive the audience, as the author plans for the character to pursue yet another option.

In the realm of espionage and warfare, choice is fundamental to deception. For the Allied landings in Normandy on June 6, 1944, the British fed the Nazis clues about plans to invade:
- Greece (Operation Zeppelin)
- Italy (Operation Ferdinand)
- South of France (Operation Vendetta)

- West coast of France (Operation Ironside)
- Pas de Calais (Operation Fortitude South)
- Norway (Operation Fortitude North)
- Spain and Turkey (Operation Royal Flush)

The Germans had many alternatives to choose from and they choose wrong, which allowed the Allies to surprise the Germans when they landed in Normandy.

Magicians love to give an audience a choice. "Pick a card, any card," might be one of the most famous magician's lines ever, and it is a choice. However, when magicians offer you a choice, they are usually not offering a real choice. A magician may ask you to pick a card from among five cards. You pick one and the magician says, "Okay, let's discard that card." Of course, depending on the trick, he could just as easily have said, "Okay, let's keep that card." Called the Magician's Choice, this is just one of hundreds of forced choices magicians use, which are outlined in Ted Annemann's wonderful *202 Methods of Forcing*, showing how a choice isn't always a choice.

Conmen also use choice to ensnare their marks. The street game is called *Three*-Card Monte to ensure choice. No conman plays *Two*-Card Monte, let alone *One*-Card Monte. When someone sends you an email claiming your computer is infected with a virus but they can fix it for $99 you face a choice: pay $99 or risk your computer freezing up. Fake IRS notices work the same way: would you rather send in a few hundred bucks or run the risk of an audit? The whole basis of cons rests on a choice for the mark between believing that the conman, who invariably seeks to make a nice, kind impression, is honest or dishonest. Would the garage mechanic really con you over a $334 set of brake shoes or did he really do the work? Would the theatre owner whose new play sold out really have given away an entire house full of free tickets to pack the seats or is the new play really good? We tend to want to believe the best of people, a choice confidence men routinely exploit.

Without choice there can be no deception. At the simplest level, if you offer readers only one version of events, then there is no choice. Readers will select that single option and will not be deceived nor will they be entertained. A story that has only two characters stranded on a barren island in which one character is murdered, leaves the reader with no choice: the survivor must be the murderer. Christie mocks this concept in her novel *Crooked House*, when a character says, "In some books person after person is killed. . .You end by spotting the murderer because he or she is practically the only person left" (unless she is one of Christie's *Ten Little Indians*).

In *Wolf to the Slaughter*, Ruth Rendell gives readers a choice between two motives for the murder of a young woman: revenge (she had just dumped her boyfriend) or theft (£500 was in her purse). In a twist von Moltke would have loved, neither turns out to be true. The woman wasn't even murdered. In *Beyond a Reasonable Doubt*, an excellent novel by Sue Grafton's father, C. W. Grafton, young rookie attorney Jess London is in danger of being arrested for the murder of his brother-in-law. Seven people claim they saw Jess just after the murder in the vicinity of the crime, his fingerprints are on the murder weapon, and the facts all point directly at him. The likable Jess, who is the point-of-view character, says he visited the victim just before the murder, but his brother-in-law was alive when he left. Readers are confronted with a choice: is Jess lying and guilty of murder or is he an innocent man trapped in a set of unfortunate circumstances? Read the wonderful novel to find out the real story.

In his entertainingly twisted historical mystery, *The Alienist*, Caleb Carr offers readers a range of choices based on facts related to:

- The identity of the murderer of boy prostitutes in 1896 New York City: A man or a woman? Native-born or a recent immigrant? Ex-soldier or civilian? A police officer? A Westerner or an Easterner? A religious zealot?
- The motive: A disgruntled customer? An anti-immigrant group? A rival brothel owner? A pedophile?
- How the boys are spirited out of their rooms when no one sees them leave and their rooms are many stories above the ground: Are the boys disguised? Are they lowered to the ground with ropes? Are witnesses lying?
- Why are powerful men blocking the investigation? Financial reasons? Conflict with reformers led by Theodore Roosevelt? Inter-gang conflicts?

Even when the team of heroes is closing in on the serial killer, Carr offers readers a choice: is the murderer Japheth Drury, Japheth's brother, Adam, or John Beecham (who sexually assaulted

Japheth as a boy)? Carr adds another choice by having Japheth take Beecham's name, making readers face the choice of whether the Beecham the heroes are pursuing is the real Beecham or Japheth Drury using Beecham's name. Readers are left with choices right up to the final scenes of the novel and, with each choice, Carr stands an excellent chance that readers will choose one of the many incorrect options and be surprised by the real story.

For every question related to the real crime in a mystery—suspects, motives, means, opportunity, and nature of the crime—you should provide at least two and, if possible four or five plausible, realistic answers. Every choice the reader has to make increases the odds your readers will make an incorrect choice and be surprised by your explanation of the real story at the end of your novel or script. Your goal is to have your readers constantly considering several options about which character is guilty and pondering which version of events fits all of the facts and is, therefore, true. If conflict is central to a good story, choice is just as central to a good mystery, thriller or conspiracy story, or to any type of fiction.

Choice is central to love stories. At its most basic level, *Gone with the Wind* is the story of the choices in a classic love triangle: the impetuous, strong-willed heroine, Scarlett, the gentleman, Ashley, and the rogue, Rhett. But Margaret Mitchell adds far more choices about Scarlett's romantic future than just between Ashley and Rhett. Scarlett flirts with several young men and then is interested in Ashley Wilkes, who spurns her. In response, she marries Charles Hamilton, before flirting with Rhett Butler and then marrying store-owner Frank Kennedy. Finally, still in love with Ashley, Scarlett finally marries Rhett Butler. More recently, the Twilight saga poses the same choice based on a romantic triangle as teenager Isabella "Bella" Swan must choose between 104-year-old vampire Edward Cullen and werewolf Jacob Black.

Fantasy novels are filled with choices. In George R.R. Martin's multi-volume fantasy saga *A Song of Ice and Fire*, readers and the television audience are repeatedly given choices about their heroes and heroines, as well as about the villains, and about the fates of the various houses. Will Eddard Stark, Lord of Winterfell, bring peace and prosperity to King's Landing as the King's Hand or will he fall victim to his enemies the Lannisters? When a civil war erupts, which house will ally with which house? Who will win on the battlefield and politically? Choices are layered on choices as Martin keeps his audience guessing about which way each character's story will go, as well as the arc of the main stories about each aristocratic house.

Literary authors offer readers choices to deceive, surprise and entertain the audience. The Pulitzer-Prize winning *To Kill a Mockingbird* is, in part, the story of a rape trial. It centers on whether the hero, attorney Atticus Finch, will successfully defend Tom Robinson, a black man accused of raping a white girl. Besides whether Atticus will win, Harper Lee offers readers choices about whether Atticus will be able to prevent a mob from lynching Tom, the identity and intentions of a reclusive neighbor, and the identity of the man who attacks Scout and her brother late one night in the woods.

Science fiction authors offer their audiences choices. In the film *Intersteller*, the audience faces a choice when young Murphy "Murph" Cooper claims someone or something is moving books and making marks in the dust in her bedroom. Is Murph doing it herself, is it a poltergeist as she claims, or is it something else entirely? Once that mystery is solved, choices continue, including the question of whom or what is trying to communicate with Murph. It is only near the end of the film that the audience learns the real story of who was/is sending her messages in the time-bending epic.

Military adventure stories and thrillers often use choice to keep readers in suspense. Tom Clancy's *The Hunt for Red October* gives readers a choice about whether Soviet Captain Marko Ramius plans to defect or to attack the United States with his nuclear-missile armed submarine. Thrillers are based on the choice of how the hero will survive and who is behind the conspiracy that may kill him. John Grisham's *The Firm* tells the story of young attorney Mitch McDeere who is offered a dream position at a Memphis law firm straight out of law school, but Mitch soon learns that two of the firm's attorneys recently died scuba diving in the Caribbean. Readers face a choice: was it an accident or murder? Mitch soon discovers that no attorney ever leaves the firm, and that the firm represents the Mafia. Mitch soon faces an increasingly life-threatening choice: cooperate with the FBI and risk the Mafia murdering him or defy the FBI and face life in prison. At each stage of the story, Mitch and the audience face choices. How will Mitch gather evidence against the Mafia? Will he use that evidence against the Mafia and, thereby, get disbarred for acting against his client's best interests? In a romantic cover story, will Mitch's wife leave him over a one-night stand he had during a business trip to the Caribbean? What role will a seedy PI play in the story? With each choice, Grisham has the opportunity to deceive and thereby surprise the audience, and he almost always succeeds, as shown by the more than 275 million novels he has sold worldwide.

The power of choice in relation to deception is based on the concept of letting the audience reach their own conclusions based on various options. Their own conclusions are far more dramatic and powerful than information that is provided to them outright. The concept is an old one. In his *Pensées*, the French philosopher and mathematician Blaise Pascal wrote more than 300 years ago, "People are more convinced by reasons they discover themselves than by those found by others." The concept is at the core of the axiom "Show, don't tell." Director Allan Dwan made the same point in an interview with Peter Bogdanovich, when he said, "Make the public work. If you do all the work for them, they sit there bored to death." In *The First Time I Got Paid for It*, writer/director Cameron Crowe discusses Billy Wilder's love of the "Lubitsch touch." Director Ernst Lubitsch was known for taking the time to allow the audience to draw the conclusions he wanted from all of the possible choices. In Lubitsch's *Ninotchka*, Greta Garbo plays a strict Russian Communist who travels to Paris to sell some jewels for the Soviet Union. She arrives at her upscale hotel, which she loathes, and spots a flamboyant hat in a shop window. She glares at the hat and tells her Communist colleagues, "How can such a civilization survive which permits their women to put such things on their heads?" Later in the film she passes the hat again, shaking her head with disdain. An American suitor, Melvyn Douglas, attempts to woo her, but appears to be getting nowhere. Will he succeed or will Ninotchka sell the jewels and return to Moscow a good little Communist? One morning Ninotchka sends her colleagues out of her suite and from a drawer takes out the flamboyant hat and tries it on. Lubitsch doesn't tell the audience she is becoming Westernized and is falling for Douglas, he lets them figure it out. The dramatic effect is far greater than if Lubitsch had directed Garbo to talk about her feelings. *In Rewrites: A Memoir*, playwright Neil Simon discussed the same principle that he applied to his writing: "You have to leave the audience some work to do on their own, because their own discovery of the truth is more interesting to them" (p.255). In his play *Plaza Suite*, a wife attempts to reignite her marriage by renting the same suite at the Plaza Hotel in which she and her husband honeymooned. The husband barely notices and complains that he wished they didn't have to be out of their house. She explains that they couldn't stay in their house while it was being painted. Simon leaves it to the audience to figure out that the painting was part of her plan and not just a chance occurrence. Simon discusses a similar concept in relation to theatre directors. He argues that the finest directors don't tell actors how to play a scene, but make suggestions so the actor can come to see for themselves the best way to play the scene (p.308). For an excellent example of letting the audience figure things out, watch *Fallen Idol*, which is told from the viewpoint of a young boy as he witnesses the disintegration of a marriage and a possible murder.

Questions for Authors:

Does the reader have a choice between:
- Two or more crimes, scandals or illicit affairs in your novel or script to determine which is the real story's crime?
- Several suspects?
- Multiple possible motives for the murder?
- Different motives for each character's behavior: some good, some less than angelic?
- Different possible means for how the crime was committed?
- Different times when the murder may have occurred? A clock smashed during a murder might provide one time, while a witness may set another time and an autopsy a third.
- Different places where the murder might have occurred? Could the body have been moved?
- Can you leave it open as to whether the death was murder, an accident or natural causes?
- If your story is a conspiracy, do you provide several possible explanations for the conspiracy? Different goals? Different motivations?

- If your novel is a love story, are there at least two plausible suitors for your heroine?
- If your story is science fiction, do you provide several different possible interpretations for what is happening?
- Whatever the genre, do you provide several possible key traits for each character? Is the police officer, priest or boy scout all good? Is the thief, Wall Street banker or conman all bad?

All such factors will provide readers with a choice, increasing the chance they will make the wrong choice and be deceived, surprised and entertained.

Common Mistakes and How to Fix Them:

Some mysteries just do not have enough choice. There are too few suspects with too few motives and too few characters with the opportunity to commit the crime. For a mystery or thriller, write down the questions related to the central crime: Who did it? How? Why? Then go through the draft of your novel or script and, as you read, note the other possible answers to these questions that your cover stories suggest to readers. If you do not have several possible answers for each question early in the story and a range of answers that continue to be believable until nearly the end, then you need to add some new logical and plausible answers. You may need to add one or more cover stories to provide more suspects with motivations, means and opportunities to commit the real crime or conspiracy.

You may need to:
- Add characters with a motive to murder the victim
- Provide motives such as greed, jealousy, lust, hatred, or envy to characters you already have to provide them with a motive
- Change the location of characters at the time of the murder to provide them with the opportunity to commit the crime
- If you have a specific means to commit the crime, make sure many characters have access to the means (a gun, knife, blunt instrument, or poison) or the physical ability (strong enough to strangle the athletic victim, having a key to the locked

room, or the ability to swim a river to reach the scene of the crime) to commit the murder.

If you do not add choices to your story, you may end up with a mystery that lacks choice, which means it will also lack deception, surprises and, worst of all, dramatic impact.

For thrillers, make sure a rival explanation for the conspiracy remains viable until nearly the end of the story. Make it appear that at least two, if not more characters might be behind the conspiracy.

For love stories, make sure you have a rival suitor who remains a viable possibility until almost the end of the story. Ashley Wilkes remains Rhett's rival for Scarlett's love until the final scene of *Gone with the Wind*.

For science fiction, make sure the other possible explanations for what is happening continue to be viable until the final pages of the novel or the last frames of the movie.

Chapter 8

Principle 6: Dole Out Clues Slowly
and Late

All authors, but especially mystery authors must dole out information (and clues) about cover stories and the real story in measured amounts at just the right time to maintain the reader's interest, build suspense and sustain the story or mystery until the end. The British author Evelyn Waugh wrote that novelist W. Somerset Maugham was "a master for creating the appetite for information, of withholding it until the right moment, and then providing it surprisingly." No one wants to solve a mystery, know who the heroine will end up with, or discover the identity of the villain behind a conspiracy in the first few pages of a novel. Patience in doling out clues, making characters work to get the clues, and providing the clues in interesting ways are fundamental virtues of a mystery writer or of any author.

The training, finesse and patience authors require to dole out information bit by bit at just the right time is similar to the skills required of the British spymasters who used double-agents to feed deceptive information to the Germans in World War II. When the British sought to deceive the Germans about the timing and location of the D Day landings, they didn't provide the Germans with information pointing to other possible landings all at once. During the months before the invasion, the British sent deceptive, yet apparently true information back to the Germans via German agents in Britain whom the British had convinced to work for them. The British managers of the deception operations were code-named "musicians and choristers." The terms suggested the need for near perfect coordination and timing to convince the Germans that the main landings would not be at Normandy and would not be on the morning of June 6, 1944. The "musicians and choristers" were in such perfect tune that their deception convinced Hitler that the Normandy landings were not the real invasion for weeks, during which he kept many of his most powerful military units in the Pas de Calais waiting for the "real" invasion.

Conmen don't provide all the information about their cover story upfront. Charles Ponzi and Bernie Madoff started paying out impressive returns. With time, people heard about the returns and the conmen slowly let the story about how they were supposedly investing in postal coupons or stocks (the cover story) spread. The schemes would have been far less effective if the conmen had explained all about their cover story right away without making their marks work to gather the information.

Magicians know the importance of doling out information slowly to build suspense and increase the surprise when the real story is revealed. Houdini didn't just climb into a water-filled cabinet and then escape from its watery confines. He stretched out the process for a tension-filled five minutes as the cabinet was rolled out, filled with water, his assistants shackled him, audience members examined the cabinet and the manacles, and he was dropped into the cabinet. At every step of the process, information (clues) was slowly provided about each aspect of the illusion to build suspense and make Houdini's escape that much more dramatic.

While doling out clues slowly in a mystery, you must provide enough clues early enough so the reader will have a chance to solve the murder mystery before your detective heroine. If crucial clues are only revealed in the final pages of a mystery, readers will feel cheated, especially if it's a puzzle-style mystery. Readers of a puzzle style of mystery want a mystery that they can solve, if they possess exceptional intelligence, before your detective hero. The same concept applies to other types of mysteries and to other genres to the extent that at the end of a hard-boiled detective novel, thriller, romance, or literary novel, readers should be able to look back and see how the ending was inevitable if only they had noticed and realized the importance of key information or clues.

An excellent example of the need to provide information at just the right time and deliver it in a dramatic way is seen in the contrast between Barry Unsworth's 1980 novel *Pascali's Island* and the 1988 eponymous motion picture based closely on the book. On a Greek island in 1908, a Turkish spy, Basil Pascali, becomes involved with an English archeologist, Anthony Bowles, a conman intent on swindling the local Turkish Pasha who oversees the island. Near the end of the motion picture, Pascali learns that Bowles is going to sneak off the island before their agreed upon joint departure time. Pascali thinks Bowles is going to double-cross him. Pascali is desperate to leave the island because he believes the Greeks have discovered that he is a Turkish spy. Fearing Bowles will abandon him, Pascali leads the Turks into position to apprehend Bowles. In the ensuing skirmish Bowles is killed. In the movie, when Pascali returns to his rooms, he finds a note from Bowles that has been slipped under his door telling Pascali to be ready to leave the island earlier than they had agreed. A devastated Pascali and the stunned audience realize that Bowles was not going to double-cross Pascali. Revealed nearly at the end of the movie, the simple but devastating note has maximum dramatic impact.

In the novel, the fact that Bowles is not going to double-cross Pascali is made clear to Pascali and the reader before Pascali leads the Turks into position to apprehend Bowles. Unsworth may have had Pascali learn that Bowles was not going to double-cross him to create a scene in which Pascali has to do the Turk's bidding even though he knew Bowles had turned out to be a true friend, or maybe Pascali still did not trust Bowles. Even if either possibility was the case, the final twist in the novel is given away just one scene too soon and the difference in dramatic impact is profound. The novel powerfully captures life on a Greek island amidst the decline of the Ottoman Empire, is wonderfully written and intricately plot-ted, but the movie made the one crucial change in when that key piece of information is revealed and delivers that information in such an understated fashion that it dramatically improves the already outstanding novel. Instead of any long or wordy explanation, the movie leaves it to the audience to realize the note's devastating impact on Pascali.

The novel and film versions of the epic western *Dances With Wolves* also highlight the importance of when key information is provided to an audience. In the film, a Pawnee war party sees smoke on the horizon on their land. The audience sees that a mule driver named Timmons and the hero, Lieutenant Dunbar, have both separately lit fires. The Pawnee ride toward the smoke. Who are the Pawnee about to attack: Timmons or Dunbar? Suspense builds until the audience finally sees the Pawnee close in and kill Timmons. In the novel, the Pawnee see the smoke, but then the reader is told the smoke is from Timmons's fire. The provision of that clue just a scene too early greatly decreases the dramatic impact of the scenes. Such subtle differences about when clues are provided continue when Dunbar meets the Native American shaman Kicking Bird, who comes to investigate Dunbar's camp with no aggressive intent. In the novel, the reader knows Kicking Bird is coming and why. In the film, Dunbar (and the audience) is surprised by a fierce-looking Native American brave who appears to be trying to steal his horse. The surprise works because the audience knows nothing about Kicking Bird or his peaceful intentions. Clues about his identity have been withheld for greater dramatic effect. The same difference between the novel and the film occurs when Dunbar meets a Caucasian female the Comanche captured and made one of their own, Stands With Fist. In the novel, the meeting is told from her point of view, taking away any surprises in the scene. In the film, the scene is from Dunbar's point of view, showing his surprise when he discovers that one of the Comanche is white, which also surprises the audience. Even Dunbar's emotions are more dramatic in the film. In the book, when a Native American brave charges Dunbar, the reader is told he is paralyzed with fear and, therefore, doesn't move. In the film, the audience doesn't know what Dunbar is feeling. They just see that he is standing stock still as the brave charges him. Dunbar appears to be the epitome of bravery. It is only after the brave has retreated and Dunbar collapses that the audience realizes that he was terrified. These are all minor points in what is an excellent novel by Michael Blake and an even better film, but they highlight the crucial nature of when information is provided to the reader or audience.

For authors, patience is a virtue. William Goldman displays admirable patience for revealing clues big and small at just the right moment in his novel *Heat*. The hero/narrator, Nick Escalante, lives in Las Vegas. Well into the novel, Nick must go to Los Angeles to investigate a ransom case. Nick mentions that he grew up on one of the biggest estates in Los Angeles. The reader assumes Nick came from a wealthy family. It is only many pages later, after Nick has arrived in Los Angeles and had a flashback about an encounter at the estate's pool with a gorgeous girl that the reader learns that Nick's parents worked on the estate. He grew up living with his parents above the estate's garage. A small detail, but it is crucial to Nick's gambling addiction, and Goldman knows to feed the information to the reader as late as possible and to make the reader work for the information. If Nick had just said earlier in the novel that his parents worked on an estate in Los Angeles the information would have been far less dramatic and memorable. Show information as late as you can without confusing your audience.

Goldman does the same thing later in *Heat* when Nick returns from his LA trip to meet a computer expert. Nick asked the expert to investigate a venture capitalist. Does Goldman have the expert just provide Nick the information in one quick sentence? Of course not, but Goldman doesn't just delay for no reason other than to add a few paragraphs of text as he builds suspense. Earlier in the novel Goldman has created a character, the computer expert, with a good reason to delay providing the key information. The expert is in awe of Nick and wants to work with him more, so to impress Nick the expert explains every step of what he did to gather the information. It takes three pages for Nick and, more importantly, the reader to learn that the venture capitalist is crooked and is in debt $1.5 million. Goldman makes the wait worthwhile; $1.5 million is a crucial figure because the kidnapper demanded a ransom of $1.5 million.

Elspeth Huxley doles out information slowly and as late as possible at the start of *The African Poison Murders*. Best known for her memoir about colonial Kenya, *The Flame Trees of Thika*, Huxley was a journalist and author of more than 30 books, including several mysteries. In the first pages of *The African Poison Murders*, Huxley takes her time in doling out information about the setting (British East Africa), the time (1930s), and even the profession of the protagonist (CID Officer Vachell). The reader is led from question to question with answers doled out slowly, but with at least one question always left open to draw the reader on. Once the reader learns in the first few pages the answer to the question of Vachell's identity and profession, the reader wonders why a CID officer has come to East Africa. Just as the reader learns that he has been sent to investigate Nazi Bund activities, Vachell visits a farm where someone is violently attacking farm animals at night. Who is behind the violent attacks? The answers keep coming, but so do the questions to keep the reader wondering and reading. Huxley could have started her novel, "CID Officer Vachell arrived in British East Africa on May 6, 1936 with orders to investigate Nazi Bund activities, but then he learned someone was attacking farm animals." Such an approach would have been far more efficient than the measured, patient approach she used, but it would have been far less dramatic and far less effective at engaging the reader. Readers do not want efficiency; they want to be entertained. Buy a copy of *The African Poison Murders* and study the first 15 pages. Take a pen and mark where key information is revealed to the reader, such as the identity and profession of the protagonist, his mission, the setting, and the first crimes. The pacing with which Huxley provides such information is masterfully done. Huxley leaves the reader constantly wondering, on the borderline of confusion, but never crossing over into it, as the reader tries to figure out what is going on from the various possibilities, and why.

In *For the Sake of Elena*, Elizabeth George displays ample patience doling out clues even about a cover story. She keeps the name of a murdered girl's lover a secret until page 333, increasing the suspicion that his identity is crucial. It isn't. He is a red herring. George also shows the greatest patience when she ends a section with a witness stating that they saw the murderer. George then waits eight pages through another important scene before revealing what the witness saw. Such a tactic is a common method of delaying the provision of clues related to the real story by switching to a scene related to a cover story before providing the seemingly crucial clue, which is often nowhere near as crucial as the reader hoped. George's witness saw a woman, which narrows the suspect list, but can provide nothing to specifically identify the murderer.

Epic fantasy and horror stories use the same real/cover story or plot-switching tactic to delay providing information about the fate of key characters. In *A Song of Ice and Fire*, George R. R. Martin handles at least four main story lines (and more as the novels progress) to ensure that most sections end in a cliffhanger. Key information is withheld as the narrative switches to another storyline before finally returning to provide a resolution to the cliffhanger a chapter, or in most cases, several chapters, later. In the wildly popular comic book and television series *The Walking Dead*, the story about zombie-apocalypse survivors shifts between various sub-groupings of characters in different locations and sometimes at different times. The TV series kept fans on edge as they waited three episodes to learn whether a popular character, Glenn Rhee, had been caught and eaten by zombies in an alley. By delaying the provision of information, the authors of the series maintained the deception that he was zombie meat, increased suspense, and ensured their show entertained their audience. In *Game of Thrones*, the television series based on *A Song of Ice and Fire*, the writers ended one season with a cliffhanger about whether a popular main character, Jon Snow, had died after being attacked by his brothers of the Night's Watch. Viewers had to wait months to learn whether Snow still lived. Whenever possible, delay providing clues for a page, a scene, a chapter or, if it's important enough, even another novel or season. As the old saw states, the first line sells the current book, but the last line sells the next book, especially if the reader is left in suspense by facing a choice about what is going to happen next to a beloved character.

Romances are best when clues about the heroine's love life are provided slowly. Margaret Mitchell keeps Scarlett and Rhett apart for much of *Gone with the Wind*, as Scarlett marries two other men and Rhett becomes rich as a blockade-runner. In every romance, such as *Emma, Sense and Sensibility,* and *Bridget Jones's Diary*, the whole point of the story is to chronicle the obstacles that stand in the way of true love, with the lovers coming together only at the very end of the novel or film. The greater the obstacles and the longer the delay, the more dramatic the story.

Delay and timing is even crucial in non-fiction. Shelby Foote, author of the monumental *The Civil War: A Narrative*, spoke in an interview about including the fact that Confederate General Robert E. Lee's home was Arlington. Lee's home was turned into a Union military cemetery and he never visited again; a touching fact that helped show the depth of his commitment to his state, Virginia. Some authors might have included it early, when Lee was deciding whether to accept command of a Union or a Confederate army, but at that stage losing his home would have been something in the future, somewhat theoretical; if the South won the war, he wouldn't lose his home. Foote chose to include that fact only when Lee was riding north, years into the war, as his army invaded the North and marched past his former home. The effect of having Lee see his home, which he had lost because of his choice of which side to fight for in the Civil War, is far more dramatic than any theoretical future cost would have been.

You must study and practice to achieve the precision and patience in doling out information that contribute fundamentally to a great mystery, thriller or any other type of story. You should study works in your genre from masterpieces to potboilers, and in all mediums. In his memoir *Rewrites*, Neil Simon argued that you learn little from works of genius, since they are too intimately tied to the individual author to replicate. He found that plays with flaws were the best to learn from since he could see the flaws and try to figure out how they could have been fixed. It may be different for you, so whatever the genre or level of perfection, when reading novels or watching films, you should analyze:

- When clues and information are provided about cover stories and the real story
- How clues and information are subtly hidden using various deceptive techniques
- What the author wants the reader to think after each scene and each chapter
- What effect different deceptive techniques have on the audience
- Which deceptive techniques are used to mask which types of clues
- How certain clues are subtly highlighted to mislead the audience

- How readers are offered choices in relation to suspects, motives, opportunities, and means related to the real crime, as well as clues related to cover stories
- For romances, how does the author make Mr. Wrong appear to be Mr. Right, and Mr. Right appear to be Mr. Wrong
- For thrillers, how the conspirators hide their plans from the hero and the audience

When studying, make notes, time lines and observations on representative mysteries from cozies to police procedurals, thrillers or whatever genre you favor. Seeing how others create masterpieces, and how and why other novels and films fall short of perfection is an excellent means of learning how to use deception to craft your own engaging stories. Novice painters study the masters to learn to paint. You should study the masters of fiction to learn to be a master deceiver and, thereby, a master storyteller.

Questions for Authors:

Since no one can keep all the clues and facts in the real story and the cover stories in their mind at once, you can save considerable time by developing a logical process to create your mystery; as Hercule Poirot repeatedly stressed, "Order and method." One relatively easy way to maintain the coordination required to dole out clues patiently is to draft time lines for the real story and each cover story with notes on when which clues will be provided in each story. The object is not just to keep the reader deceived, mystified and guessing, but also to build the novel or script to a satisfying climax. If you don't work with an extensive plot before you start writing, you should at least keep track of many factors, including:

- What do you want the reader to believe at each point in the novel, especially about the crime in a mystery, conspiracy in a thriller or love triangle in a romance?
- What choices related to various characters' motives, opportunities, and means, as well as the nature of the real crime have you suggested to the reader?
- When a cover story is exposed as false, make sure at least one other cover story continues to appear to be plausible until the final scene. This is crucial so the audience will be faced with a

choice until the end of the novel and will be surprised by the final solution of the crime, conspiracy or love story.

- When do you provide key clues and information to the reader about the real story and each cover story?
- Is key information doled out slowly and at fairly regular intervals throughout your novel or screenplay?
- How are the clues presented? Do you offer readers a choice as to how to interpret each clue? Does each clue point to more than one suspect, motive, and means, or to more than one crime?
- What do you want the reader to think after each clue is revealed?
- Do you use deceptive techniques to mask your clues, both for cover stories and the real story? Are some of the clues related to your cover stories subtly highlighted to mislead readers by having the detective hero or his sidekick focus on the deceptive clue?
- If you are writing a puzzle mystery, are enough clues provided early enough so readers have all the clues they need to solve the crime before the final scenes of your novel or script?

Common Mistakes and How to Fix Them:

Go through your novel or screenplay and note when clues and key information are provided, and how clearly it is provided. Marking scenes by what type of information they have in them will help you avoid making the mistakes of providing too much information about the real story too early, too late or too obviously. If a scene does not advance any of the stories, cut it. The best scenes provide clues about multiple stories. Clues about the real story should be doled out throughout your story and, whenever such information is provided, it should be deceptively embedded in scenes that also provide clues about various cover stories. This technique ensures that clues about the real story are masked by clues about the cover stories.

Chapter 9

Principle 7: The Longer the Cover Story, the Greater the Surprise

The longer someone is deceived, the greater the surprise and dramatic effect when the deception is revealed. The revelation that an individual is a double-agent has far greater impact the longer they have held positions of importance. Kim Philby, a British double agent, is famous in large part because he deceived his colleagues and friends for almost thirty years from 1934 until he defected to the Soviet Union in 1963. American naval Warrant Officer John Anthony Walker was famous because he passed information to Moscow for almost twenty years, from 1968 to 1985. The British created fictional units in North Africa in 1941 that would later be used as part of deceptive cover stories for Operation Bodyguard, which masked the D Day landings three years later. The effect of the three years of deceptive planning was a successful surprise invasion of France.

In a similar fashion, confidence games that last for years have far greater impact than short cons that are far briefer. Bernie Madoff is famous because his con lasted years and involved billions of dollars. The *$64,000 Question* scandal in 1958-59 revealed that answers were given to popular players of the game show to ensure they stayed on the show longer. The longer they were on the show, the more money they made and, with more money at stake, the suspense for the audience increased. When the scandal finally broke, the public's surprise at the deception was great because it had gone on for so long.

Magicians understand the importance of maintaining a cover story for as long as possible to build suspense. Magicians never just come out on stage, do their illusion and leave. They add showmanship in the form of a monologue, music, lights, and assistants to entertain and distract the audience during the build-up to their illusions. In 1983 David Copperfield made the Statue of Liberty disappear before a live audience of 20 lucky tourists. Copperfield took almost an hour to build up to the illusion, ensuring that when he dropped the curtain and the statue disappeared, the tourists were suitably awed.

Just as deceptive cover stories used by spies, conmen, generals, and magicians are more powerful the longer they are believed, mysteries, thrillers and other fiction that have twist endings demonstrate the power of keeping a cover story believable almost to the end of a novel or script. Excellent examples of maintaining cover stories include several already discussed, Scott Turow's *Presumed Innocent*, Ross Macdonald's *The Zebra Striped Hearse* and Agatha Christie's *Witness for the Prosecution*. Richard Hull's *Murder of My Aunt* is a masterfully written black comedy about a murder told from the murderer's point of view. The ending has a wonderfully creative twist, which as one reviewer wrote, "Would be a sin to reveal," so I will not sin. Read it and see how a master keeps a cover story alive until almost the end of a novel for maximum dramatic and comedic effect.

Twist endings are used in every genre and every form of fiction. In Ambrose Bierce's short story, "A Horseman in the Sky," a Union soldier shoots a Confederate scout from a horse. Only at the end of the story does the reader learn that the rebel scout was the Union soldier's father. Authors maintain cover stories until the end in literary novels, such as in Yann Martel's *Life of Pi*, which won the 2002 Man Booker Prize. Martel spins a yarn about a 16-year-old boy sharing a lifeboat with a tiger, a hyena, a zebra, and an orangutan after their freighter sinks. After an adventure-filled story, the novel ends with the boy explaining that the animal-filled tale he has been telling for several hundred pages may be a cover story. Readers are surprised to learn that in another story (cover or real?), the boy shared the lifeboat with his mother, a cook and a sailor with a broken leg. The later story explains all of the preceding events as well and possibly better than the original story. The reader is left to wonder which story is "real": the tale of the boy and the Bengal tiger or the story solely populated by humans.

Motion pictures often reveal the real story in a dramatic twist at the end. Besides the movie versions of *Witness for the Prosecution* and *Presumed Innocent* mentioned above, *The Usual Suspects* features a crippled character that tells a cover story for most of the film. In the final scenes the real story is dramatically revealed. The crippled character is not crippled and is the cover story's elusive and mysterious criminal mastermind, Keyser Söze, who is also the villain in the real story. In *The Sixth Sense*, the psychiatrist protagonist helps a young boy who claims to see ghosts. Only near the end of the film do the psychiatrist and the audience realize the real story: the psychiatrist is dead and is a ghost. The twist ending works because it explains certain oddities earlier in the film, such as why the psychiatrist's wife doesn't appear to pay any attention to him, well beyond the audience's assumption that their marriage is in trouble.

Brazil is a film about a young man who lives in a dystopian future where workers rebel against the grossly inefficient government by actually fixing things, such as buildings' heating and cooling systems. The hero joins the rebels and following the usual trope, it seems that the rebels will be victorious. Near the end of the movie government forces capture the hero and torture him. Rebels break in and free him, with the final shots of the film showing the hero and his lady love fleeing to a new land where they can live free, but it is a cover story. The movie's final scene reveals the real story: the tortured hero is still in prison. The hero's rebel-assisted escape is just a hallucination.

Whether a novel or a motion picture, the key to craft a satisfying story with a twist ending is to remember that once the final page is read or the final scene shown, the real story must make more sense than the cover story. If it doesn't, the audience will feel confused or, worse, cheated. The TV series *Dallas* is famous for its heavily criticized dream season (1985-86). Patrick Duffy, who played Bobby Ewing, left the show so his character was killed in an accident. Duffy changed his mind and returned the following season to reveal that the entire previous season was a dream of Pamela Ewing. The audience felt cheated since there were no clues during the preceding season that it was all a dream. In the film *Fight Club*, the action starts when the two main characters, Jack and Tyler, are fighting outside a bar and two men ask to join the fight. At the end of the movie, the real story reveals that Tyler is a figment of Jack's imagination, so why would two guys ask to join a fight when it is just Jack punching himself? David Lynch's *Mulholland Drive* and *Twin Peaks* are either loved or hated for their convoluted plots which, many argue, make little or no sense when the real story is revealed at the end. The 2001 film *Planet of the Apes,* a remake of the 1968 classic, featured an ending in which the hero finally manages to return to Earth only to discover that apes have taken over the planet. There is no explanation for why this has happened, so the ending felt tacked on with no real relationship to what preceded it.

The best twist endings explain all that went before and follow logically from all the clues and events in the cover stories, just with a different interpretation. In *Pascali's Island*, Unsworth doesn't just spring Bowles's apparent change of character out of the blue to make a twist ending. From the start, apart from his con game, Unsworth makes Bowles appear to be honest, forthright and decent. Bowles acts disapproving when Pascali says his mother was a whore, argues a moral position when they discuss politics, and for an ethical approach to painting, as well as appearing honest compared to Pascali. All of which makes Bowles's moral behavior and the twist at the end plausible and believable when Bowles acts to protect the kouris he has discovered instead of stealing it to sell to the highest bidder.

In *The A.B.C. Murders* Agatha Christie offers a plausible ending to explain the murders of four people with names starting with A, B, C, and D living in towns with names starting with the same letters. On page 175, Alexander Bonaparte Cust is arrested with blood on his jacket and a knife used in the murders is found in his lodgings. He has epileptic seizures and blackouts, so even he fears he is the killer, committing murder while he is blacked out. All the evidence points to Cust. Someone offered Cust a job by mail selling hosiery across Britain and sent him a list of possible customers, the first four of whom were murdered. Cust worked through the list, so he visited each victim in turn just before they were murdered. When Cust explains this odd occurrence, the police find the letters, which confirm his story, but they also find the typewriter on which the letters were typed in his lodgings. It appears that Cust is the murderer. The twist in the final pages is wonderful as Poirot unmasks the real story—the explanation that explains everything. An heir has murdered his rich relative, but to mask the crime he created the ABC story, sent Cust the letters, framed Cust with the job, the list of customers, and the typewriter, and murdered three other people to mislead the police and the audience, but not Hercule Poirot.

Questions for Authors:

Can you move the revelation that exposes a cover story as false later in your story? Can you move the clue back a chapter, a scene, a page, a paragraph, a line? Every line that you can move the revelation later in your story will increase the dramatic impact.

Do you have at least one cover story remain believable until nearly the end of your novel or script?

In a romance, does your heroine have at least two viable, believable suitors until the final scenes?

In a thriller, does the hero still face a choice between two explanations of the conspiracy until nearly the end of the novel or script? Or is he certain about one cover story until the revelation of the real conspiracy in the final scenes reveals that he is wrong?

Common Mistakes and How to Fix Them:

The most common and egregious error authors commit in creating a story with a twist ending is that the final explanation of the crime or conspiracy does not fit all of the preceding facts. If you have a twist ending, go through the draft of your novel and note each event, character motivation and action, and major question related to the crime in your mystery or thriller. Carefully read your final explanation of the crime or conspiracy and honestly determine whether your twist ending answers all of the questions and provides logical, rational explanations for all of your characters' motivations and actions. Even better, let some trusted writers, reviewers or editors read your novel or script for feedback. If the twist ending is lacking, devise new answers and explanations that fit what has gone before or change what has gone before to match the ending, although doing the later risks making characters do things just to fit your plot requirements in an often fatal deux ex machina.

One solution in some cases in which the twist ending is unsatisfactory is to reverse the two endings; if A is the "false" cover story ending and B is the unsatisfactory "real" twist ending, then make B the cover story ending and A the new "real" twist ending. If you do this, you can have your detective hero point out the problems you found with the twist ending you originally devised (B) as the reason why that explanation does not work, only to then reveal the real story of the crime (A). Sometimes it is easier to remedy any problems with the original false ending and make it the new, real ending than to fix problems with what was the original real story.

Another common error is having all of the cover stories revealed as cover stories long before the end of the novel or script. Keep at least one plausible cover story viable until the end to maintain suspense. Once the real story is revealed, end your novel or script promptly.

Part II: The 10 Techniques of Deception

Chapter 10

Framing

Frames are a cognitive tool that allows us to make sense of a complex world by breaking it down into smaller, understandable parts. Military officers, diplomats, spies, conmen, magicians, and writers use framing to deceive. Presenting a story or issue in terms of a frame based on geography, time or a topic area can lead the target to focus on what is in the frame, while ignoring everything outside the frame. When the deceiver then uses something outside the frame to achieve their goal, the target is surprised.

You can frame an issue in one way so that certain options are considered, while others are ignored. In 1941, the United States and Japan held talks over Japan's invasion of China. The United States framed the issue as a negotiation. The Japanese, however, had decided by late 1941 that the issue could not be resolved by diplomacy. They re-framed the issue as a military crisis. Even as Japanese aircraft carriers sailed across the Pacific to attack the US fleet, the Japanese kept the Americans convinced that the issue was best framed diplomatically, not militarily. The Japanese succeeded in their framing deception and caught the Americans by surprise when they attacked Pearl Harbor on December 7, 1941.

A few months later, framing worked against the Japanese. As the Imperial Japanese Navy planned to invade Midway Island in the central Pacific, the Japanese held war games to determine how the battle might play out. The Japanese admiral playing the American side sank several Japanese aircraft carriers. The Japanese naval leadership did not believe that such an outcome could happen. Intellectually they framed the exercise as ending in a Japanese victory. The "sunk" Japanese carriers were raised and the exercise continued to eventual (inevitable) Japanese victory. A few months later, when Japanese and American fleets met at Midway, the Americans scored a stunning victory by sinking four Japanese carriers at a cost of only one of their own, turning the tide in the Pacific war.

If you think such framing is a thing of the past, it isn't. In the summer of 2002 the US military staged Operation Millennium to wargame a possible war against Iraq. The wargame was framed as ending in a US victory. The clever Marine general in command of the stand-in for Iraq's forces acted unconventionally and sank several US warships, including an aircraft carrier. Just as the Japanese had done 60 years before, the US judges ruled that such a thing could not occur, "raised" the lost warships, and the exercise ended in a (inevitable) US victory. Although the US did not outright lose the 2003 war against Iraq, less stringently framed exercises beforehand might have helped the United States more accurately predict the course of the conflict and its aftermath.

Magicians understand the power of framing. Houdini performed a clairvoyant act in which he would tell the audience amazing details about their families and themselves. The crowd framed the show as starting when they took their seats, but Houdini framed the show much more broadly. His assistants would visit a town days before Houdini's show to collect information at the cemetery (for any recent deaths), coffee shops (for gossip), and to read the local newspaper for information Houdini could use in his clairvoyant act. At the entrance to the show, Houdini's assistants watched what was in women's purses as they paid for their tickets. Houdini then amazed his audience by describing what was in certain audience member's purses, and mentioning recent deaths and other personal details. By framing the show as starting well before he took the stage, Houdini deceived and amazed his audiences. Steve Martin's underrated *Leap of Faith* shows how this works with a con-man/preacher who uses information gathered before a revival meeting to amaze his audiences, until God really does intervene—or does he?

Conmen use the power of framing to deceive marks. Bernie Madoff did not seek investors on street corners. In what is called an affinity con, he sought clients through Jewish groups in which he was active. By framing his investments as offered by a co-religionist, the positive tenets of Judaism helped frame Madoff's investment plan as honest when it was really a giant Ponzi scheme. Most people are surprised that crooked games of chance are far more common at church, school and little league casino nights than at a racetrack or in a boxing ring. The frame of a friendly, local church or group operating the casino night makes people far less aware that they may be marks in a confidence game.

In a murder mystery, framing is used to cause readers to focus on certain aspects of a story, such as clues or suspects, while excluding other clues or suspects that are crucial to solving the mystery. In a conspiracy, the conspirators are usually outside the frame of the cover story. In a love story, framing is used to focus readers on Mr. Wrong who is in the frame and to make sure that Mr. Right, who is outside the frame, is not even considered as a potential suitor.

The setting can frame a novel or film so that the murderer is outside the frame, making it far less likely that the audience will consider that character a suspect. You can use a geographic location as a deceptive frame. Agatha Christie's *4:50 From Paddington* uses a frame of a country house. An extended family in the house appears to offer the full range of suspects when a poisoner strikes, but the murderer turns out to be someone outside the country house frame. He visits the country house but does not live there, nor is he a member of the family. The murderer is the family doctor. Christie used the same framing technique in *The Murder of Roger Ackroyd*, with another country house setting and another murderer who turns out to be the family doctor. (Did Christie ever trust doctors?) The frame extends to a list of suspects on page 201, which even includes the butler, but not the doctor. In *For the Sake of Elena*, Elizabeth George has a murderer strike at a Cambridge college, which frames the story. The murderer is Sarah Gordon, an artist, who is neither a student nor a professor, and therefore is outside the frame of the story. George doesn't stop with just one frame. The novel involves the murders of two girls in the Hare and Hounds running club, a second deceptive frame, since the murders have nothing to do with the running club. In the *Midsomer Murders* episode "Murder on St. Malley's Day," a student member of the Pudding Club at an elite English public school is murdered. DCI Barnaby and Sergeant Troy focus on the club and its members as they seek to unravel the identity of the murderer. The murder is framed by the club, but the murderer isn't a member; he's the sergeant at arms of the club and gatekeeper at the school, Mr. Ludlow.

Not only the murderer can be outside the frame of a murder mystery; the murderer's motive can be outside the frame. In *A Mind to Murder*, P. D. James frames her murder mystery within the confines of a psychiatric clinic. All of the characters work or are patients at the clinic, but the motive for the crime does not relate directly to psychiatry or to the clinic. The familial relationship between Nurse Bolam and Administrative Officer Enid Bolam is the key. Enid is Nurse Bolam's aunt and an inheritance is involved, but that relationship is outside the frame of the clinic.

You can use a profession to frame a story. Scott Turow in *Presumed Innocent* tells a story of lust, ambition and corruption in a District Attorney's office. The murderer, however, is outside the frame of the attorneys' working world in which most of the action occurs: the main attorney's wife is the killer and she works at a university. The gifted QC turned author Sir John Mortimer wrote "Rumpole and the Bright Seraphim," about a soldier who is stabbed at a British base in West Germany. Apart from Mortimer's lovable but curmudgeonly barrister Horace Rumpole, almost all of the characters are soldiers, including several who deceptively cover up the murder. The murderer, however, is outside the frame of the regimental barracks: a soldier's wife is the murderer. Spouses make excellent cover stories since they often share motives, opportunities and means with their better half, but are usually outside the frame of the story.

Time can serve as a frame. You can deceive by providing clues early in a novel or film before switching to another scene set at a different time and place. The reader will probably forget the initial scene that happened outside the time and place frame of the main story. Agatha Christie provides a masterful example of this technique in *Evil Under the Sun*. The first scene of the 1982 movie is of a young woman discovering a woman's body on England's Yorkshire Moors and then running off for help. Then the scene shifts to years later as Hercule Poirot travels to a Mediterranean island to help determine how a millionaire purchased a phony diamond. Christie probably hoped that the reader will forget the incident in England or, if it is remembered, not realize its importance because it is in a different frame. Crucially, the initial scene foreshadows what happens on the island when a woman is murdered. The first scene is key because it focuses on the key variable of when the murder occurred, and both murders were committed in such a way that the character that discovered the body provided an alibi for the murderer.

In the *Midsomer Murders* episode "Judgement Day," the first scenes filmed in black and white show a 7-year-old girl becoming upset when her parents leave her at home so they can go out for an anniversary dinner. The housekeeper scolds the child and sends her to bed after she throws her dinner on the floor. Later, the child takes a knife from the kitchen and murders the housekeeper. The next scene is in color and it is now many years later as a story begins about a perfect village competition in England. A local rogue and then one of the competition's judges is murdered. The initial scene is crucial to solving the murders. The little girl in the initial scenes has grown up, changed her name, and married a local man. She murdered the rogue in a psychotic rage over the possibility that he might marry her daughter and murdered the judge because the judge knew her before she changed her identity.

You can use a theory of a crime, conspiracy or love story as a frame to deceive the audience. Stories with twist endings, such as *Witness for the Prosecution, The Zebra Striped Hearse, The Usual Suspects, The Sixth Sense*, and *Identity,* use one explanation of the events to frame the main cover story and then near the end of the novel or film reveal the real story based on another frame to explain all that has gone before in an entirely different, yet dramatically satisfying way.

You can frame a character in one way, only later to reveal that the character is not bound by that frame. In *Pascali's Island*, Barry Unsworth frames the English archeologist Anthony Bowles as a conman. In that frame, Bowles is not to be trusted. It is only at the end of the novel that Bowles breaks out of that frame and proves to be a true friend to Basil Pascali and to value a kouris more for its historical and aesthetic value than for its monetary value. In Christie's *Evil Under the Sun*, the married victim, Arlena Marshall, is framed as an adulterer who is hated by her step-daughter. The audience will conclude that of all the characters, she deserves the most to die. When the real story is revealed, however, Christie creates a new frame around Arlena that paints her as a lonely victim. Her newest love interest cynically bilked her out of a fortune and murdered her because her husband was on the verge of discovering the loss.

One way to use a frame is by doing what Raymond Chandler argued was the key to deception in mysteries; "The most effective way to conceal a simple mystery is behind another mystery. This is literary legerdemain. You do not fool the reader by hiding clues or faking character á la Christie but by making him solve the wrong problem." In *Wolf to the Slaughter*, Ruth Rendell sets readers to solving the wrong problem or crime. A young woman goes missing and is presumed murdered. For three-quarters of the novel the scenes focus on the apparent murder of the young woman, until she turns up alive and well. The real crime is the murder of her ex-boyfriend, yet the frame of the story doesn't even include the possibility that the ex-boyfriend was murdered until the last quarter of the novel. In the movie *At Bertram's Hotel*, Agatha Christie adds a string of burglaries as a frame to distract the audience from the real story about a murder, again setting readers to solving the wrong problem.

Agatha Christie brilliantly framed *The A.B.C. Murders* around the wrong question of why someone has murdered four people with names starting with the letters A, B, C, and D in towns with names starting with the same letters. Poirot and readers focus on this puzzle when the key question is outside the A-B-C frame. The key question is why the killer sent letters about the crimes *before* they occurred to Poirot. The murderer sent the letters to ensure that the murders would appear to be related, not just four random murders spread across England. The linking of the murders is key to the murderer's plan to frame the murders as a cover story about a madman killing his way through the alphabet and not the real story of a murder for an immense inheritance from the third victim, the wealthy Sir Carmichael Clarke. Without the cover story frame, the murder of Sir Carmichael would have been far easier to solve, since only one relative stood to financially benefit significantly from his early demise and that relative is the murderer.

Questions for Authors:

When you're developing your real story, can you frame the story in such a way as to deceive and later surprise the audience? Can you use the setting (geography, time, profession) or a single theory of the events in the story to mislead the audience?

If it is a mystery or a conspiracy, can the villain be outside the frame of the main cover story?

If your story is a romance, can the real Mr. Right be outside the heroine's frame, such as her profession, geographic location or even time period, such as in Diana Gabaldon's Scottish *Outlander* series?

Can one trait or context frame a character, which turns out to be inaccurate?

Common Mistakes and How to Fix Them:

In a murder mystery, conspiracy or love story, the villain or Mr. Right should not be so far outside the frame of the story that the reader feels cheated when he pops up seemingly out of nowhere at the end of the story. Dorothy L. Sayers has a character in *The Five Red Herrings* tell Lord Peter Wimsey, "See here, Wimsey, you're not going to turn around now and say that the crime was committed by Mrs. Green or the milkman, or somebody we've never heard of? That would be in the very worst tradition of the lowest style of detective fiction." Even so, some authors still use a villain from far, far outside the frame of the story or someone who is barely even in the story. In the 1989 film *Sea of Love*, a burnt-out New York police detective, Frank Keller, is assigned to solve the murder of three men. Each man was murdered in a similar fashion and appeared to be lured to their deaths via a lonely hearts newspaper column. The police have the murderer's fingerprints from one of the crime scenes, so Keller places his own ads in the column and begins to meet women as his partner surreptitiously collects their fingerprints to determine if they are the murderer. Keller falls in love with one of his dates, Helen Cruger, but then learns that she saw each of the three murdered men. Keller fears she is the murderer, but when the real story is revealed, Helen's ex-husband, Terry, is the murderer of her three former lovers. Unfortunately, as film critic Roger Ebert pointed out, Terry is barely in any scenes before his entrance as the murderer near the end of the film. The audience feels as if the screenwriter has not played fair, providing no chance for them to have solved the mystery. Make sure your villain is in your story early and often, even if he is outside the story's frame.

Chapter 11

Dazzle

Humans need light to see, but if the light is too bright, it can dazzle and blind us. In a form of deception called dazzle, you can achieve the same blinding effect as a bright light by supplying readers with information that appears to be crucial but is actually unrelated to the real story. Cover stories—extra information that dazzles the audience—make a story of a crime a mystery. Your goal is for your reader, amidst the mass of irrelevant information or noise to miss crucial clues about the real crime. In every genre authors use cover stories to dazzle readers to increase the chance they will be surprised when the real story is finally revealed.

In everyday life, we routinely face dazzle. In the supermarket, we confront dazzle as we peruse dozens of brands, types, prices, and sizes of everything from toothpaste to bread. Similarly, in selecting investments for retirement accounts, we must choose from hundreds of companies offering thousands of funds, stocks, bonds, ETFs, TIPs, and all manner of investment options. Having so many options makes deciding far more challenging than if we only had to choose between a stock fund, a bond fund and a money market account.

Military officers often use dazzle. In World War I, the Germans used dazzle by giving their reserve units the same unit numbers as front-line units. The British and French gathered information about the German units, but each unit appeared to be in two places at once. In World I and II, the British painted some of their ships with false bow waves, providing the enemy with two bow waves—the real and the false—to increase the chance an enemy ship or submarine would misjudge how fast the British ship was cruising when they attacked to throw off their aim. During the Cold War, some Soviet spies complained that American society by its very nature was a form of dazzle. In attempting to determine US policy, the spies had to determine who spoke for the government: the president, Congressional leaders, the Secretaries of State or Defense, the National Security Advisor, or some combination of them all? It was just too much information to figure out which information was important.

Magicians use sexy assistants, upbeat music and flashes of light to dazzle and distract their audience from what is really happening as they perform their illusions. Conmen running a Ponzi scheme have reams of documents showing their investments, returns, trends, risk analyses, and all manner of financial material to dazzle their marks. This blizzard of apparently important information means that most such investment cons take years to unravel, even when financial experts become involved. In 1999, a financial analyst informed the SEC that the returns Bernie Madoff was reporting were impossible. Given all of Madoff's dazzle, it took until 2008 for the authorities to unravel what had really happened and for the FBI to arrest him.

Dazzle is especially useful if an adversary already knows the deceiver's plans and the deceiver wants to confuse the issue, which is the case when a mystery novelist attempts to deceive a reader who knows they are reading a mystery, when a romance reader knows the heroine will end up with the handsome rogue, or when a general is leading an army to relieve a surrounded garrison. During the 1944-5 German winter offensive that led to the Battle of the

Bulge, the Germans knew that General George S. Patton's Third Army would move to relieve the encircled "battered bastards of Bastogne": the US 101st Airborne Division. Patton's dazzle-ruse was to issue five sets of orders over the radio to his army. Only his officers knew which set was correct, so although the Germans knew Patton's army would attack, they didn't know when or by which routes.

Many mystery writers understand dazzle and some even have their detective character comment on its use by the villain. In "The Adventure of the Reigate Squire," Sir Arthur Conan Doyle has thieves searching a country house use dazzle to mask the object of their search. The thieves take two plated candlesticks, an ivory letter-weight, an oak barometer, a volume of Pope's *Homer*, and a ball of twine. The reader is left to wonder what these objects mean. In reality the thieves took them at random to mask the fact that they were searching for an important document, which they failed to find. As Holmes states, "It is of the highest importance in the art of detection to be able to recognize out of a number of facts which are incidental and which are vital." In "The Naval Treaty," Holmes offers a concise definition of dazzle when he concludes, "The principal difficulty in our case lay in the fact of there being too much evidence. What was vital was overlaid and hidden by what was irrelevant." Edgar Allan Poe has his detective hero, Auguste Dupin, comment on the way information overload dazzles the police in "The Murders in the Rue Morgue." Dupin explains that when the police succeed it is "brought about by simple diligence [at collecting information] and activity. When these qualities are unavailing, their schemes fail." If a novelist or villain uses dazzle, police (and readers) who merely collect information will stand little chance of unmasking the culprit, since gathering more information, if anything, makes determining which information is important and which is superfluous dazzle even more difficult.

At a basic level, all cover stories are dazzle. However, there are several other ways to dazzle your audience. The human mind can only keep about seven facts in short-term memory at once, so if you provide more than seven clues or key facts in your novel you stand an excellent chance that your readers will be unlikely to remember all seven, let alone discern which clues are crucial to the solution of your mystery. Philip Macdonald uses dazzle in *The List of Adrian Messenger* by focusing the story on a list of more than seven men. Messenger's list has 11 names on it. The audience is confronted by dazzle as ex-MI-5 agent Anthony Gethryn attempts to figure out what connects the apparently unrelated 11 men, almost all of whom appear to have died either naturally or by accident.

If a novel has more than seven main characters, it is the dedicated reader indeed who can keep all of them straight to stand a reasonable chance of solving the mystery. Agatha Christie's *Thirteen at Dinner* (14 main characters), *Towards Zero* (11), *And Then There Were None* (10), *The A.B.C. Murders* (10), and *Peril at End House* (9) all have more than seven main characters, thus relying in part on dazzle to deceive readers. In *After the Funeral*, Christie includes so many members of the murdered Richard Abernethie's family that she provides a family tree to assist readers in keeping everyone straight. Of all her novels, the plot is probably the most convoluted and an example of dazzle possibly taken too far to the point where readers are just confused, not entertained.

Even though it is a short story, Conan Doyle's "The Adventure of Silver Blaze" adds characters as dazzle to what is a relatively simple story about the theft of a race horse. Conan Doyle adds several extra characters to dazzle readers, including a group of gypsies who were seen near the estate where the horse was stolen. The gypsies have moved on the morning after the theft, increasing the chance that readers will focus on them as the horse thieves, even though they are innocent of the crime.

You can use subplots as well as characters to dazzle readers. Jed Rubenfeld populates his bestselling 2006 historical mystery *The Interpretation of Murder* with a dazzling cast of characters and subplots. In 1909 Sigmund Freud arrives in New York on his first and only visit to the United States. A stunning debutante is found bound and strangled in her penthouse apartment. The following night another beautiful heiress, Nora Acton, is found tied to a chandelier in her parents' home, viciously wounded and unable to speak or recall her ordeal. Freud and his American disciple, Stratham Younger, are asked to help Miss Acton recover her memory and discover the killer's identity. The story involves real famous people, including psychologist Carl Jung, New York Mayor George B. McClellan, and millionaire Henry Thaw (who murdered his wife's lover, architect Stanford White, on the roof of Madison Square Garden), as well as many fictional characters, including George Banwell, who murders a bridge worker (a red herring) as he disposes of evidence that links him to the murder of a young woman, and Banwell's wife, Clara, who is having an affair with the father of Nora, who was attacked (another red herring). The long list of some 40 characters with all their related sub-plots provides ample dazzle to mask the real mystery related to Nora. Even determining which mystery is the real story is a challenge.

To use dazzle in a romance add love interests to keep the reader guessing the identity of the heroine's true love. In *Gone with the Wind*, Margaret Mitchell made Ashley Wilkes Scarlett's first love interest and a strong rival to Rhett Butler, but she added romantic dazzle in the form of Scarlett's best friend's brother, Charles Hamilton, and wealthy merchant Frank Kennedy, who appeals to Scarlett's overriding need for cash to rebuild her beloved plantation Tara. Having Scarlett marry three men in succession adds layers of deception to the novel that would be absent without Scarlett's many dazzling suitors.

You also can use multiple motives to dazzle readers. In Isaac Asimov's *Murder at the ABA*, a young, rising star novelist, Giles Devore, is found dead in the bathtub of his hotel room at the 75th American Booksellers Association convention. The hero, Darius Just, concludes it was murder, and characters with motives abound, including:

- Just is suspected of being jealous of Devore, who was Just's protégé, but sold more books and was far more famous than Just.
- The couple who own the small press that first published Devore are angry with him for moving to a larger press.
- A store owner who first promoted Devore's books and was interested in him romantically is upset with him for not appearing at a book signing arranged by her store.
- Devore stood-up a public relations woman who had arranged for him to present a talk.
- Devore was brusque and rude to almost everyone at the convention.

All of these characters with various motives dazzle the reader and mask the real motive for the murder, which has nothing to do with the publishing frame: the need to conceal a heroin smuggling ring.

Authors dazzle their readers by providing a long inventory of the items at the scene of a crime to camouflage crucial clues. After a suspicious death on an airplane in Agatha Christie's *Death in the Air*, an empty match box, a white physician's coat and a dead wasp pass without notice in a long list of items found amongst the passengers' effects, even though they are crucial. The match box held the dead wasp that was meant to appear to have caused a sting-like mark on the victim. The murderer used the white physician's coat to appear to be an airline steward as he walked up unnoticed and administered the poison to the victim in their seat. Amidst the other coats, bags and assorted belongings of the passengers she mentions, Christie ensured that the three key objects are well and truly hidden.

Even just two items can dazzle the audience and distract from a crucial clue. In *A Mind to Murder*, rubber gloves are a key clue, since they explain why no fingerprints were found on the murder weapon, a chisel. When Inspector Dalgliesh sees rubber gloves fall out of Nurse Bolam's pocket, he expresses surprise such gloves are used at a psychiatric clinic. Bolam's reply is weak, but James seeks to dazzle the reader by adding that a rubber apron is also missing. The apron, unlike the crucial gloves, is a red herring, since they have nothing to do with the murder; Cully, a porter at the clinic, borrowed the apron to keep his clothes clean when he painted his flat. Just as with cover stories, extra clues, characters, plots, and motives added to dazzle readers must be just as interesting, well thought out and creative as the clues, characters, plots, and motives in the real story.

To dazzle your audience, you can use one crime to hide another crime. Clues about the cover-story crime distract the reader from the real story's crime, such as the corruption case that masks the murder in Scott Turow's *Presumed Innocent*. In *A Mind to Murder*, P. D. James uses blackmail to mask a murder.

You can even use the number of murderers to dazzle your readers. Instead of having one or two murderers, Agatha Christie's *Murder on the Orient Express* has 13 murderers. This plethora of killers means that any reader attempting to cull the murderer from the suspects is awash in clues that point to many of the suspects, since they are all guilty. In the main cover story, the murderers also add clues about a suspicious stranger on the train to further dazzle Hercule Poirot and mask their crime.

The length of a novel or movie can dazzle audiences. The longer a novel, the more difficult it is to remember all of the key events, characters and clues. Since a novel is usually read over a week or more (except by my wife who can read a novel in a single night), it is a challenge to remember all of the characters and events to figure out the murderer's identity. Mysteries of the Golden Age of detective fiction were much shorter and therefore easier to solve, at least in terms of dazzle, compared to most mystery novels published today. Agatha Christie's *Murder in Three Acts* (1934) and *Peril at End House* (1932) are only 177 pages. Dorothy L. Sayers's *Strong Poison* (1931) is 272 pages, while three unabridged John Dickson Carr novels, *The Three Coffins* (1935), *The Crooked Hinge* (1938) and *The Case of the Constant Suicides* (1941) were included in *A John Dickson Carr Trio* (1957) in 31 fewer pages (472) than just one P.D. James novel, *Devices and Desires* (503 pages in paperback) published in 1990. Today, most mystery novels are far longer than novels published during the Golden Age, which were brief, in part, because of newspaper shortages during the Great Depression and the Second World War. Elizabeth George's *A Banquet of Consequences* (2015) is 592 pages, Patricia Cornwell's *Depraved Heart* (2015) is 480 pages and Sue Grafton's *X* (2015) is 416 pages. This trend toward longer novels usually leads to greater depth of characterization than for the most part existed in the shorter novels of the Golden Age. All manner of subplots have become common, especially romantic entanglements for the detective character or personal issues for the heroine, such as addictions and family dramas. This very depth, however, adds dazzling information that makes it more difficult to winnow out the clues from the characterization chaff to try to solve the real story's mystery.

Mystery movies today are also longer than they were in the 1940s and 1950s, which adds dazzle and makes it harder to solve the mystery. In 1945, the film version of *And Then There Were None* ran 97 minutes, *The Maltese Falcon* (1941) was 101 minutes, and *Charlie Chan in Panama* (1940) was a brisk 67 minutes. The 1957 movie *Witness for the Prosecution* was 116 minutes. In contrast, the murder mystery movie *Gone Girl* (2014) is 149 minutes, the mystery *The*

Girl with the Dragon Tattoo (2011) is 158 minutes, and the religious-conspiracy movie *The da Vinci Code* (2006) is 146 minutes, all far longer than movies in the 1940s and 1950s.

You can use a setting to dazzle readers. Christie's *Death on the Nile* with its portrayal of a scenic cruise on the Nile and her *Appointment with Death* set amidst the ancient wonders of Petra, Jordan, have settings that dazzle the audience with information that doesn't help the reader solve the mystery. Peter Hoeg's *Smilla's Feeling for Snow* (*Smilla's Sense of Snow* in the US) makes Copenhagen and Greenland part of the story, especially in relation to snow, which help mask the mystery. In Dan Fesperman's fascinating *Lie in the Dark*, Inspector Vlado Petric investigates a murder in the grim, chaotic city of Sarajevo during the 1990s siege. All of the details about war-torn Sarajevo distract readers from the relatively basic real story's mystery. Remember that simple stories are far from a negative. Shakespeare wrote more simple stories about revenge, jealousy, loyalty, evil, good, ghosts, and the division of estates than anyone. More recently, Marshall Moore used the beauty and otherworldly nature of Antarctica in *Tantalus Zero* to dazzle readers. The key is to make the information about the setting fascinating and new to most readers, so you don't commit the capital crime of boring the reader as you try to dazzle them.

Translating novels set in other countries often increases dazzle and the deceptiveness of a setting. Foreign readers notice the things that are different in each scene, which are usually not clues, thereby adding a deceptive layer of dazzle to the real story. Masako Togawa's *A Kiss of Fire* is set in 1990s Japan and involves the investigation of an arson and murder 30 years before, while Keigo Higashino's award-winning *The Devotion of Suspect X* is the story of a murder played out in today's Japan. Both novels add a layer of deceptive dazzle via the Japanese setting for non-Japanese readers. Stieg Larsson's Millennium trilogy of mysteries centering on journalist Mikael Blomkvist and investigator/computer expert Lisbeth Salander, are set in modern Sweden, which can distract foreign readers from each novel's real mystery.

You can use a historical setting to dazzle readers. Lindsey Davis's Marcus Didius Falco novels set in the Roman Empire during Vespasian's rule use the ancient setting to dazzle the reader. (Davis is an excellent speaker; entertaining, funny and enlightening, especially for an ex-British civil servant. See her if you ever get the chance.) Barry Unsworth's 1992 novel *Morality Play*, which was short listed for the Man Booker Prize and later made into a movie (*The Reckoning*), is set in Medieval England at the end of the 14th Century. Centered on a troupe that performs religious morality plays, the setting is crucial to the story as one of the players suggests the troupe perform a play about a recent murder to unmask the killer. At that time, a play based on real events was unheard of. The Medieval way the characters think and what they believe dazzles the audience and ensures surprises about what happens next.

Thrillers are the masters of using exotic locales to dazzle and distract the audience from the conspiracy ensnaring the hero. James Bond, Jason Bourne and the Mission Impossible team travel the world on their adventures to unravel evil conspiracies. Spy stories, such as tales penned by John Le Carré, Len Deighton and Alan Furst, often are set in exotic locations around the world or in notable periods of history. Especially in films, such settings distract from the real mystery or conspiracy. Heist films, such as *The Italian Job*, and romances, such as *Under the Tuscan Sun*, often use foreign settings to add dazzle to mask their real stories.

Adding characters, clues, cover stories, and exotic settings are not the only ways to dazzle readers. You don't have to do it all yourself as the author. Your characters, especially the villain, also can use dazzle. In *A Mind to Murder*, P. D. James has the murderer add a carved fetish (an object believed to embody a potent spirit) to the crime scene at a psychiatric clinic. Inspector Dalgleish learns that the fetish was carved by a violent patient: is he the murderer? The fetish has nothing to do with the murder, but adds a layer of dazzle to the mystery. In *The A.B.C. Murders* Agatha Christie has the murderer add a layer of dazzle by having four murders appear to be tied to a railway guide, a copy of which is left at each murder scene, and to victims whose names and cities of residence progress through the alphabet beginning with A. The police, Hercule Poirot and the reader are, to one degree or another, dazzled by Christie as she has the murderer use dazzle to deceive everyone about the murders and hide his murder of a rich relative for money. Ellis Peters in *One Corpse Too Many* also has the murderer use dazzle to mask his crime. It is 1194 and England is riven by civil war. In Shrewsbury, 94 rebel prisoners are executed, but when Brother Cadfael arrives to bury the 94 unfortunates, he counts 95 corpses. When he raises the issue with King Stephen, his highness is far more interested in prosecuting the civil war than an extra corpse. The murderer almost gets away with his attempt to hide his crime with dazzle. Only Cadfael's perseverance leads to the culprit's arrest.

Dazzle can be used in similar fashions in thrillers, romances, literary, sci-fi, fantasy, and horror stories. The key is to layer cover stories over the real story, include exotic settings, and provide interesting information to distract the audience from the real story. In *The Da Vinci Code*, Dan Brown does a marvelous job of layering apparently factual information throughout his novel, which is essentially a chase, to distract the audience from the conspiracy at the heart of the real story. Brown also uses exotic settings, the Louvre, a French country house, Westminster Abbey, and a chapel in Scotland, to dazzle the audience and distract them from the real story, all while entertaining them.

Setting your story against epic historical events is a well-proven method of making a story more dramatic, as well as serving as dazzle to distract your audience from the real story. In *Gone with the Wind*, Margaret Mitchell sets her love story against the backdrop of the US Civil War and its aftermath. The beginning of the war, Confederate victories followed by gradual defeat, and then the destitution of the South after the war distract readers from the real love story and help surprise the audience with deceptive plot twists. Boris Pasternak's *Doctor Zhivago* is a love story set against the backdrop of World War I and the Russian civil war. The momentous events add depth to the love story and dazzle the audience as they try to figure out whether Dr. Zhivago and Lara will ever be together. Herman Wouk's *Winds of War* is the story of US naval officer Victor "Pug" Henry's family set against the events of 1939 and World War II. The historical events serve as dazzle to make Pug's family dramas that much more entertaining and the plot twists that much more surprising.

Horror films are often set at idyllic summer camps with pretty, bikini-clad girls and suntanned, handsome boys to add a layer of sex appeal, lust and romance, as well as dazzle to the psychotic activities of the mass murderer in the real story. Romantic and sexual scenes also serve as deceptively calm periods between the scenes of bloody mayhem and gore.

Fantasy novels and films create whole new worlds to dazzle audiences with unique races, languages and cultures. *Lord of the Rings, Dune, Wheel of Time, Earthsea Cycle*, and *A Song of Ice and Fire* (*Game of Thrones*) are excellent examples of such world-building, which add layers of fascinating dazzle to relatively basic quest or epic fantasy stories.

If you are writing science fiction, you can use dazzle to add interest and to mask the real story. Robert A. Heinlein's *Starship Troopers* is a coming of age story (the real story), but combined with its futuristic setting (dazzle) of mobile infantry and a galactic war against the bugs, it has become a classic. The television series *Star Trek* was pitched as *Wagon Train* in the stars. The plots were often basic, yet the otherworldly settings added a layer of dazzle that made the real stories that much more interesting, leading to the rebirth of the series in movies that have attracted legions of new fans. *Star Wars: A New Hope* borrowed from classic story lines or tropes about a lonely, obscure young man discovering he is crucial to a galactic fight against evil. George Lucas set the story in a galaxy a long time ago and far, far away with light sabers, Jedi and death stars to dazzle the audience so they wouldn't notice the basic real story and very few did.

Even literary stories add dazzle to mask basic real stories. *The English Patient* is a love story, but set against World War II in North Africa and Italy, with fascinating information about early Twentieth Century desert exploration, Michael Ondaatje crafted a Booker Prize winning novel. Ken Follett (*The Key to Rebecca, Century Trilogy, Kingsbridge* series) and James Mitchener (*Hawaii, Mexico, Texas*) are masters at writing sweeping tales set against major historical events, which help dazzle the audience and mask the real stories.

Questions for Authors:

For your mystery, do you have seven or more suspects?

Do you have seven or more clues that are required to identify the murderer?

Can you add extra objects to any scene or list that includes a crucial clue?

Does every major character have a different motive to murder the victim?

Does more than one character have the opportunity to commit the crime?

Can you add cover stories about another crime, affair or seedy arrangement that will make the participants wary of the police, thus giving them a reason to lie and to appear nervous, even though they are innocent of the real crime?

Is there an opportunity for the murderer to use dazzle when they commit the crime by leaving "extra" evidence? Murdering more than one person? Leaving a clue that points to another character?

If a special talent or skill is needed to commit the crime, such as strong hands or a certain stature, make sure that several suspects have strong hands or are short or tall, as required by the crime.

Is your novel long enough to dazzle readers? If not, can you add a fascinating cover story or enhance the interesting exotic or historical setting?

Whatever the genre, can the story be moved to a setting that will dazzle the reader with new and interesting information? This doesn't have to be a geographic location, but can be an exciting business, historical period or subject area.

If you are writing a love story, does the heroine have several suitors, not just two?

Common Mistakes and How to Fix Them:

A common mistake is to cram a huge amount of information into the start of a novel or screenplay. Often this makes the opening scenes far too dense, slow and confusing. Read the start of your novel or screenplay.

- How many characters are introduced in the first few pages?
- How many cover stories are introduced in the first few pages?
- How much information about each cover story is shown in the beginning?
- How much information about each character is included when they are introduced?

Too many characters and plot lines at the start of a novel or script can leave the audience awash in a mass of indistinguishable characters and confusing plot lines. If you find this is the case, consider whether some characters can be introduced later in your story, as well as starting some of the cover stories later in your novel or screenplay. In the age of sound bites and shortened attention spans, readers expect a fast-paced start to your novel or screenplay, so don't bury them with a crowd of characters or a library's worth of stories in the first chapter of your novel or the first five minutes of your screenplay.

The opposite problem is when authors provide too little information and clues are too apparent, the villain too evident, and there are too few cover stories or believable suspects with powerful motives. Avoid having the real villain motivated by a strong motive, such as gaining control of a family fortune, while the other suspects are driven by love, revenge or jealousy. Money is usually seen as stronger than other motivations, so it is often prudent to have several characters share the motive of the villain in seeking a mountain of cash.

Avoid providing tangential information in your novel or script that is not central to a cover story or the real story. Avoid lectures and long speeches. Try to think of interesting ways to deliver information, such as when characters are doing a fascinating activity, such as mountain climbing, attending a rock concert or having some creative form of sex.

Chapter 12

Conditioning

Conditioning is when you establish a pattern your target comes to expect and then you surprise the target by changing the pattern. The classic example is the boy who cried wolf. Each time he warned of a wolf in the area, the townspeople paid him less and less attention until they ignored him entirely. The target is desensitized to what the deceiver is doing, thereby making it easier to deceive the target and, when the wolf really does appear, surprise the target.

Conditioning is often used to deceive enemies in wartime. A classic case of conditioning occurred when the German warships *Scharnhorst, Gneisenau* and *Prinz Eugen* broke-out from German-occupied Brest on February 12, 1942. For months the Germans jammed British radar sites every day at the same time to condition the British into believing that the atmosphere was disrupting their signal reception. The British became so conditioned to the "atmospheric" problems that the German ships had 12 hours of unmolested sailing past the jammed British radars before the British reacted, allowing the warships to safely reach Germany.

Leo Marks's excellent and humorous *Between Silk and Cyanide*, chronicles British attempts to send agents into German-occupied Holland during World War II. British agents reported forming cells and provided useful intelligence. In reality, the Germans had captured almost every British agent and turned them. The Germans used the agents to send carefully selected accurate information to London to condition the British to believe the agents were free and still working for the British. The Germans convinced the British to drop more agents, which the Germans intercepted and either turned or shot, and critical supplies, which the Germans used themselves.

The Germans didn't have a monopoly on conditioning. The British Royal Air Force used conditioning to mask bombing raids. In 1943, before the British planned to attack the German rocket complex on Peenemunde, they sent Mosquito fighter-bombers repeatedly along the route a raid on Peenemunde would take, but had the planes attack Berlin instead. Over time, the Germans were conditioned to believe that this route meant an attack on Berlin, so when they detected aircraft on that route, they focused their air defenses on Berlin. On August 17, the British yet again sent eight Mosquitoes along the same route. The Germans were certain they were the vanguard of yet another attack on Berlin and sent fighters to defend the capitol, but the RAF aircraft behind the initial eight Mosquitoes attacked Peenemunde instead. The conditioning was highly successful. At the cost of one aircraft lost to German fighters, the eight Mosquitoes used in the diversion lured 203 enemy fighters to Berlin. Of 597 British bombers sent to Peenemunde, only 40 were lost and 32 damaged, and Peenemunde was severely damaged. If the conditioning ruse had been unsuccessful, it is quite possible, as one German postwar account claimed, that an additional 160 bombers would have been shot down.

In 1973 over several months the Egyptians repeatedly moved troops up to the Suez Canal to threaten to attack Israeli forces holding the canal's east bank. Each time the Israelis mobilized their armed forces in response and each time the Egyptian troops returned to their bases and the Israelis demobilized. Then in early October the Egyptians again sent their forces to the canal. On the eve of the Jewish holy day of Yom Kippur and having mobilized so many times before to no effect, Israel decided not to mobilize for several crucial hours. This time the Egyptians attacked. The Egyptians had conditioned the Israelis to expect them to pull back and when the Egyptians broke the pattern and attacked, the Egyptians delayed the Israeli response, achieved surprise and almost won the war.

Conmen are well aware of the power of conditioning. Ponzi schemes are based on conditioning. At first investors receive impressive returns on their investment. It is only after many months that the returns stop. In most cases the investor, conditioned to believe the returns will continue, takes a long time to accept that the returns will never resume and, worse, they have also lost their initial investment. Almost all cons start with the mark making money, conditioning the mark to believe the conman. Only then does the conman change the game and take the mark's money.

Magicians also use conditioning. A magician throws a ball up in the air once, twice and then the third time it disappears. How? The magician palms the ball before he throws the third time, yet makes the throwing motion and looks up at where the ball would be if he had thrown it. The audience has been conditioned to expect the ball to be in the air and completely misses seeing the magician palm the ball.

Mystery authors have murderers use conditioning to fool detective characters, such as in *The A.B.C. Murders*. Agatha Christie has the murderer condition the police and Hercule Poirot, at least at first, to conclude that a psychopath is murdering his way through the alphabet using a railway guide. The real story is related to the third murder, which appears to fit the pattern, but was committed for a far different motive than any psychotic one: greed. Similarly, in P.D. James's novel, *Devices and Desires*, a murderer uses the killings of a serial murderer, the Whistler, to mask her murder of another woman by copying his modus operandi.

You also can have villains in thrillers use conditioning. In *The Manchurian Candidate*, the Chinese communists brainwash (condition) an American soldier to assassinate a US presidential candidate. The deception continues as the audience expects the ex-prisoner of war, Sergeant Raymond Shaw, to shoot the US presidential candidate, but Shaw shoots his Communist-agent mother instead. Unseen by the audience, the hero has reconditioned Shaw.

You can use characters other than the villain to condition your audience. You can have your characters focus on one aspect of a story, which conditions readers to focus on that aspect, and then surprise your audience by changing the focus. In his novel *A Simple Plan*, Scott Smith spins a dark tale of two brothers and their friend who discover a crashed plane in northern Ohio with a dead pilot and a duffle bag containing $4.4 million aboard. Distrust and suspicion soon leads to multiple murders. As the story progresses the focus is on the money and the possibility that the authorities or a hit-man will find the three friends and the money. Eventually, the narrator, Hank, has survived and he and his wife have the money. His brother and their friend are dead. The reader has been conditioned to assume that Hank, who was portrayed at first as the nicest of the trio, will finally be able to enjoy the money. Smith then changes the focus of the story. Instead of the authorities or the hit-man imposing some sort of justice on Hank for what he has done, Smith has Hank burn the money, feeling that what he has done, including murder, doesn't justify his financial windfall. Changing the source of justice is an unexpected twist for readers, which, in part, led to the novel being made into a 1998 movie that earned two Academy Award nominations.

Characters can use conditioning, but so can authors. Conditioning can be thought of as a form of foreshadowing, where you pay off the foreshadowing again and again until the end of the novel or script when you foreshadow an event which then doesn't happen. In *Pascali's Island*, Barry Unsworth does a masterful job of conditioning. Throughout the novel Pascali, a Turkish spy, Bowles, an English archeologist, Lydia Newman, an artist, a German agent, Greek rebels, and the Pasha work their deceptive ways. The story is told from Pascali's point of view, so the expectation of double-crosses is reinforced, since Pascali views the world as one in which deception reigns. Everyone lies to everyone else. The reader is conditioned to expect the final double-cross to be Bowles and Lydia double-crossing Pascali. After setting up the conditioned pattern of double-crosses, the twist is that, while Pascali double-crosses Bowles and Lydia because he expects them to double-cross him, they do not double-cross him.

Character traits can be used to condition the audience. If a character's behavior based on a key trait changes for a good reason, it can surprise the audience. In *Star Wars: A New Hope*, the audience is conditioned to believe that Han Solo (Harrison Ford) is motived primarily by money. He only agrees to take Luke Skywalker and Obi-Wan Kenobi off Tatooine in the *Millennium Falcon* in exchange for an exorbitant fee. He agrees to rescue Princess Leia only because she is wealthy and he expects to be richly rewarded. Throughout the movie the audience is conditioned to believe he is motivated only by money, until the end when he rides to the rescue in the *Millennium Falcon* to help destroy the Death Star. You can't just have a character change for no reason, however. Han changes because he has come to value his friendship with Luke and Leia more than money.

All genres use conditioning. In the movie *The Shawshank Redemption* (based on Stephen King's novella "Rita Heyworth and the Shawshank Redemption"), set in a Maine prison, an elderly inmate, Brooks, is released. He tries to fit into society on the outside but he has been incarcerated so long he can barely function and becomes depressed. Brooks hangs himself in his hotel room. Later in the movie, Red, the main character's closest friend, is also finally released after most of a lifetime in prison. Like Brooks, Red also struggles to adapt to life on the outside, pausing at one point to stare at a revolver in a store window. The audience is meant to conclude via conditioning that Red will do just what Brooks did, commit suicide, but Red does not, surprising the audience.

In science fiction conditioning can be effective. In C. M. Kornbluth's imaginative short story "Little Black Bag," a highly advanced medical bag from the future ends up in the hands of a pair of disreputable sorts in the 1940s. The pair use scalpels that never cause pain or even bleeding, and drugs beyond imagining to make a fortune, mostly on cosmetic surgeries. Kornbluth conditions readers to conclude the pair are going to get away with their unearned, newfound wealth but then, when a patient refuses to believe a scalpel will not hurt them, one of the disreputable sorts draws it across her own neck to prove its unbelievable qualities. Unfortunately for her, in the future the missing bag has been noticed and has been deactivated. The scalpel slices into her throat and kills her.

In George R. R. Martin's *A Song of Ice and Fire*, a popular character, Rob Stark, fights and wins every battle in a war. Readers are conditioned to believe that he will, therefore, win the war. Martin then breaks the pattern by having Rob murdered at his wedding banquet, the famous Red Wedding. The TV series *The Twilight Zone* often used conditioning. In one 1959 episode, "Escape Clause," a hypochondriac makes a deal with the devil to live forever. He becomes more and more reckless, eventually committing murder as the audience becomes conditioned to expect that he will avoid punishment and live forever. Confident he won't die even if convicted of murder and sent to the electric chair, all seems well for the hypochondriac. Then the author breaks the conditioned pattern: the hypochondriac's attorney saves him from the electric chair and instead secures him a sentence of life in prison.

Questions for Authors:

Can you use conditioning in your story to establish a pattern and then surprise your audience by breaking the pattern?
    Can you foreshadow an event or behavior and then make it appear it will happen again, but it doesn't or it does in a different way?
    Can your murderer or conspirators use conditioning to deceive the police or the hero? Can your murderer commit multiple murders to mask their key murder?
    Can you focus your story on one goal, such as cash, revenge, jealousy or lust, only to switch that goal at the end of your story? Can you give a dishonest character a reason to act honestly at the end of your story, or a reason for an honest character to lie, cheat or steal?
    In a romance, can your heroine gravitate to one type of man repeatedly before a twist at the end causes her to realize that a different type of man is really perfect for her?

Common Mistakes and How to Fix Them:

If you create a story using conditioning, the greatest sin is to make the story too repetitive. Although events must repeat to create a situation that leads to conditioning, each time the event repeats, make it different enough to be interesting to the audience. Don't overdo it, as Stephen King showed in *The Shawshank Redemption*, establishing a pattern even with one character is often enough for readers to expect the pattern to repeat with a second character if the two characters share similar traits or backgrounds.

Chapter 13

Break the Rules

If you do something unexpected, such as going against expectations or the implicit rules of a situation, you're likely to deceive and thereby surprise your opponent. In real life, generals, spymasters, conmen, and magicians break implicit rules or go against expectations to deceive adversaries, marks or their audience.

Julies Caesar wrote, "The most powerful weapon of war is the unexpected," and breaking the rules is always unexpected. In 1939, the Germans broke the rules of war. Instead of parceling their tanks out to each infantry division, they concentrated their tanks in highly mobile, powerful tank divisions. Controlled by radio and supported by dive bombers, the Germans created a new form of warfare called Blitzkrieg (lightning war). Instead of the long static lines of trenches and broad, frontal attacks of World War I, the Germans in World War II attacked on narrow fronts with overwhelming forces of tanks, artillery and dive bombers to punch a narrow hole through the enemy's line. The new method that broke all the old rules brought rapid victories for the Germans in Poland, the Low Countries, France, and at first in the Soviet Union.

The Germans weren't the only ones to break the rules in World War II. At the time, the accepted wisdom was that for an amphibious landing to succeed, the invading force had to land at or near a port. The landing force needed a port so it could land reinforcements faster than the defender could reinforce the defenders overland. Without a port, the defender would build up forces faster than the attacker and the invasion would fail. On August 19, 1942, more than 6,000 infantrymen, mostly Canadians, supported by 237 ships and 74 RAF squadrons landed at the French port of Dieppe to test the feasibility of capturing a port. The German defenders repulsed the raid with relative ease, inflicting 60% casualties on the invaders. The Allies concluded that landing at a port would be suicidal, but they still needed a port, so they broke the rules. They would bring their own port. The British created Mulberries, portable harbors they could tow across the Channel, which allowed them to deceive and surprise the Germans when they landed on the beaches of Normandy.

Magicians often break the rules. Magicians mark decks of cards and angle mirrors in the backs of cabinets to make them appear empty. The well-known illusion of sawing an assistant in half usually relies on a visual illusion related to the size of the box, allowing the assistant to place her legs beneath or behind where the saw is about to bite. While magicians break the rules to entertain, all conmen break the rules (and the law) for personal gain. Computer criminals send emails that claim to be from your bank, the IRS or an ex-Nigerian dictator, while Ponzi and Madoff used new investors' cash to pay fraudulent returns to previous investors.

Breaking the rules can lead to new schools of fiction or art. With his novel *One Hundred Years of Solitude*, Gabriel Garcia Marquez helped create magical realism by breaking the rules of fiction when he introduced magic into the rational world of his novels. The Impressionists broke all the accepted rules of painting in late 19th century Paris leading to one of the most popular art movements in history.

In fiction, while conditioning takes advantage of patterns and expectations established in the story, breaking the rules takes advantage of expectations established before the reader even opens your novel or sees the first scene of your film. Readers expect murderers to be cold personalities with anger issues, albeit often well hidden. Agatha Christie used this belief in *Murder is Easy* to lead readers to believe that wealthy Gordon Whitfield is the killer. He is said to have killed his fiancée's canary, is seen arguing with other characters just before their demise, and has motives to murder the various people who die in the story. Whitfield appears to fit the image of a cold-blooded killer, yet he is not. His former fiancée, with whom he broke an engagement, decided in revenge to frame him for a series of murders, all involving people who had wronged him.

Most readers don't expect the detective hero to be the criminal, even though it is a very old deception. In 1907 in "The Mystery of the Yellow Room," Gaston Leroux had the detective turn out to be the criminal. By the 1920s the idea had become a cliché, which S.S. Van Dine warned against in 1928 in his "Twenty Rules for Writing Detective Stories": "The detective must not himself commit the crime." Even so, Agatha Christie had a police officer turn out to be the murderer in "Hercule Poirot's Christmas" and in her long-running play, *The Mousetrap* (1952-), Sergeant Trotter, the policeman in charge of the case, is the murderer, although he isn't really a policeman. The key to remember is that if you are the first author to break a rule, such as having a police officer or the narrator the murderer, it is deceptive and entertaining, but if others have used it, the trick becomes a cliché. You should not rest the deceptive core of your novel solely on the twist that the narrator or detective is the murderer, unless you give it a new twist. Agatha Christie gave the detective-as-murderer twist a new take in *The Murder of Roger Ackroyd*, which tells the story of the death of Mrs. Ferrars, a wealthy widow. Since Dr. Sheppard is the first-person narrator and is Hercule Poirot's neighbor and friend, readers are likely to see the doctor as Poirot's new Captain Hastings. Poirot even says, "You must have indeed been sent from the good God to replace my friend Hastings." Christie doesn't make the detective the killer, but makes his new sidekick, Dr. Sheppard, the murderer.

The narrator dying at the end of a story has been done so often as to become a cliché. Therefore, if you decide to kill your narrator or point-of-view character, make sure you add a dramatic twist. Billy Wilder famously had his narrator dead at the start of his motion picture, *Sunset Boulevard*. In the first scene, screenwriter Joe Gillis is dead floating face down in a Hollywood mansion's swimming pool. In a creative twist, the film *The Sixth Sense* had the point-of-view character that appeared to be alive turn out to be a ghost.

In murder mysteries, readers assume that when someone dies, they will remain dead, and that if there is only one character left alive, they are the murderer. In *And Then There Were None*, Christie has all of the characters appear to be murdered, so when there are two characters left alive, one of them, Vera Claythorne, (and the audience) conclude that the other must be the murderer. She is wrong. A confession in a postscript reveals the real story. Wanting to cause the death only of the guilty and finding himself with only a short time to live, Justice Lawrence John Wargrave, a retired judge, lures nine people who have been responsible for a death but escaped justice, to an island to be murdered. He pretends to be one of the guests and fakes his own death with another character's help (Dr. Armstrong) and then kills Armstrong once the doctor's verdict of his death is accepted by the others. Wargrave murders the others, drives the last survivor into committing suicide, and then shoots himself using a rubber-cord contraption to drop the weapon away from him to fit the description of his death in several of the guest's diaries. Christie broke the rules of a murder mystery by having a character come back from the dead and the sole apparent survivor not be the murderer, and, by doing so, sold more than 100 million copies of *And Then There Were None*.

The audience expects characters to be real people, at least in the fictional world the author creates. In the excellent psychological mystery/thriller *Identity*, written by Michael Cooney and modeled on *And Then There Were None*, ten characters are stranded in a torrential rain at a motel when they begin to be murdered one by one. The movie appears to be a basic mystery playing by the accepted rules as the audience tries to figure out who is committing the murders from among the ten characters. But the murderer is not among the ten, at least not in the sense anyone in the audience expects. The characters are the extra facets of a vicious murderer's divided mind undergoing psychiatric treatment to avoid execution. As the psychiatrists manage to banish each of the split personalities, one after another of the characters at the motel are murdered. The story isn't real, but it isn't fiction in the usual sense of a novel or film. Cooney creates a masterfully deceptive story that breaks the rules of the mystery.

Although not a mystery, "fictional" characters deceive and then surprise the audience in *A Beautiful Mind*. A young John Nash, a future Nobel Prize winner in economics, arrives at Princeton University and meets his roommate Charles Herman. Later Nash meets William Parcher, a supervisor at the Pentagon. It is only later in the movie that the audience learns that Nash has paranoid schizophrenia and Herman and Parcher are figments of Nash's imagination.

Most murder mysteries have one or maybe two murderers, but Christie broke this convention in *Murder on the Orient Express* when she had not one, not two, not three, but a train carriage full of murderers. Mr. Ratchett is murdered on the Orient Express. Poirot discovers that Ratchett, who had asked Poirot for help since he believed his life was in danger, was really a man called Cassetti, who kidnapped a child in the United States. The ransom was paid, but Cassetti murdered the child anyway. At a trial, which many believed was rigged, Cassetti avoided punishment and then fled the country. Poirot learns that all 13 people in the train coach had ties to the case and reasons to hate Cassetti, and all 13 are the murderers.

In most murder mysteries or thrillers, the murder of children (and pets) is rarely, if ever, described or shown. Often, children are not even killed in situations where their deaths would be completely logical. In *Jurassic Park*, dinosaurs eat many of the adults, but the two children escape from several close encounters with carnivorous dinosaurs and survive. Even so, Alfred Hitchcock broke this rule in his film *Sabotage*. A terrorist gives a box to his young step-nephew to deliver. The audience knows there's a bomb in the box and, as the boy boards a bus, expects the boy to somehow avoid being blown up. Hitchcock shatters that expectation with an explosion that kills everyone on the bus, including the boy. Hitchcock later said he should have had the boy die off-screen, but it was not just a gratuitous death, since Hitchcock uses the death to motivate the boy's mother to murder her husband, the terrorist, when she discovers what he has done. Until fairly recently, children were rarely, if ever, the murderer. Agatha Christie went against this rule in *Crooked House*. An old, wealthy man is murdered. The victim's 12-year-old granddaughter turns out to be the murderer. Be warned: having a child be the murderer has become too common to use as your sole deceptive twist.

Readers expect the murderer to be human, but Edgar Allen Poe broke the rules when he cast an orangutan as the murderer in "The Murders in the Rue Morgue." In "Silver Blaze," Sir Arthur Conan Doyle broke the rules by having a non-human murderer. A prize racehorse is stolen and a man is found dead on the moor nearby. It turns out that the murderer is the horse, which kicked the man who was trying to steal him, to death. In a deceptive twist on the rules of a murder mystery, the horse is the murderer and the victim is a thief. Most victims are good people, worth the time spent finding their murderer, but in the case of "Silver Blaze," the victim is a thief, which may be why Conan Doyle made his murderer a horse. It would have been difficult for Conan Doyle to justify catching and punishing a human for murdering a thief.

Readers expect the murderer to commit the crime himself, but Agatha Christie found creative ways to break that rule. She created a murderer who tried to use the state to commit his murder for him in *Towards Zero*. A handsome tennis player, Neville Strange, frames himself for murder with weak evidence, then frames his wife with much stronger evidence. Britain at that time had the death penalty, so if she is convicted, she will hang, and only Superintendent Battle is able to deduce that Neville is the murderer. In Curtain, Christie has a murderer use the power of suggestion to convince others to murder for him, including almost convincing Captain Hastings to commit murder.

In keeping with the common belief in a just world, readers expect evil murderers. But in Harry Kemelman's *Thursday the Rabbi Walked Out*, the murderer is a small-town bank president who appears to be kind and thoughtful. He even takes in a young man with a troubled background for no apparent reason other than altruism. Often authors use characters with careers that evoke respect as their murderers, since readers are less likely to suspect successful characters of murder. Edward D. Hoch's "The Most Dangerous Man Alive," has an attorney turn out to be the murderer.

Audience also expect that, although their detective heroes may be wrong early in a novel or show, in the end the hero is always right. The TV series *Perry Mason* featured the brilliant attorney Perry Mason who invariably defeated his rival DA Hamilton Burger

(Hamburger?). Therefore, audiences were deceived and surprised when Perry lost three cases; "The Case of the Terrified Typist," "The Case of the Witless Witness," and "The Case of the Deadly Verdict."

Even the great Sherlock Holmes could surprise his audience when he was wrong. In "The Adventure of the Yellow Face," Effie Munro asks her husband, Grant, for £100 and begs him not to ask why she needs the money. Two months later, Grant sees Effie secretly meeting the occupants of a neighboring cottage in Norbury, England, which includes a mysterious yellow-faced person. Overcome with jealousy, he breaks in and finds the cottage empty. The room where he saw the mysterious figure is well-furnished with a portrait of his wife on the mantelpiece. Holmes learns that Effie was married before in America and, although the husband is supposed to be dead, Holmes believes the mysterious figure is Effie's first husband. Holmes theorizes that the husband has come to England to blackmail her. When the cottage is reoccupied, Holmes, Watson and Grant enter the cottage, brushing aside Effie's entreaties. They find the strange yellow-faced character. Holmes peels that face away, showing it to be a mask and revealing a black girl. Effie Munro's first husband was John Hebron, a black man. He did die in America of yellow fever, but the couple's daughter Lucy survived. Afraid that Grant would abandon her if he knew she was mother to a mixed-race child, Effie hid Lucy. Effie used the hundred pounds to bring Lucy and her nurse to England. Holmes says, "Watson, if it should ever strike you that I am getting a little overconfident in my powers, or giving less pains to a case than it deserves, kindly whisper 'Norbury' in my ear, and I shall be infinitely obliged to you." There is no crime and Holmes is wrong, a powerful deception for avid readers of the brilliant Holmes.

Authors who develop unusual motives can deceive and surprise readers. In *Smilla's Sense of Snow*, author Peter Hoeg deceives readers into thinking that the object the villains are seeking is extremely valuable. Partly this plays on the unwritten rule that mysteries and thrillers are about a "MacGuffin," as Alfred Hitchcock called the object the character in a thriller are desperately seeking, which is usually worth piles of money, such as the *Maltese Falcon*. In Hoeg's novel the object the villains seek is only of value in a certain way. The lead villain wants to be famous for having discovered a rare meteorite. Nicholas Meyer's *The West End Horror: A Posthumous Memoir of John H. Watson, M.D.*, a Sherlock Holmes mystery, has a murderer kill two people so they avoid a "horrible death" caused by a disease.

In *Towards Zero*, Agatha Christie breaks the rules by creating a mystery that appears to be a locked-room mystery, but is not. The murder occurs in a house on a promontory between the sea and a river. The investigation focuses on the characters in the isolated house, but the murderer was not in the house. He swam to the house on the night of the murder, maintaining his alibi that he was across the river at the time.

As Chekhov advised, "Remove everything that has no relevance to the story. If you say in the first chapter that there is a rifle hanging on the wall, in the second or third chapter it absolutely must go off. If it's not going to be fired, it shouldn't be hanging there." This principle is known as Chekhov's gun, even though he broke his own rule in *The Cherry Orchard*. Since most readers have come to expect it to be followed, breaking it can deceive audiences. You could have a rifle on the wall and then a murder committed with a rifle, but not that rifle. Or maybe the rifle was used not to shoot the victim, but to bludgeon the victim to death.

Fantasy novels increase suspense by breaking the rules, such as the traditional fantasy rule that main characters rarely, if ever, die. Following the rule, in *Lord of the Rings*, of the original Fellowship of the Ring, all save one survive. David Gemmell breaks the rule in *Against the Horde* when his hero Druss the Legend falls trying to defend a great fortress against the Nadir people. In George R.R. Martin's fantasy novels *A Song of Ice and Fire*, main characters die with deceptive and surprising regularity, including Eddard Stark, Stannis Baratheon, Tywin Lannister, Drogo, Robert Baratheon, Ygritte, Robb Stark, Shae, Barrister Selmy, Viserys Targaryen, and many more. With each death Martin conditioned his audience to expect major characters to die, so the degree of surprise decreased with each death; thereby serving as a warning to writers not to overuse a single deceptive technique.

In a technique similar to Martin's, Derek Robinson creates characters that readers begin to like, only to have them die. Robinson writes novels about the World Wars for the most part, such as *Piece of Cake*, *The Eldorado Network* and the Booker Prize-nominated *Gos-*

hawk Squadron. In most war stories when a character is introduced who later dies, they are secondary and not much time is spent on their background and thoughts. In *Piece of Cake*, a main character, Dickie Starr, is killed trying to fly under a bridge in France on a bet. In another of his flying novels, Robinson introduced a pilot character. He spends pages describing the pilot's background, fears and dreams, and then, after a chapter focused on the pilot, has a German shoot him down and kill him.

In fiction, according to the two-time Academy Award winning scriptwriter and novelist William Goldman, most audiences want to be told a truth they already know or a falsehood they want to believe in. In *Jerry Maguire*, the old reliable truths that if you're a good, moral person, fate will smile on you, and that love will find a way to win out are at the core of the film. Both may be far from reality, but at least for 90 minutes in a darkened theatre we want to believe those "truths." If you can tap into such a belief or trope and then twist it to deceive and surprise your audience, you just may strike artistic gold. In *Ever After: A Cinderella Story*, Prince Henry, a stand-in for Prince Charming, rushes to save Cinderella from the clutches of an older letch bent on having her as his wife. By the time the prince arrives, breaking the fairy tale trope, Cinderella has already rescued herself. Richard Matheson's sci-fi/horror novel *I am Legend* goes against the trope that zombies are mindless monsters. In Matheson's novel, the zombie-like monsters taking over the post-apocalyptic world are beginning to develop their own society and become something far from monsters.

Questions for Authors:

Does your story break any "rules" of the genre? Do you break a rule, stereotype or trope (a common story line) in a creative, new way? Read and watch other novels and movies to make sure your twist hasn't been done before.

Can your story have multiple murderers? Can an animal be the murderer? Creativity is crucial; let your mind roam and develop a hundred possibilities, a couple of them just may be deceptively great and may not have been done before.

Does your real story, cover stories or any characters go against reader's expectations? Can you create a stereotype character that late in the story belies your audience's expectations? The moral thief, the prudish whore, or the simple-living Wall Street banker. Make certain you show a motivation for the change in behavior or audiences will not believe the change.

Common Mistakes and How to Fix Them:

The most common failing of aspiring authors is to break one of the rules of a genre, such as having the narrator turn out to be the murderer or the love story turn out to have been a dream, in the belief that it has never been done before. It probably has, and probably with more dramatic effect than your first attempt. Read (or watch) extensively in the genre in which you write so you know when and how rules have been broken before, and to ensure that you are not copying what has been done before. Readers and movie audiences are desperately seeking a unique story, not a repetition of something they have read or seen before.

Chapter 14

Manipulate Time

Spymasters, generals, magicians, conmen, and writers alter time to deceive their adversaries, marks or audience. In the 1930s, the Germans manipulated time to deceive Stalin. The Germans used documents about meetings between German and Soviet military officers from the 1920s when the two countries were cooperating as evidence of treasonous meetings in the 1930s when the two were adversaries by changing the dates on documents related to the meetings. The deception worked and Stalin ruthlessly purged his military, weakening it just before the German invasion of the USSR in 1941.

During the operation to deceive the Germans about the timing of the Normandy landings, the Allies manipulated time to deceive the Germans. The British fed information to the Germans that the rehearsals for the landings were just beginning, so the Germans would conclude that the landings would be late in the summer. In reality, the exercises the Germans were seeing evidence of in the spring of 1944 were the final rehearsals for the June 6 landings, early in the summer.

Magicians often deceive their audience by using the mind's inability to live in the moment. The brain takes about a tenth of second to process information, so we always live ever so slightly in the past. Magicians use this time lag to deceive their audience. The most common example is when a magician makes a coin disappear as he passes it from his left hand to his right. The time lag in our brain means we miss the magician palming the coin in his left hand. Our brain just assumes the coin is being passed and when it doesn't appear in the other hand, we are deceived.

Some con games rely on manipulating time. A common con is to buy a lottery ticket with the previous day's winning numbers. The conman alters the date on the ticket and, after devising a plausible reason why he can't collect the winnings such as the need to avoid appearing in the media because of a litigious ex-wife, offers to sell the "winning" ticket to someone else for a fraction of the ticket's supposed winnings.

Because of the need to tell two stories at once, mystery authors are the authors who most often manipulate time to deceive their audiences. In one story, which is usually told chronologically, the detective character gathers clues and interviews suspects to solve the crime. The second story is often told in part at the start of a novel, when a murder is shown, and then in bits and pieces, usually not in chronological order, as the detective pieces together the story of the crime. Usually the second story is told in its entirety only at the end of the novel when the great detective explains what really happened leading up to the murder. You can tell the two stories in any order you want, jumping back and forth in time between the stories to increase suspense and surprise readers.

It is easier than you may think to deceive using time, since most readers don't closely follow where all the suspects are minute by minute at the crucial time of the murder, especially if your story is moving along at an entertaining clip. Director Howard Hawks highlighted the lack of the audience's attention to detail when he discussed *The Big Sleep* with Peter Bogdanovich. While filming the movie, Hawks could not figure out who had committed one of the murders. He cabled the author, Dashiell Hammett, to ask. Hammett replied, but Hawks pointed out that the character Hammett said had done it was at the beach at the time of the murder and could not have done it. Even so, *The Big Sleep* remains a much-loved classic. Hawks later said, "I realized that you don't really have to have an explanation for things, as long as you make good scenes you have a good picture—it doesn't matter if it isn't much of a story." David Lynch would probably agree.

Within the two stories—the murder and the detection—you can have characters, usually the villain, manipulate time, especially in relation to when a murder occurred. John Dickson Carr's *The Three Coffins* (also called *The Hollow Man*) is probably one of the most famous novels that have a murderer who tries to manipulate time in relation to the time of a murder. Grimaud appears to have been shot by his brother, Fley, who called on Grimaud at his home on a snowy evening. Grimaud is wounded, but Fley is later found dead in the snow, shot in the chest, as if from a self-inflicted wound. It appears that Fley called on Grimaud, shot his brother and then, returning to his lodgings, shot himself in anguish over what he had done. The novel is a locked-room mystery and from the start Carr seeks to have the reader increasingly certain that the only explanation is that Fley shot Grimaud and then committed suicide. It is only at the end of the novel that the real story is revealed: Grimaud shot Fley first. Then Grimaud disguised himself as Fley, called at his own house, faked his own shooting using a paper disguise and a mirror, and then had the duplicate "Fley" disappear. The murders occurred in the reverse chronological order from which Carr describes them in the novel. Fley didn't try to murder Grimaud and then shot himself; Grimaud murdered Fley and then staged the scene where "Fley" shot Grimaud.

Manipulating the time of the murder is an old idea. In 1907 in "The Mystery of the Yellow Room," Gaston Leroux has an attempted murder occur long before it appears to have happened. A woman is found seriously injured in her locked bedroom. Disoriented, she can't answer an investigator's questions. It appears she was assaulted during the night, but how and by whom? The investigator eventually deduces that the woman's ex-husband assaulted her the day before. The woman concealed signs of the attack since she didn't want her father to know she was married and locked herself in her room. During the night, traumatized by the event, she fell out of bed and hit her temple on the corner of her bedside table, making it appear the attack happened during the night.

The reader gets an entirely distorted view of when the assault took place.

Authors still have murderers manipulate time. In the *Death in Paradise* TV series, the 2015 episode "Until Death Do You Part" features the murder of a bride-to-be who is drowned in her hotel room's bathtub. The time of death is tied to how long a candle took to burn down, since the candle is still burning when the body is discovered. The candle is rated to burn for a set period of time. The killer, however, sprinkled salt on the candle, which makes candles burn much slower, thus changing the apparent time of the murder and allowing the murderer to engineer an apparently unbreakable alibi until DI Humphrey Goodman deduces the truth.

You can have your murderer use poison to manipulate time, especially in relation to alibis. A death caused by poison can be long separated from when the poison was administered to a bottle, pill or food. In *The Mysterious Affair at Styles*, Agatha Christie in her debut novel used her knowledge of poisons learned from working in a pharmacy during World War I to deceive and entertain readers. Three drugs are used to murder Mrs. Inglethorp. The old lady is taking a strychnine tonic, which is tampered with by having bromide powders added. This addition causes the strychnine to concentrate in the bottom of the bottle, so a lethal quantity is delivered in the final dose. Therefore, there is a delay between when the poison was added and when the victim died. But another drug, a narcotic, is also added to slow the effect of the poison, thereby causing confusion as to when the poison was taken.

In her novel *At Bertram's Hotel*, Christie has her murderer manipulate time in relation to a locked door to create a challenging mystery for Miss Marple. When a door is forced open and a dead body is found in the room, the police notice that the chain on the door has been ripped out of the door frame. The chain appears to have been ripped off when the door was forced open. However, the chain was ripped off before the murder in the room so the murderer could leave and make it appear that the room had been locked from within. In the 2007 movie of *At Bertram's Hotel*, three women wear similar hats. One of the women is murdered, making the police and the audience conclude she was murdered by mistake since another woman, wearing a similar hat, was shot at earlier in the story. The murderer, however, has manipulated time by adding the hat to the victim's head after the murder to cast doubt on the identity of the intended victim and, thereby, cast suspicion on other characters. In *A Pocketful of Rye*, the murderer attempts to mislead Miss. Marple by creating a letter with the wrong date on it to make it appear that a wayward son had been invited home by his father, when he had never been invited at all.

Authors often have murderers tamper with watches to alter the apparent time of death. In the television program *Father Brown*, the episode "The Sign of the Broken Sword" involves a murder at an army base in England. A major is murdered and the watch on his wrist, apparently shattered in a struggle with his killer, sets the time of death as 12:40 pm. The false time of death allows the murderer to establish an alibi. However, Father Brown notices when searching the dead major's room that the officer's wrist watch is on his desk. Father Brown is able to identify the murderer, in part, because he is missing his wrist watch, which he put on the dead major.

You can use bodies to manipulate time. In Agatha Christie's *Evil Under the Sun* the murder is not committed until after the victim's "body" appears to have been found. The murderer and another character arrive by rowboat at a secluded beach. A woman is sunbathing with a sun hat covering her face. When the murderer approaches, he checks the body and announces that the sunbather is dead. He sends the other character back to a nearby hotel to alert the authorities. The time of death then appears to be before the real murderer even arrived at the beach. After finding the "body" of his accomplice, the murderer then kills the real victim who is waiting for a romantic assignation with the murderer in a beachside cave. In a similar fashion, in *For the Sake of Elena* Elizabeth George has the murderer kill a jogger, return home to be seen, and then return to "find" the body. A witness has seen the murderer finding the body as she came from her home, so it seems that she could not have committed the murder.

The murderer or an accomplice can use a second murder to mask the time of another murder. In Keigo Higashino's award-winning *The Devotion of Suspect X*, the murderer switches the bodies of two victims murdered on March 9 and 10, so the alibis and clues related to one murder are deceptively shifted 24 hours (Technique 5). Tetsuya Ishigami is a talented mathematics teacher who lives next door to Yasuko Hanaoka and her daughter Misato. When Yasuko's abusive ex-husband, Shinji Togashi, arrives to extort money from Yasuko, the situation escalates and Yasuko and Misato kill Togashi. Overhearing the commotion, Ishigami, who secretly loves Yasuko, offers his help, disposing of the body and plotting the cover-up of the murder. Ishigami can't just dispose of the body, since if the body is found, the police will trace the murder back to Togashi's ex-wife, Yasuko. Instead, Ishigami pays a vagrant to stay in Togashi's apartment the day after Togashi is murdered, so the vagrant's DNA will be in the apartment. Ishigami removes from the apartment all of Togashi's clothes, possessions and anything that would assist identification. Ishigami then murders the vagrant, whom no one will notice is missing, and dresses the corpse as Togashi. Ishigami smashes the vagrant's face so the police will think the vagrant was Togashi and then steals a bicycle, which will be reported stolen, to ensure the body is found rapidly, ensuring an accurate determination of the time of death the day after the murder of Togashi. Yasuko had no alibi for that night, but Ishigami engineers a weak alibi for the next night for the women—they went to the movies—but an alibi the police can't break. An iron-clad alibi would have aroused suspicion. The vagrant, who the police believe is Togashi, was murdered on a night when his ex-wife and daughter have an alibi. An apparently unrelated body of a vagrant, which is really Togashi, found near the river, was murdered on a night the women do not have an alibi, but they have no motive to have murdered the vagrant. If the plan falls apart, Ishigami can just confess to the murder, since he did it in the sense that he did murder the man the police think is Togashi.

As Christie showed with the body on the beach in *Evil Under the Sun*, you can have murderers use disguises to alter the apparent time of death. In *Double Indemnity,* insurance salesman Walter Neff strangles the husband of his lover, Phyllis Dietrichson, as she drives her husband to the train station for a trip to Palo Alto, California. To establish alibis (and to collect double on an insurance policy for accidental death), Walter disguises himself as the husband, boards the train and jumps off to make it appear as if the husband died later than he did and that it was an accidental death caused by falling off the train.

Authors have developed other creative ways to mask the time of death. In *The Murder of Roger Ackroyd*, Agatha Christie has Dr. Sheppard leave Roger Ackroyd's office. A servant later hears Ackroyd talking to someone, which sets the apparent time of death after Sheppard left, but Hercule Poirot realizes the phrasing of the "conversation" sounds like the dictation of a letter, not a conversation. Dr. Sheppard used a Dictaphone recording to make it appear that Ackroyd was alive after he murdered Ackroyd. Christie also has her murderer/narrator manipulate time merely by skipping 10 minutes in his narrative during which he committed the murder.

You can also manipulate time by using flashbacks. Audiences tend to believe flashbacks are true and forget they can just be one character's memories, which may be purposefully or mistakenly distorted. Hitchcock's *Stage Fright* begins with actor Jonathan Cooper telling aspiring actress Eve Gill in a flashback about a murder in which he helped his former lover after she murdered her husband. Cooper asks Gill for her help. The flashback is a cover story and it is not until near the end of the film that the real story is revealed: Cooper murdered his lover's husband. Hitchcock was criticized for the flashback, but he asked, "Now, why can't a man tell a lie? I don't know. But people complained, 'Ah, you cheated us on the flashback.' Can't he be a liar?"

Time can be manipulated in adventure stories, probably most famously in Jules Verne's *Around the World in Eighty Days*. Phileas Fogg makes a £20,000 (about $1.6 million in today's money) bet with his Reform Club friends that with modern transportation circa the 1870s he can travel around the world in 80 days. Fogg and his valet race around the world, only to arrive back in London one day late. Fogg will be ruined financially. In the final scenes, the day after they arrive home, the valet meets a minister to arrange Fogg's marriage to an Indian woman they met on their journey and discovers they have gained a day by traveling eastward around the world. Fogg arrives at the Reform Club in the nick of time, wins the bet, avoids destitution, and marries his lady love. In a way Verne didn't manipulate time, he just used a real phenomenon to deceive and surprise the audience.

Playing with the linear structure of a story is another way to manipulate time to deceive an audience. In William Goldman's novel *Brothers*, an assassin working for a shadowy US government department sneaks into the Belgrave Square, London home of the director of his organization and surprises the director as he takes a shower. Instead of describing how the assassin gained entry and hid in the mansion flat first, Goldman has the director come home, check the flat with his bodyguards and then, after positioning guards outside, settle in to take his shower, only to be surprised by the assassin. Only then does Goldman flash back to show how the assassin gained entry. By reversing the order of events, Goldman ensures the reader is surprised when the assassin appears outside the director's shower, yet is also shown how the assassin cleverly gained entry.

In a more complex example, the film *Memento* includes a series of black-and-white scenes that are shown chronologically and a series of color scenes shown in reverse order. The two series converge at the end of the film to create one cohesive story. The main character, Leonard Shelby, has anterograde amnesia and can't store recent memories. In searching for one of the men who raped and murdered his wife (he killed the other one but was struck during the fight causing his amnesia), Leonard uses tattoos on his body to remember key clues. Only at the end do viewers learn the real story: Leonard has already killed the other man and continually searches for a man with a common name as the rapist/murderer to continue to have a goal in his life or...who knows why?

Questions for Authors:

Can you change the order of scenes or of time in your real story or any of your cover stories to mislead readers, yet still make a logical, plausible and interesting novel or script?

Can you use a flashback to mask clues about the motive, means or the identity of the murderer? Can you start your story with a flashback to bury a key clue early by setting it in a different time frame so the audience is likely to forget the clue by the end of the novel or film?

Can the murderer use a watch, video, computer, cell phone, candle, body-double, or some other method to alter the apparent time of death and establish an alibi? Can your murderer use slow-acting poison to establish an alibi? Can the poison be added to something that is taken much later?

Can the order of two deaths be switched? Can a body be moved so the victim appears to have died at a different time, such as hit by a train, bus or car at a specific time?

Can your murderer use a body double to appear to "find" the victim before the murder even happens?

To increase the dramatic impact, can you show the climax of a series of scenes before showing what led to the climax?

Common Mistakes and How to Fix Them:

Playing with time can be fun and interesting, but doing it too much can lead to confusion for your audience, as well as for you. If you plan to manipulate time, a chart of what happens when can be useful. It's easy to become confused during the writing of a novel or script that involves the manipulation of time. (A chart of *Memento* looks as confusing as a diagram for the construction of a space shuttle). One trick is to write the story in chronological order chapter by chapter or scene by scene and, once the structure is established, reverse or rearrange the order of the chapters or scenes. Then you can edit the story to ensure that appropriate introductory information about each character and setting occurs when the character or setting is first mentioned, and to check for other problems related to the flow of the re-ordered story. The search feature on word-processing programs can help you easily find the first mention of each character and setting.

If you're having trouble keeping track of your plot in terms of time, then your readers could face a nightmare and give up. If you are playing with time, go through your draft and make note of when scenes occur chronologically and when you have them in your novel or script. Ask yourself why certain scenes are out of order and why they occur when they do. You should have dramatic reasons for manipulating time. If not, a more linear structure may serve your story better. If it is difficult to follow your story, you might add a tag line before each section with a time reference, or use a descriptive device such as the age of a character to highlight when a scene occurs to make it easier for readers to follow.

Chapter 15

Red Herrings

In the real world a red herring is a smoked fish with a strong scent that is said to throw hunting dogs off the scent of their quarry. (The TV show *The Mythbusters* in "Fool the Bloodhound" used red herrings to throw a bloodhound off a "fugitive's" scent and, although the bloodhound stopped to eat the fish, the dog back-tracked, found the trail, and located the "fugitive.") In a mystery, red herrings are used to divert attention from a key clue or suspect and focus attention on another clue or suspect. Red herrings seek to make the audience certain, but wrong that an innocent suspect is the villain, or a clue is crucial when it is irrelevant to the real crime.

Red herrings are not only used in fiction. Diplomats, spymasters, generals, conmen, and magicians use red herrings to deceive adversaries, marks or audiences. In the fall of 1940, the Japanese continued negotiations with the United States over Japan's invasion of China even after they had begun military planning to seize the

Dutch East Indies, Singapore, and the Philippines, and to attack the US Pacific Fleet at Pearl Harbor. The negotiations were a red herring to distract US attention from the coming Japanese attack. In 1944, as the Allies prepared to invade Western Europe, their various deception plans to convince the Germans that the landings would be anywhere and anytime but Normandy on June 6 were all red herrings. In the 1980s, the Iranians developed a covert deception operation to convince the US government that there were moderate Iranians in the Tehran government who could arrange the release of Western hostages in Lebanon in exchange for arms. The "moderates" in the Iranian government did not exist. They were red herrings.

Magicians' use of misdirection is similar to red herrings. Misdirection is the art of having the audience focus on one thing (the cover story), while the magician does something crucial to the trick somewhere else (the real story). When a manacled Houdini was lowered into his water-filled cabinet, his assistants dropped him in so the water would splash. It looked dramatic, but the splash was misdirection (a red herring). The real story was that the assistants dropped Houdini in with a splash so some of the water from the full cabinet would slosh out, leaving an air gap for Houdini to use to breath while he performed his escape.

Conmen use red herrings in con games. When conmen salt a mine, they want the mark to focus on the amount of gold in the sample (the red herring) and not consider how the gold got there. Various Who's Who directories charge a small fee to include your name with the promise of appearing next to top people in your field (the red herring), hoping you never research how rarely, if ever, such directories are accessed.

Just as generals, diplomats, magicians, and conmen deceive their adversaries, audience or marks with red herrings, authors use red herrings to deceive their audiences. Red herrings work because a red herring looks the same as a clue to the real story. In *The Mysterious Affair at Styles*, Poirot finds ashes in a fireplace grate on a hot summer day. Who would have a fire on a hot day? The ashes are a crucial clue in the murder of a wealthy woman. The ashes, however, could just as easily have been a red herring. They still would have been just ashes in a fireplace. The fact is the same; the interpretation is what makes the fact a red herring or a clue to the real crime.

Authors sometimes play with the very name of this deceptive technique. The character Bishop Aringarosa in Dan Brown's *The Da Vinci Code* is a red herring. The bishop is presented in such a way that readers suspect him of being the mastermind behind the conspiracy in the church. Aringarosa helps the murderer, Silas, travel, and facilitates Silas's pursuit of the hero, American symbologist Robert Langdon. Later it is revealed that Aringarosa is not the man behind the conspiracy. Readers might have got a hint of the character's purpose if they spoke Italian; Aringarosa translates as "red" (*rosa*) "herring" (*aringa*). If Brown had wanted to add another deceptive twist to his character's name he would have called the bishop Falsapista, since the Italian name for a red herring is *falsa pista* or false track.

Agatha Christie uses a similar ploy in *And Then There Were None*. When there are four people left alive on the island, Dr. Armstrong goes missing. The remaining three and the audience assume Armstrong is the killer. Later his body is found on the shore. Astute readers might have referred back to the poem about the 10 little Indians at the start of the novel in which it states: "Four little Indian Boys going out to sea; A red herring swallowed one and then there were three." Dr. Armstrong was the fourth last to die, so the audience might conclude his death is a red herring and he is the murderer. Christie doesn't make it that simple. The real murderer, Judge Wargrave, convinced Dr. Armstrong to help fake Wargrave's death in an attempt to unmask the murderer. Wargrave's death is a red herring and it costs Armstrong his life when Wargrave murders him; just as the poem foretold, a red herring did "swallow" Armstrong.

You can have your villain use red herrings to achieve their nefarious goals. In Conan Doyle's "The Final Problem," the criminal mastermind Professor Moriarty uses a red herring to isolate Sherlock Holmes. Dr. Watson and Holmes are walking in the Swiss mountains. A messenger arrives to say that a woman has fallen ill at the hotel and she will only consent to be seen by an English doctor. Watson returns to the hotel only to find there is no medical emergency. Moriarty has isolated Holmes for a final confrontation during which the pair fall off Reichenbach Falls.

You also can have your villain use a red herring to try to clear themselves. In Christie's *And Then There Were None*, Judge Wargrave's fake death is a red herring that appears to remove him from the suspect list. In *Crooked House*, Christie has the murderer, a young girl, fake an attempt on her own life as a red herring. The girl balances a heavy doorstop on the top of a door of a little-used shed, on which everyone in a country house knows she often swings. The weight hits her head but does not kill her. Everyone concludes that the murderer has attempted to kill her, clearing her of any suspicion. In the *Midsomer Murders* episode "Judgement Day," the murderer adds poison to a wine bottle, which she then uses to pour wine at an event for her victim. Even as the victim drinks her wine, the murderer takes a sip of her own wine, which is also poisoned. The murderer then wretches, spins around and crashes down onto the table holding wine glasses filled with the rest of the wine from the poisoned bottle, as well as from all the other bottles. The murderer thereby makes it appear that she was also a victim even as she destroys any chance the police have of determining how much poison was used and in how many bottles. Was the poisoning meant for one, two or dozens of victims?

Often the villain uses a red herring to direct suspicion toward another character. Grimaud frames Fley in John Dickson Carr's *Three Coffins* and in *Towards Zero*, Christie has Neville Strange frame his wife. In *The Murder of Roger Ackroyd*, Christie has her murderer, Dr. Sheppard, use another character's stolen shoes to make boot prints on the window ledge outside the room where the murder occurred to frame the other character.

Authors often use another character as a red herring to direct suspicion away from the villain, even if the villain has nothing to do with creating the red herring. In *The Bodyguard*, Whitney Houston plays singer Rachel Marron. When a stalker's obsession appears to reach dangerous levels, former Secret Service agent Frank Farmer (Kevin Costner) is hired to protect her. Someone makes an attempt on Rachel's life and Frank (and the audience) assumes the stalker and the person trying to kill her are the same person. It is only later that Frank realizes the stalker and the killer are not the same individual: the stalker is a red herring.

In *Peril at End House*, Agatha Christie makes it appear the wrong woman (a cousin) has been murdered because she borrowed the shawl of the supposed "right" woman, who someone had already attempted to murder. The red herring is that the "wrong" woman was the murderer's real target. By changing the apparent target of a murder, Christie directs suspicion away from the murderer and adds a deceptive layer of suspects while following Raymond Chandler's advice to set the reader to solving the wrong mystery.

Elizabeth George in *For the Sake of Elena*, created a suspicious character, Justine Weaver, to distract readers from the real murderer. Justine is the second wife of a man whose daughter, Elena, is murdered. Justine is neat, unemotional and cold, the perfect description to make readers dislike her and think her capable of murder. "Cold" is one of the most negative words you can use to describe a character. George piles on the incriminating evidence against Justine:

- She hated the victim because her husband loved his daughter, taking time away from her
- She was supposed to run with her step-daughter that morning, but said she got a call no one heard from Elena saying she was not going, even though Elena did go running
- Justine usually ran with her dog, but did not that morning, suggesting she needed to be dog-free to murder Elena
- She knew where, when and for how long Elena ran

The stack of clues pointing to Justine as the murderer is designed to make readers certain, but wrong. They are all red herrings designed to distract readers from the real murderer.

Sometimes a character other than the villain makes another character a red herring. In Ross Macdonald's *The Chill*, Helen Haggerty, a visiting professor at a university, is murdered. Lew Archer, Macdonald's detective hero, learns that a college dean, Roy Bradshaw, was seeing Helen. Lew discovers that Helen was blackmailing Roy over an old previous marriage. It appears that Roy murdered Helen, but Macdonald has laid a careful trail of red herrings leading away from the murderer. In the real story, Roy fell in love with Laura Sutherland, dean of women, but Roy lives with his mother, Letitia, who years before murdered her sister's husband because they were having an affair and Letitia was jealous of her sister. In reality, Letitia is not Roy's mother, but his wife. (Remember, novels need not be likely, just plausible). When Roy falls for Laura, he fears Letitia will murder her, so he feigns interest in Helen, making

Helen a red herring. Roy's jealous wife Letitia mistakes Helen for
Roy's real love interest and murders her.

Another type of red herring is an infinite clue; a clue that rules
out few, if any suspects. In Agatha Christie's *Towards Zero,* old Mr.
Treves tells a story about a boy who killed another child with a
bow and arrow years before. The death was ruled an accident, even
though Treves said he heard that the boy who shot the arrow was
seen practicing with the bow days before the accident. The boy had
a distinctive physical characteristic, which Treves does not describe.
That night Treves dies of a suspected heart attack. The apparent
clue of a distinctive physical characteristic is an infinite clue, since
several characters have distinctive physical characteristics, such as
a lock of white hair, a stiff right arm and an oddly shaped skull. In
fact, the physical characteristic, which Treves said he would be able
to recognize even in the adult, was the murderer's little finger on
the left hand is shorter than the right, not exactly the most apparent
physical characteristic. (Christie also made Treves's story a red herring in another way. The flashback is key not because it helps identify the murderer through some physical trait, but because the old
murder had the same motive as the current murder: pride. Neville
Strange murders his first wife because she left him and she is about
to remarry, something his pride cannot abide.)

Authors often use a detective's sidekick to divert attention away
from a crucial clue, a type of red herring. Dr. Watson and Captain
Hastings often perform this function in the Holmes and Poirot
stories. As Poirot says in *The Mystery of the Spanish Chest*, "What
ineptitudes he (Hastings) would have uttered" if he had been present. Often the detective will point out a clue that later turns out to
be crucial, but the sidekick then asks a question or makes a statement that takes the audience in an entirely new direction, masking
the real clue. This phenomenon is much like a magician diverting
the audience's attention by tossing a ball in the air with one hand
while performing the trick's crucial sleight of hand with the other.
In *Murder on the Links*, Hastings views the old clothes that the victim, Paul Reynaud, planned to use to disguise himself with after
faking his own death. The clothes are crucial to solving the mystery,
but Hastings dismisses them by asking whether they are the gar-
dener's. Since Hastings is only in eight Poirot novels and plays, local
police often fill the sidekick role for Poirot. In *The Murder of Roger*

Ackroyd, Agatha Christie has Inspector Raglan say that a chair that has been pulled out from the wall in the room in which Ackroyd was murdered is of no importance. In truth, the chair is crucial. It was moved to hide a Dictaphone machine that played back the victim's voice after his murder to alter the apparent time of death. Sometimes a sidekick mentions a clue, but the clue is a red herring. In *The West End Horror*, Nicholas Meyer has Watson suggest that when a dying man pulled a copy of *Romeo and Juliet* off the shelf, it suggested the murder was related to two warring newspapers: *The Morning Courant*, edited by the murdered man, and *The Saturday Review*, edited by a rival. It is, however, a red herring and has nothing to do with the murder.

You can have a sidekick point at a crucial clue, but obliquely or with an incorrect interpretation so the key meaning is hidden. In Agatha Christie's *The A.B.C. Murders*, Hastings says something crucial, but not in the way he means. Hastings says the third letter of warning from the murderer, which was misaddressed, may have gone "astray intentionally." The key question for Poirot is not Hasting's question—why the letter went astray—but why the letters were addressed to Poirot in the first place? Sending the letters to Poirot and not to Scotland Yard is crucial. A letter misaddressed to the famous Scotland Yard would still be delivered on time, while one misaddressed to Poirot would be delayed. Therefore, the third letter arrives late and the third victim, the wealthy Sir Carmichael Clarke, is not warned and is murdered—and his murder is the key crime. The other three murders are dazzle masking the greed-driven murder of Sir Carmichael Clarke.

You can mislead your audience by just not mentioning a key fact; a red herring by omission. In Agatha Christie's *Towards Zero*, a key part of the mystery involves the isolation of a house on a promontory between a river and the sea. The mystery centers on who arrived and left via the single path/road to the house. The reader never thinks to question the house's isolation and the locked-room mystery Christie has created, yet the key to the solution rests on the fact that someone who was across the river from the house swam the river to reach the house to commit the murder. Christie plays fair by mentioning how fit the murderer is, since he is an ex-professional tennis player, but she never mentions the key clue that someone could swim across the river; a red herring by omission. (This red herring is strengthened for North America readers, since many rivers in North American are far from swimmable, while most in England are much narrower.)

Red herrings include misattributions, in which the reader concludes that a character is reacting to one thing when they are really reacting to something else, or when a behavior or words are misinterpreted. With words or phrases that have double meanings, the reader will invariably jump to the more common meaning or the meaning that appears to fit the context better, leaving ample room for deception. In Ruth Rendell's *Wolf to the Slaughter*, the key suspect is a woman's husband. Unfortunately for the detectives and the audience, the woman has two "husbands": a current husband and her ex-husband. The police and most readers focus on her current husband, but the more important "husband" for solving the mystery is her ex-husband.

In Ngaio Marsh's short story "Death of a Fool," a man is murdered during a masked and costumed folk dance. One of his son's yells that she's "the one what (sic) done it" and points at a Mrs. Bunz. Readers may jump to the conclusion that Bunz is guilty of murder. Bunz is guilty, but not of murder. The son was not referring to murder when he made his accusation. Bunz bribed one of the folk dancers so she could participate in the male-only costumed dance. The superstitious son yells because he believes that by violating the male-only tradition of the dance, Bunz caused the death.

In the *Midsomer Murders* episode "Judgement Day," the wife of a vet, Gordon Brierly, finds a pair of blood-splattered trousers in his closet. She confronts him, asking if it is blood from the recent murder of Peter Drinkwater, a local rogue. Before he can answer, she asks if it is animal blood. He grins and replies with a malicious grin that yes, it is animal blood from a vile little creature that he had to put out of its misery. Since Gordon knows his wife was having an affair with Drinkwater, the implication is that Gordon murdered Drinkwater. Even his wife believes he did it. Gordon has purposely misled his wife, however. Later he admits that he didn't kill Drinkwater. He just wanted her to think he did so she would suffer for cheating on him.

Even having a dying character point at his murderer can be misinterpreted. In the *Midsomer Murders* episode "Death in Disguise," a dying Iain Craigie points at his killer, but the room is crowded.

Almost everyone in the room believes he is pointing at the ruthless businessman Guy Gamelin, with whom he had recently argued. It takes DCI Tom Barnaby some time to realize that Craigie was pointing at the man standing just to the side of Gamelin, the young and popular Chris Wainwright, who is the murderer.

Behavior other than pointing also can be misinterpreted. In the 2013 British mini-series *The Guilty* a boy goes missing. The prime suspect is a handyman. After his arrest it appears that the case is solved, but then the father recalls that his older son held his younger son's head under water in the bathtub just before the younger son disappeared. The father (and the audience) jump to the conclusion that the older son murdered his little brother. When he later found his son's body, the father, wanting to protect his surviving son from a murder charge, hid the younger boy's body. Then the older son explains that a neighbor's boy showed them a game in which children half-strangled themselves to see stars and hallucinate. The younger son was fascinated and asked the older son to start to drown him in the bathtub, which the father witnessed and misinterpreted as attempted murder. When the father later found the younger son's strangled body, he thought his older son had murdered the younger boy. The truth is the younger son was playing the "game" of strangling himself and died by accident.

An often used type of red herring is based on the fact that an alibi provides an alibi for the person alibied, as well as for the person providing the alibi. In Ruth Rendell's *Wolf to the Slaughter*, Linda Grover tells the police she was at a party the night of a murder when she spotted Alan Kirkpatrick, the victim's recently dumped boyfriend, lurking outside the party, apparently waiting for the victim. Her claim is a red herring. Alan was nowhere near the party, but Linda is both framing Alan and providing herself with an alibi.

Some authors even use a title as a red herring. Stanley Kubrick and Jim Thompson's film *The Killing* is the story of a recently released convict who assembles a gang to rob $2 million from Landsdowne racetrack. The title primes the audience for a single killing, but in the finest tradition of red herrings that assumption is shattered when there are far more than just one killing. In a taut 83 minutes, the story winds tighter and tighter to a wonderfully powerful final three-word sentence by the anti-hero; see it if you can. Richard Hall's wonderful *Murder of My Aunt* also uses the title as a red herring with a double meaning. I am willing to spoil the surprises in most novels and movies to teach about deception, but not for *Murder of My Aunt*. To find out how Hall's title is a red herring, read it and enjoy.

Red herrings are not only used in mysteries. In *Great Expectations*, Charles Dickens created the character of Pip, a young man with a secret, wealthy benefactor. The reader assumes the benefactor is Miss Havisham, an elderly eccentric who kindly takes Pip into her home. Only later does the reader learn that Miss Havisham is a red herring who helped Pip to exact revenge on a man who left her at the altar. Pip's real benefactor is an escaped convict, whom Pip helped as a boy.

William Goldman makes full use of red herrings in his excellent coming-of-age novel *The Color of Light*. Charley "Chub" Fuller is a blocked writer, who meets a rain-soaked girl on his doorstep one night. They begin an affair and she moves in, even though he has an on-and-off girlfriend, an ex-model nicknamed The Bone. The new girl talks about suicide, even perching on a windowsill of Fuller's high-rise apartment one night. One day at 12:30 pm, she is found dead on the pavement, having fallen or been pushed out of Fuller's window. Besides the possibility of suicide, Goldman has established two possible murderers: an ex-boyfriend and a violent ex-student of Fuller's. All three possibilities are red herrings and, reminiscent of von Moltke's quote, the real story is a fourth possibility. Fuller refuses to believe his lover committed suicide. She appeared happy and loved watching TV game shows and soaps. She would never miss them, yet she died when such shows air and the TV was even left on. Having ruled out suicide, Fuller discovers his ex-student wasn't even in town when his lover died. Fuller also rules out the ex-boyfriend, who talks to Fuller about marrying the girl, since he doesn't appear to even know the girl is dead. Since the novel is more of a coming-of-age story than a murder mystery, readers may conclude the mystery will remain just that, a mystery, with the preponderance of evidence coming down on the side of suicide. Then, in the final scene Goldman reveals the real story when Fuller meets his girlfriend, The Bone. In a dramatic twist and an excellent example of withholding information as late as possible for maximum dramatic impact, the second to last sentence of the novel has The Bone recall that yes, the television was on in

Fuller's apartment when his lover went out the window. The Bone murdered her boyfriend's lover.

If you write science fiction your characters can create red herrings. In the film *Intersteller*, Matthew McConaughey stars as Joe Cooper, a widowed former NASA pilot who is recruited for a mission to find mankind a new home. Blights have made farming increasingly difficult on Earth and mankind's existence is threatened. Twelve volunteers have journeyed through a wormhole to find new potential home planets for humans from among a dozen potential new home worlds. Cooper leads a mission to investigate three planets about which the volunteers have sent encouraging reports. They investigate one planet, which turns out to be uninhabitable, due to massive tidal waves. With two left to choose from, Joe chooses one first explored by Dr. Mann (Matt Damon), a hero and the leader of the first group of volunteers. After landing on Mann's world, Joe and his team learn that Mann and his data are red herrings. Not wanting to be abandoned to die, Mann has been faking data to make his world look more habitable.

Thrillers, spy, con-game, and heist stories often use red herrings. If a group of characters is planning an operation, such as robbing a bank, rescuing a kidnapped heiress or overthrowing a government, an author faces a choice: explain the plan up front or show the plan unfolding as it happens. If the former, then the plan must not go as planned or the audience will be bored, in effect seeing the same story twice. In such cases the explanation of the plan as discussed by the group is a red herring, in that the operation does not go as expected. *The Sting* involves a con game centered on a horse-racing betting parlor. The audience learns what is supposed to happen from the point of view of the lead character, Johnny "Kelly" Hooker (Robert Redford), but then author David S. Ward has several things go wrong, including the arrival of a female hitman, to deceive and surprise the audience. If the author doesn't explain the plan, then everything can go as planned and no red herring is involved. In 1949's *White Heat*, as a gang prepares to rob a train, the lead robber asks one his henchmen if he knows what to do. The henchman starts to explain, but since the robbery goes according to plan, the leader barks not to bother talking and just do it. The heist largely goes as planned. Even if the plan goes smoothly, it should be creative and dramatic, such as in the 1955 French crime film, *Rififi*. The audience watches a gang break into a jeweler's store. The thieves creatively use an umbrella inserted through a drilled hole to catch debris as they chisel through the floor from an apartment above the jeweler's store, so the debris will not set off the alarm system. The entire sequence is packed full of creative and entertaining touches.

Questions for Authors:

Are there red herrings throughout your story to direct the audience to other explanations of the crime? Other suspects? Other means, methods and opportunities?

Does your villain set false clues (red herrings) for the detective hero? Does the villain frame another character or two? Can the murderer fake an attempt on his own life?

Can you create a scene, action, line, or reaction that has multiple possible interpretations, which will deceive your audience?

Can your detective hero's sidekick divert the audience's attention after the hero mentions a crucial clue? Can the sidekick focus attention on a red herring?

Can you make the target of a murder appear uncertain, as if the victim might have died in a case of mistaken identity?

If you are writing a love story, do you have rival love interests for the heroine who appear as if they could be the real Mr. Right? Does Mr. Right have another suitor who appears to be his Mrs. Right?

Can your title be a red herring with multiple meanings?

Can a character be other than what he or she appears to be? An unsavory character who act honorably? An honorable character that lies, cheats or steals?

Common Mistakes and How to Fix Them:

Red herrings should not be so obvious that readers see through them upon first reading. Just as with cover stories, your red herrings should be as well developed, plausible and realistic as your real clues and suspects. Make sure your red herrings have a subtle flaw that your detective heroine can notice to show their brilliance and reveal the truth.

Chapter 16

Camouflage and Disguises

Camouflage is used to hide something of importance by making it blend into the background, while disguises make something look like something else. Individuals, buildings, machines, beliefs, motivations, behaviors, and practically anything else can be camouflaged or disguised.

Camouflage and disguises are common in warfare. The Mongols raised dust clouds with their horses to disguise the size of their armies. During the Boer War (1899-1902), the British discarded their famous red coats for khaki to camouflage their men. In World War II, the British developed explosives disguised as dog and horse excrement to distribute to partisans to disable German vehicles on roads in occupied Europe. In 1982, during the Falklands War, the British bombed the air strip at Stanley and, based on craters visible in reconnaissance photos, believed they had disabled the airfield. It was only after they landed when their troops heard the sound of cargo plane engines at night that the British realized the Argentines had used fake craters to disguise the operational field as damaged. The Argentines only used the airfield at night to maintain the deception. Submarines use the vast oceans as camouflage to hide, while soldiers today wear multi-colored uniforms to blend into the terrain.

Spies are known for their disguises. CIA officer Antonio Mendez was a master of disguise. Using disguises, he helped hundreds of people escape from perilous situations in operations called exfiltrations, including helping six Americans trapped in Tehran during the 1979-80 Iranian hostage crisis escape, which was dramatized in the movie *Argo*. A mole uses their fellow employees, who look and appear to act the same as the mole, as camouflage. Kim Philby, Aldrich Ames and Oleg Penkovsky did not look any more like double-agents than their loyal colleagues.

Buildings can be disguised. In December 1942, a German agent landed in Britain, was captured and agreed to work for the British. Code-named Fritz, the agent started sending information vetted by the British back to Germany. To ensure he was believed, the British had Fritz sent reports on a fictitious spy ring he was developing, and even planned and carried out an attack on an aircraft factory. With the judicious use of paint and debris from building sites, the British created scenes on the roof of several of the aircraft factory's buildings that appeared, at least from the air, to confirm that Fritz had successfully led an attack on the factory. German aerial reconnaissance confirmed the attack and from then on the Germans placed great credibility in every piece of information Fritz sent them.

Conmen use shills in the crowd disguised as regular people. The shill may be the first to buy a questionable product or the one in a three-card Monte game who bends the corner of the Queen when the dealer appears to be distracted. The shill then places a large bet, apparently certain he will be able to spot the Queen, which convinces the marks around him to put their money down on what appears to be a sure thing, but isn't.

Magicians use confederates in the audience and often disguise or camouflage objects. A confederate in the audience can assist in a mind-reading experiment or check that manacles are tight around the magician's wrists when they are not. Props can be painted black and set against a black curtain so they are camouflaged and appear to disappear. A magician can make a heavy metal ball float. In reality, the ball is a helium balloon painted metallic to disguise it as a metal ball. Conversely, a magnetized metal ball can be covered with a soft fabric to make it appear to be entirely made of cloth. The magician can then make metal magically stick to the "cloth" ball.

Just as con men, magicians and spies use disguises and camouflage, mystery writers sometimes have their detective heroes don disguises to further their investigations, as well as deceive other characters and the audience. Conan Doyle has Sherlock Holmes use a range of disguises, including an old clergyman ("A Scandal in Bohemia"), an opium addict ("The Man with the Twisted Lip"), an elderly Italian priest ("The Adventure of the Final Problem"), a bookseller ("The Adventure of the Empty House"), a plumber ("The Adventure of Charles Augustus Milverton"), and even a dying man ("The Adventure of the Dying Detective"). In Dorothy L. Sayers's *Murder Must Advertise*, Lord Peter Wimsey uses a disguise to go undercover at an advertising agency. In *The West End Horror,* Nicholas Meyer has Holmes disguise himself as a Plymouth estate agent who tells Watson that Holmes has lost all his money when land he owned in Torquay fell into the ocean, showing that you can use a disguise for comedic purposes.

In one sense, mystery authors always camouflage their murderer as just another character to deceive other characters and their audience. Beyond that universal technique, some authors also have the murderer use a disguise to commit a murder. In Agatha Christie's *Sparkling Cyanide,* the murderer disguises himself as a waiter to put poison unnoticed in a drink at a dinner party. She used a similar technique in *Death in the Clouds.* On an airliner, the murderer dons a white jacket to impersonate a steward in order to stab a passenger with a poisoned thorn as he passes by. In her long-running play *The Mousetrap,* Christie has the murderer disguise himself as a police detective to escape from one murder and find out information to attempt to commit another murder. In Ellery Queen's *The Egyptian Cross Mystery,* the villain had a limp as a child, so Queen searches for a suspect with a limp. The murderer, however, has been cured of his limp and to throw the authorities of his trail only limps when he is committing his crimes.

Murderers can use disguises to mislead detectives (and audiences) about alibis. In Christie's *Lord Edgware Dies*, actress Jane Wilkinson is suspected of murdering her husband so she can marry another man, but she has an alibi. At the time of the murder she was attending a dinner party with 12 friends, even though a witness places her at the scene of the crime. Poirot discovers that Carlotta Adams, another actress who has impersonated Jane on stage, attended the dinner as Jane while Jane went to murder her husband. In a similar fashion, in *One, Two, Buckle My Shoe*, Christie has an actress impersonate another woman to deceive the reader about who was where, when. The victim is also misidentified because medical records have been switched, which is another now common method of disguising the identity of a body.

Murderers can also use disguises to frame another character. In Alfred Hitchcock's *I Confess*, the murderer wears a priest's cassock when he leaves the scene of a murder in Quebec City, Canada. A priest becomes the prime suspect, especially when the murderer, who is not a priest, hides the cassock he wore stained with the victim's blood in the suspected priest's room. In *The Mysterious Affair at Styles*, Christie has a woman dress like a man to buy poison from a chemist to incriminate the man she is disguised as.

Murderers can also use disguises to hide previous murders. In the *Midsomer Murders* episode "Judgement Day," a child-murderer has grown up, married and settled down in an English village. Her disguise as a normal, well-adjusted wife and mother is shattered by the appearance of a woman who was at a local psychiatric home with her years before who might recognize her and reveal her bloody past. The child-murderer murders again to preserve her disguise.

Murders can fake their own death and assume a disguise. In Agatha Christie's *Murder in Mesopotamia*, a woman's second husband is really her first husband in disguise. He used the opportunity of a train wreck to fake his own death and, disguised, keep his former wife from marrying again and, finally, to remarry her years later before killing her. The motive for the murder is tied to the disguise, since the motive, jealousy, only makes sense if the reader realizes the second husband is the first husband.

Not only murderers but other types of criminals can use disguises. In Christie's *At Bertram's Hotel*, a criminal gang uses actors to pose as gang members to provide alibis for a string of burglaries. In the 1988 motion picture *Die Hard*, terrorists take over a new high-rise building in Los Angeles and make a list of demands about releasing their terrorist brethren or they will blow up the building. The terrorist angle turns out to be a disguise to mask the criminals' true purpose of robbing a safe in the building of $640 million in bearer bonds. In the *Midsomer Murders* episode "Faithful Unto Death," a woman stages her own kidnapping and then has a makeup-expert friend disguise her as a victim of a beating. Photos of her "beaten" face are sent to her husband to convince him to pay a ransom.

Twins are an old form of disguise that can cause readers to mistake a character's identity. Twins are often used in comedies. Shakespeare's *Twelfth Night* features a female twin who disguises herself as a man, and his *Comedy of Errors* has twin masters and twin servants who switch identities causing no end of confusion and comedic misunderstandings. Although S.S. Van Dine warned as long ago as 1928 that no self-respecting detective story writer would pin the crime on a twin, twins are still used occasionally as a form of disguise for murderers. In the poorly received 2004 television movie *Sherlock Holmes and the Case of the Silk Stocking*, twin brothers collude to murder several young women. You should avoid twins as a deceptive twist unless you can develop a new take on twins for your novel, play or script.

Even without using twins, you can use resemblances between two characters to deceive readers. "Twinned" characters can be similar in appearance, personality, behavior, or some other trait. In Conan Doyle's *The Hound of the Baskervilles*, a man with a black beard follows Holmes and Watson. Watson (and probably readers) concludes the man is Barrymore, the caretaker of Baskerville Hall, because he is the only character in the story with a black beard. The man following the detective duo is in fact a man called Stapleton wearing a beard as a disguise. He is a neighbor and distant relative of the Baskervilles, and the murderer. In Christie's *Peril at End House*, a woman is killed and the reader is led to believe erroneously that it was not only because she looked like her cousin (a "twin"), who had been the target of several previous murder attempts, but she was also wearing her cousin's jacket (a disguise). In this case the murderer got it right; the victim was the target of the murderer, although authors can have murderers deceived by characters who look similar. In Elizabeth George's *For the Sake of Elena*, a second murder is committed after a young woman in Cambridge is murdered while jogging. Inspector Lynley and Sergeant Havers attempt to tie the second girl to the first, but get nowhere. There is nothing to find because it turns out the murderer killed the second girl by mistake. The murderer meant to kill a witness who was also jogging and bore a resemblance to the unintended victim.

A disguise need not just be clothing or appearance. Characters can disguise their feelings, motivations or even their health from other characters and the audience. In Christie's *The Mysterious Affair at Styles*, a real loving couple acts as if they hate each other and are not even a couple so no one will believe they acted in concert to murder the man's older, wealthy wife. The couple use hate to disguise love. Christie's *Witness for the Prosecution* used the same basic idea: the loving wife is disguised as a wife who loathes her husband so a jury will believe her testimony, which then helps get him acquitted of a murder charge. In Christie's *Hickory Dickory Dock*, a British student at a boarding house fakes a neurosis to try to attract the romantic attentions of a young psychologist. The disguise has little to do with the murder in the novel, but it serves as a deceptive cover story. In *Curtain: Poirot's Last Case*, Hercule Poirot disguises the state of his health so no one will think he can walk. Poirot even dismisses his long-serving valet to ensure the effectiveness of his disguise. His apparent incapacity is crucial to Poirot's plan to execute a murderer who persuades others to murder for him and, therefore, will never be brought to justice.

In films, perhaps the greatest and most extensive use of disguises was in the 1963 movie *The List of Adrian Messenger*, based on Philip Macdonald's entertaining eponymous 1959 novel. Some of the most famous actors and actresses of the time don disguises to play various characters, including Kirk Douglas, Tony Curtis, Burt Lancaster, Frank Sinatra, and Robert Mitchum. The disguises are not central to the mystery, but they add a deceptive layer to the movie, since part of the fun is trying to determine which character is which famous actor. More recently, *Face/Off* told the tale of an FBI agent and a psychopathic terrorist who each undergo a face transplant to look like the other; the agent is disguised as the villain and the villain is disguised as the agent.

Camouflage and disguises are used in romances, thrillers, horror, science fiction, film noir, and even epics. In the play *Cyrano de Bergerac*, Christian borrows Cyrano's poetry to woo Roxane, disguising himself as a witty wordsmith. In the 1996 romantic-comedy *Bridget Jones's Diary*, Helen Fielding masterfully disguises the moral attributes of Bridget's two main love interests: Daniel Cleaver and Mark Darcy. Mr. Right is disguised as Mr. Wrong and Mr. Wrong as Mr. Right. Daniel tells Bridget that his university friendship with Mark broke up when Mark slept with Daniel's fiancée. The information appears to confirm that Daniel, despite his womanizing reputation, is moral and may truly be in love with Bridget, while Mark is amoral and not the staid, sober and serious man he appears to be. It is only late in the novel/film that Bridget learns the real story: the men's friendship broke up when Daniel slept with Mark's wife, not the other way around. Romantic heroines can also assume disguises. The romantic-comedy *While You Were Sleeping* is based on a lonely subway token collector (Sandra Bullock) disguising herself as the fiancée of a handsome commuter who has an accident and falls into a coma. Her disguise leads to comedy and romance, but not with her secret crush; she falls for his brother.

In conspiracies, the conspirators always try to blend into the background (camouflage) and avoid attention. By definition, if a conspiracy becomes public it is no longer a conspiracy. At the end of the thriller *Three Days of the Condor*, the hero played by Robert Redford awaits his fate after taking information about a conspiracy to seize Middle Eastern oil fields to the media: if the media reports the story, he will live because the conspiracy that has ensnared him will be public; if the media doesn't, the conspirators will murder him. The law firm in John Grisham's *The Firm* assumes the disguise of a normal, small, albeit very successful, law firm, when in fact it its major clients are in the Mafia.

Thriller authors often have characters, both heroes and villains, use disguises to mislead and confuse their adversaries, as well as the audience. The Saint and the Mission Impossible team often use disguises as they fight conspiracies and bad guys around the world. In William Goldman's thriller novel *Brothers*, an assassin nicknamed The Blond dons a black wig and limps as a disguise to fool the protagonist. In *The Killing*, small-time crook Johnny Clay wears a clown mask when he robs a racetrack, while the bank robbers in *Point*

Break don masks of various US presidents to hide their identity. In the Jack Higgins thriller *The Eagle Has Landed*, set during World War II, German paratroopers disguised as British soldiers takeover an English village to kidnap British Prime Minister Winston Churchill. In the final pages as the German paratroopers are surrounded by British troops, their leader manages to reach Churchill at a nearby country estate and kill him. Higgins' deceptions continue when he reveals that the "Churchill" who was shot was actually an actor disguised as the prime minister. The real Churchill is at the historic Tehran conference in Iran. Even more creatively, in writer Michael Cooney's psychological/horror/thriller motion picture *Identity*, ten characters serve as facets of multiple murderer Malcolm Rivers' personality as he undergoes a psychiatric hearing. The characters are disguised as real people when they are really just parts of Rivers' psyche. Thriller authors can also camouflage a character. In *The Manchurian Candidate*, the Chinese camouflage their assassin as a US serviceman, which he is, although he has been brainwashed to murder a presidential candidate.

Science fiction authors also use camouflage and disguises. Darth Vader may be the most famous character in science fiction who donned a mask, which disguised his identity, as well as helping to keep him alive. Luke and Han disguise themselves as Stormtroopers when they rescue Princess Leia on the Death Star in *Star Wars: A New Hope*. In his science fiction Foundation series, Isaac Asimov created the Mule. Brilliant, yet awkward and ugly with pointy ears and a three-inch nose, the Mule's appearance is a most effective disguise, since no one expects him to become the greatest conqueror the galaxy has ever seen. The Mule's power has nothing to do with physical prowess. He can adjust the emotions of others, singly or by the thousands. In yet another deceptive disguise, the Mule uses his appearance to masquerade as The Clown.

Horror authors often have their villain don a disguise. Ghostface in *Scream* wears a distorted white mask to hide the fact that the mass murderer is two people: Billy Loomis and Stu Macher. In *Friday the 13th*, Jason famously hides his identity behind a hockey goalie's mask.

Not only villains wear masks to hide their identity. Superheroes also hide their real identity. Clark Kent uses a mask and costume to become Superman, Bruce Wayne becomes the masked Batman and Peter Parker dons his spider suit to become Spiderman. In *The Princess Bride*, a mask allows each new succeeding Dread Pirate Roberts to assume the mantle of the "terror of the seas" when his predecessor retires to a life of leisure. The mask also helps hide the fact that the newest Dread Pirate Roberts is Buttercup's true love, Westley. Even fairy tales use disguises. The wolf uses a disguise to appear to be Little Red Riding Hood's grandmother, while the queen appears to be an old, wizened woman when she gives Snow White the poisoned apple. In all such cases the audience knows about the disguise, so the deception is practiced on other characters, not on the audience.

Comedy authors use disguises, although much of the comedy relates to the audience knowing who is behind the disguise, while the other characters do not. Shakespeare uses disguises and mistaken identity in several of his comedies, including *The Comedy of Errors* and *Twelfth Night*, mentioned above. In Billy Wilder's *Some Like it Hot*, Tony Curtis and Jack Lemmon play characters that witness the St. Valentine's Day Massacre and are on the run from the Mob. The pair don disguises as women to join an all-girl band so they can escape to Florida. Dustin Hoffman in *Tootsie* and Robin Williams in *Mrs. Doubtfire* wore female disguises for comedic effect and to deceive other characters, if not the audience. In Eddie Murphy's *Coming to America*, a crown prince from a wealthy fictional African nation comes to America disguised as a poor student to find a wife. Only at the end of the movie is the deception revealed to his lady love, although the audience knows all along, which only adds to the comedy.

Adventure story authors use disguises to deceive and entertain audiences. In the rousing adventure film *The Three Musketeers*, when D'Artagnan is led to the chopping block, the audience is surprised when two of the executioners are the disguised musketeers Porthos and Aramis. They rescue D'Artagnan with help from Athos, who arranges the escapee's transportation by appropriating the nefarious Cardinal's carriage.

In film noirs, the femme fatale is always evil disguised in a gorgeous body. Barbara Stanwyk plays just such a disguised embodiment of evil in *Double Indemnity* convincing insurance salesman Walter Neff to help her murder her husband. Jane Greer plays an equally delicious femme fatale in *Out of the Past*, enticing Robert

Mitchum's character to do evil deeds. (The dialogue in the film is wonderful.)

Authors of dramas and literary stories also use disguises. In *Yentl*, a Jewish woman uses a disguise to appear to be a man so she can continue her studies after her father dies. In the Academy Award-winning *Shakespeare in Love*, the female protagonist, Viola, use a male disguise so she can act in her beloved Elizabethan theatre. Even Shakespeare used camouflage and disguises. In *Macbeth*, Shakespeare has Malcolm's soldiers cut down tree limbs to camouflage their numbers as they march to attack Macbeth's forces, while also fulfilling the prophesy that Macbeth will be safe until Great Birnam Wood comes to Dunsinane Hill. Bossanio in *The Merchant of Venice* disguises his poverty by appearing to be wealthy, while Portia disguises herself as a man so she can be heard in court and save Antonio. Hamlet feigns insanity, a disguise, to attempt to expose the guilt of Claudius and Hamlet's mother. One of the greatest stories ever told, *The Iliad*, includes the use of a disguise: the Trojan Horse is disguised as a gift. Homer continues to use disguises in *The Odyssey*. Circe is disguised as a beautiful woman when she really is a witch who turns Odysseus' men into animals.

Questions for Authors:

Can you use a disguise or camouflage in your real story or one of your cover stories? Don't just think of clothing. Is there a way to mislead the audience with two characters who share a common characteristic, physical trait or mannerism?

Can you disguise the main trait of a character, which is only revealed when the real story comes to light? A good thief, an evil philanthropist or a moral assassin?

Can characters other than the murderer use disguises or camouflage to achieve their goals in the real story or cover story? A character that feigns a disease to get attention? A couple who feign dislike for each other when they are really in love or the reverse? A handicapped character that really isn't?

Can the murderer use a disguise to commit a murder, make his escape, mask his relationship to the victim or another character, or cast suspicion on another character?

Can your murderer use camouflage to conceal their real nature or profession? If you are writing about a conspiracy, can your conspirators use disguises or camouflage to mask their conspiracy? Think beyond just clothes and consider how the villains might be able to misrepresent themselves as something they are not.

Common Mistakes and How to Fix Them:

If you have many disguises, your story will seem false, since in reality disguises are rare. The exceptions are romantic comedies, comedies, spy stories, thrillers and stories focused on con games in which audiences expect characters to use disguises and assume the identities of other characters.

In relation to disguises or camouflage, don't overdo it. Just one or two disguised characters with one or two key similarities mentioned a couple of times are enough to stick in readers' minds that one character may be another character. In The Hound of the Baskervilles just a simple black beard is enough to cast suspicion on Barrymore.

Avoid the use of twins unless you are especially creative. If it's been done before, don't do it again.

Chapter 17

Use Characters to Deceive

As S.S. Van Dine argued in "Twenty Rules for Writing Detective Stories," the reader must have a fair chance of discovering the culprit and can justifiably feel cheated if the author has blatantly lied about what happened. Even if you can't lie to readers directly, you can create characters to lie for you. Since the most effective deception is based on the truth, your characters can be your agents of deception without uttering a single even white lie.

Espionage and warfare are full of examples of leaders who used individuals to deceive. In 1788, King Gustav III of Sweden wanted to start a war with Russia but needed the approval of the Riksdag of the Estates (the Swedish national assembly) and they were opposed. King Gustav decided to use his troops as his agents of deception. An order for Russian military uniforms was sent to the head tailor at the Royal Swedish Opera. Swedish soldiers wearing the Russian uniforms as disguises staged an attack on Puumala, a

Swedish outpost on the Russo-Swedish border, on June 27, 1788. The "attack" caused outrage in Stockholm and the Riksdag agreed to declare war on Russia. King Gustav got his war.

In August 1939, the Nazis used their troops and concentration camp inmates to deceive their own people. The concentration camp inmates were dressed as German soldiers and shot by the Gestapo to make it appear they had been killed by Polish soldiers as the Poles attacked a radio station in Gleiwitz, Germany. The operation helped mobilize German support for the invasion of Poland. In a similar case, on November 26, 1939, the Soviet army shelled Mainila, a Russian village near the Finnish border. The Soviets blamed Finland for the attack and used the incident as a pretext to invade Finland four days later, starting the Winter War.

During World War II, the British captured every German agent who attempted to operate in Britain. The captured spies were given a choice: cooperate or be hanged. Almost all cooperated and became British agents of deception, feeding information the British wanted the Germans to have back to Berlin. During the Cold War, the East German Stasi intelligence service used agents called Romeos to deceive. As a disguise, the Romeos pretended to be members of West German peace groups and romanced West German female civil servants to persuade them to steal classified documents.

Magicians often use an assistant to aid them, as well as confederates in the audience for certain illusions. Conmen use shills in the crowd to make their cons appear more believable or to be the first to buy a product or place a bet. All such assistants are agents of deception of the magician or conman.

Just as spy masters use secret agents to pass misinformation to their adversaries, your characters are your agents of deception to pass misinformation to your readers. In a mystery your goal is to have the villain deceive all the other characters, as well as the audience. In a thriller, the conspirators are your agents of deception, while in a romance the heroine acts deceptively, usually because she doesn't know who is right for her.

In a mystery, you can have your murderer act deceptively in many ways. You can have your murderer stage a murder attempt on himself to divert suspicion from themselves. In *A Murder is Announced*, *The Mirror Crack'd from Side to Side* and *Crooked House*,

Agatha Christie has the murderer stage a murder attempt on her to divert suspicion.

You can have your villain make murder look like an accident. In Isaac Asimov's *Murder at the ABA*, a murderer makes it appear that a writer fell in a shower, hit his head on the faucet and died. Only Darius Just, another writer, notices that although the victim was always neat and tidy, his clothes are strewn around the hotel room. Something is not right and the murderer's attempt to make murder look like an accident fails.

Villains can lie to distort relationships and to mask their crimes. A lying villain can be doubly deceptive since statements are remembered long after the source is forgotten, so the villain can send an investigation off in an invalid direction with a few well-placed red herrings and often readers will forget who planted the red herrings in the first place. The clever plot of Michael Lewin's short story "The Reluctant Detective," set in England, is driven by a deceptive villain. A solicitor hires a couple of private investigators to investigate his sister's husband, whom he says is having an affair. He also accuses his sister's husband of burning down his own mattress factory to collect the insurance. The solicitor fears for his sister's safety and wants evidence to convince his sister to get a divorce. It is not until late in the story that Lewin has the P.I.s learn that the solicitor has been deceiving them (and the reader). He is not the woman's brother. He is her lover. He burned down the mattress factory so the husband would get the insurance money. Then the solicitor planned to have the wife divorce her husband to get half the insurance money in a divorce settlement before she and the solicitor ran off together. Relying on a bedrock principle of deception Lewin has the solicitor use facts to deceive (Principle 4). The sister *is* having an affair, albeit with the solicitor, and the mattress factory *was* burned down, albeit by the solicitor not by the husband. Lewin tells his story with a light, comic touch, but his deceptive character of the fake solicitor is at the heart of the clever story.

In other genres authors often have villains lie and act deceptively. In the adventure story *Kidnapped*, Robert Louis Stevenson has David Balfour's uncle, Ebenezer Balfour, lie when he claims that he is the older son so he can keep an inheritance. Ebenezer also tricks David into accompanying him on a visit to a ship captain, whom the uncle convinces to kidnap David. In the space-opera epic *Return of the Jedi*, the Emperor Palpatine and Darth Vader send information to the rebels that their new Death Star's weapon systems are not yet operational. The information is a lie. The Death Star is fully operational and the rebels are lured into a trap. In the romantic comedy *Bridget Jones's Diary*, Helen Fielding has Daniel Cleaver lie about his history with Mark Darcy, making it appear that Mark slept with Daniel's fiancé, when in reality Daniel slept with Mark's wife.

You can have characters other than the villain act deceptively by donning disguises, acting suspiciously, using deceptive techniques, or holding back parts of the truth to mislead your detective hero and, thereby, readers. As Agatha Christie has Chief Inspector Japp say in *Murder in the Mews,* "People hold their tongues, sometimes out of the most honorable motives." Motives abound for such behaviors. Characters may be hiding an affair, concealing a past indiscretion or misdemeanor, or covering for someone they love who they think committed a murder. A character may even lie to a private investigator out of personal dislike or to the police because of a hatred of authority.

Benjamin Schutz's short story "Mary, Mary, Shut the Door" is a prime example of an author using a character other than the villain as a tool of deception. A hard-boiled private detective attempts to keep a wealthy young woman from marrying a conman who is after her money. The P.I. tells the conman the woman's uncle changed the terms of her trust so she won't receive any money. It appears the conman believes him, but goes through with the wedding anyway. Schutz intends the reader to conclude that the conman truly loves the girl. But later the conman tells the P.I. he was shaken at first when the P.I. told him about the changed trust but, having worked in a law office and knowing the terms of the trust, he realized the uncle couldn't change the terms. The conman later murders the girl in a diving "accident." The P.I. reopens the case and the story ends leaving the reader to wonder if justice will ever be done. The P.I.'s lie about the uncle changing the terms of the woman's trust did not fool the conman, but probably deceived most readers.

You can have characters other than the villain make a suicide look like murder. In "The Market Basing Mystery," a Poirot short story, a blackmail victim commits suicide. His housekeeper makes the suicide look like murder to implicate the blackmailers. The same plot device is used in another Poirot story, *Murder in the Mews,* which features the death of Mrs. Allen. Readers later learn she committed suicide and that her friend made it look like murder to frame the blackmailer.

You also can have characters unintentionally mislead other characters. In Philip MacDonald's creative *The List of Adrian Messenger,* a Frenchman reports Adrian Messenger's last words as they float on debris after a passenger aircraft is blown up over the Atlantic. The Frenchman recalls that Messenger said, "Only one brush. All the brushes, clean sweep." The mystery of the dying man's words are only resolved when an investigator asks the Frenchman to go over the words yet one more time and the Frenchman remembers that Messenger said "broom," not "brush." The Frenchman doesn't even realize that there is much, if any difference in English between brush and broom, but to the English investigator it makes all the difference: broom is the sigel of a wealthy landed English family. The realization helps the investigator make sense of a list of deaths Messenger had been investigating, which is related to the inheritance of an aristocratic title and the extensive estate that goes with it.

Even characters in love can deceive. William Goldman's novel *Heat* begins with a beautiful, well-endowed woman waiting for her nerdish boyfriend at a bar. She is debating whether to accept what she knows will be a forthcoming invitation to move from Las Vegas to Atlantic City and marry him. She likes him, but is hesitant since he is so unlike the more manly men she has dated. He is also late, even though he is always punctual. A muscular, drunk Mexican asks to buy her a drink and clumsily hits on her. She puts him off, but he is hard to get rid of. The bookish boyfriend arrives. The Mexican keeps bothering them. The couple leaves but the Mexican follows them and continues to harass the boyfriend, who has had enough. The pair fight and the Mexican loses, badly. The couple leaves and the woman decides. They make passionate love and she agrees to go to Atlantic City with him and marry him. The bookish boyfriend has used the Mexican as an agent of deception. He hired the Mexican to stage the fight to convince her that he was a real man.

In love stories and literature, characters can be your agents of deception. In *Romeo and Juliet*, Shakespeare has Juliet fake her own death. The audience knows she is faking, but Romeo does not, leading to his—and then her—death. In O. Henry's "The Last Leaf," a girl is dying of pneumonia. She comes to believe she will die when the last leaf falls from a vine tree outside her bedroom window. One night, in the midst of a storm, an artist paints a leaf on her window; a leaf that will never fall. His deception succeeds and the girl lives, but having caught pneumonia during his night of painting in the storm, the agent of O. Henry's deception, the artist, dies.

The authors of dramas create characters that deceive other characters and the audience. In the excellent 2013 Academy Award winning film *Omar*, screenwriter Hany Abu-Assad tells the story of three Palestinians who want to join the fight against Israel in the West Bank. Omar, Tarek and Amjad are best friends, but Omar and Amjad have both fallen in love with Tarek's sister, Nadia. Omar appears to be foremost in her affections, but when their anti-Israeli plans lead to Omar's arrest due to an informer, Omar eventually figures out that Amjad is the informer. In an attempt to explain himself, Amjad tells Omar that he had to cooperate because the Israelis blackmailed him with the secret that Nadia is pregnant. Omar forces Amjad to confess the pregnancy to Nadia's brother, Tarek, but in a fight, Tarek is killed. Omar arranges for Amjad to marry Nadia and then distances himself from the couple. The sad, twisted story appears to be at an end, but then two years later in a devastating ending, Omar visits Amjad and Nadia. She is home alone with her two children. The eldest, however, is less than two years old; Amjad lied to Omar about Nadia being pregnant to justify his collaboration with the Israelis and to convince Omar to help him marry Nadia. Amjad was a most effective agent of deception for Hany Abu-Assad.

Many authors use unreliable narrators to deceive audiences. Chaucer's the Wife of Bath was far from reliable, and Baron Munchausen continued the unreliable tradition with his wild tales of adventures around the world and beyond, although he told outlandish tales more to poke fun at the foibles of others than to deceive. Ford Maddox Ford's *The Good Soldier* uses Edward Ashburnham as an unreliable narrator to mask a loveless marriage, affairs and other unhappy aspects of his life, which readers slowly discern.

In Carolyn Parkhurst's creative *The Dogs of Babel*, the narrator appears to be reliable and telling a straight-forward story about his wife's suicide. It is well into the novel when a police detective tells the narrator his wife was pregnant when she died. The narrator only then admits that he knew his wife was pregnant, which is crucial to the mystery of why his wife committed suicide; she felt she was incapable of being a good mother. Parkhurst has the narrator tell so much personal information that readers are deceived and surprised when he leaves out that one crucial fact. Gillian Flynn's blockbuster novel (and movie) *Gone Girl* features alternating husband and wife narrators, Nick and Amy Dunne, both of whom prove unreliable. Early in the novel, Amy disappears. Her husband Nick becomes the prime suspect and soon reveals to readers that he is unreliable. Much later in the novel readers learn that Nick's deceitfulness pales in comparison to Amy's deceptions. Harlan Ellison in the short story "Mefisto in Onyx" also uses two unreliable narrators. Near the end of the story it appears the narrator is a mass murderer who has been suppressing the information, even from himself. It is only at the very end of the story that the reader learns the real story. The real murderer has used telepathy and mind control to convince the narrator he is the murderer.

Narrators do not need to lie by commission to be effective agents of deception. Leaving out one fact can be dramatically powerful and supports Principle 4: base deception on the truth, not lies. In P. D. James' "Moment of Power", the narrator is a clerk in a law office. While cleaning out the desk of an attorney who has died, he finds a stash of pornography. He sneaks into the office at night to view his find and sees in an apartment across the way a couple meeting for a tryst. The narrator returns and sees the couple meet every Friday night. Then the woman is raped and murdered. On that night, the narrator sees the boyfriend arrive at the apartment, knock, get no response, and, finally leave without entering. When the boyfriend is arrested for the crime, the narrator debates whether to go to the police. He fears losing his job for sneaking into the office at night and viewing the pornography. As the boyfriend is charged and convicted, the narrator gives logical, heartfelt reasons for not coming forward, such as being criticized for waiting so long, although he dreams of his great day when he comes forward to save the innocent man. He does not and the boyfriend is hanged. It is only at the end of the story that the narrator, telling the story 16 years after the fact, explains that he slipped across the street and raped and murdered the woman just before her boyfriend arrived. The reader likes the apparently honest narrator, even if he does have a negative view of women, and James' deception is well done. More importantly, James plays more than fair with the reader, in that everything the narrator says is true. He only leaves out the part where he committed the crime in his description of the night of the murder. The reader might have felt cheated if James, to accomplish her deception, had had the narrator lie by commission, instead of by omission.

In a similar vein, Agatha Christie's *The Murder of Roger Ackroyd* has an unreliable narrator, again albeit only by omission, not commission. The story Dr. Sheppard tells is accurate, save for 10 minutes that he fails to describe: "The letters were brought in at twenty minutes to nine. It was just ten minutes to nine when I left him, the letter still unread. I hesitated with my hand on the door handle, looking back and wondering if there was anything I had left undone." Sheppard murdered Roger Ackroyd during those missing, albeit mentioned, 10 minutes, and he does say the letters were unread. Maybe Sheppard was a reliable narrator.

Questions for Authors:

Does your villain lie by omission or commission? Lying by omission is usually far more deceptive and harder to uncover than lying by commission. Does he/she use any of the other deceptive techniques discussed in this book to deceive other characters? Misrepresent his/her motives? His/her whereabouts when the crime was committed? Lie about their past, relationships with other characters, or their occupation, name, gender, nationality, skills, family relations, marital status, loves, goals, interests, health, economic status, or social position? Use disguises? Distort the truth? Why does he or she lie?

Do other characters lie by omission or commission, deceive others or distort the truth about their motives, feelings about the victim or about each other? Provide false information or leave out parts of the truth in relation to the crime? Act suspiciously because of other crimes, affairs or immoral activities? Lie about where they were when the villain was committing his dastardly act?

Write down each of your characters including the villain and list why they deceived others. Is the deception based on facts (better) or lies (weaker)? Are their reasons logical and realistic? Would your friends believe such motivations? Ask them. Sometimes being forced to say out loud the motivations of your characters can reveal how strong and believable those motivations are to other people and to yourself.

Common Mistakes and How to Fix Them:

Do you lie directly to the reader about what happens in a scene? DON'T! As an author, never lie by commission. A character can commit such a deception, but you must not. Although different characters can perceive a scene differently, such as in the movie *Rashomon* about different perspectives of a rape in feudal Japan, you must not outright lie when you describe a scene to your audience. Play fair.

The most common mistake related to characters acting deceptively is that authors make characters deceive readers just for the sake of plot requirements. Whenever a character lies, acts deceptively or even just bends the truth, you must have a believable and logical reason for them doing so. If you find characters acting solely to advance your plot, STOP. Go back and develop realistic, believable reasons for why characters are practicing deception on others so the reasons are related to either the real story or a cover story. If you have trouble doing this, brainstorm a range of motivations for each character's behavior. Write them all down without judging the ideas. The first idea that comes to mind is rarely the best, in part because it is likely you have seen it before. As Alfred Hitchcock often said, your job as a writer is to avoid clichés. Put the list aside and come back to it a few days later. Waiting a few days lets you look at the list objectively. Patience is a virtue when a story is not working. Give your brain, especially your subconscious, time away from your story to devise a better plot, more plausible motivations and a more deceptive mystery.

Some authors have characters lie in a way that is too easily exposed. If you have a character claim to have spent the evening of the murder in a pub, yet your detective hero checks and no one in the pub that evening remembers the character, you have wasted a chance to mislead readers effectively. For every lie, try to use as much of the truth as the basis for the lie as possible (Principle 4). In that way, your detective character can check parts of the lie and find it supported before, after much diligent sleuthing, finally figuring out that the lie is, indeed, a lie. If a character is going to lie about having been in a pub the night of the murder, it is far better if they were at the pub, yet left briefly to commit the crime, were at the pub the night before, or their brother who looks like the murderer was in the pub the crucial night. Conversely, if they are innocent, they may not reveal their alibi because they were at the pub for another reason that they are trying to hide, such as an illicit tryst, buying drugs or to slash the tires of a hated rival's Mercedes. The better your characters are at deception, the better your novel or script, so make your characters masters of deception.

Chapter 18

Deceptive Storytelling: Increasing Ambiguity, Increasing Certainty or Both

Authors can tell a story in a deceptive way. If you use the way you tell your story to deceive your readers, then you face a choice for each part of your real story: whether to increase ambiguity or certainty. To increase ambiguity, you offer the reader many choices about various aspects of the story (what is the central crime in a story; who did it, why and how), increasing the reader's uncertainty about which one of several possible explanations is correct. Conversely, to increase certainty, you focus the reader's attention on one possibility—a false one—about the identity, motivation and/or means by which the crime was committed, which distracts the reader's attention from the real story and the real murderer. The reader becomes certain, but wrong.

The same decision is involved in all genres. In romances, will you increase certainty that one man is the heroine's true love, only to find in the end he is not; or increase ambiguity by having several possible suitors, one of which she ends up with in the final climactic scene? Thrillers share the same structure: increase certainty about one cover story and villain, only to reveal the real story and real villain at the end; or increase ambiguity as the hero struggles to figure out which among several competing theories (cover stories) explains what is happening to him (the real story) and which of several characters is the real villain.

For the D Day landings, the British sought to increase ambiguity about where and when they would land in Europe. They fed the Germans clues about many different landings sites from Norway to the south of France, as well as many different dates, thereby increasing ambiguity and uncertainty about where and when they would invade.

Conmen always try to increase certainty. Conmen want you to be certain about what you think is going to happen so you will hand over your hard-earned cash. The conman's goal is to make the mark certain he can pick out the Queen in a three-card Monte game, that the box he is handed off the back of the truck really does contain the Bose stereo system for the unbeatable low price of forty bucks, or that the investment in Kenyan bonds will return 90% a month. Ambiguity can lead to questions and the last thing a conman wants are questions that might expose the cover story and reveal the real story. Magicians tend to be similar. Magicians do not want their audience to be confused about which of several stories is the real one, so they usually offer one cover story to increase certainty. The magician wants you to be certain there is no way he can pick the card you selected from the deck of cards after you shuffled the deck seven times and sealed your card in a Ziplock bag, which was then encased in concrete. Houdini wanted the audience to be certain that he would drown before he could escape from his water-filled cabinet. The greater the certainty, the greater the surprise when the magician completes the illusion.

Increase Ambiguity

Agatha Christie was a master of the increasing ambiguity method of deception. Almost all of her stories involve multiple characters, most of whom have a motive, the opportunity and the means to commit the murder. *Death on the Nile* has a boatload of suspects, while *Lord Edgware Dies* has 13 main characters, all suspects. In almost all her stories the reader is faced with a choice (Principle 5) from among a plethora of plausible suspects. All the choices increase the ambiguity surrounding the suspects, the crime, the motive, and often even the means, ensuring readers will make the wrong choices and be deceived, surprised and entertained.

Authors who use the increasing ambiguity method of deception usually create victims who are disliked, thereby allowing them to create a large cast of characters with powerful motives for committing the murder. Agatha Christie took this idea to the extreme in *Murder on the Orient Express*, which features the murder of a man named Cassetti. He was involved in the kidnapping of a three-year-old heiress. Even though the ransom was paid, Cassetti murdered the girl. The crime harmed every other character riding in the coach, so everyone has a motive to murder Cassetti. Murder mystery novelists today continue to make victims horrible individuals to increase the number of suspects and, thereby, ambiguity. In Jonathan Kellerman's When the Bough Breaks, the victim is a psychiatrist who practices fraud, extortion and sexual manipulation on the side.

If the victim is too disliked or reprehensible, even though there may be plenty of suspects, there is little incentive to solve the mystery, unless you later show that the victim was not really that bad. In Agatha Christie's *Evil Under the Sun*, the victim, actress Arlena Marshall, appears to be a flirt, cheating on her new husband, and is despised by her step-daughter, but it turns out she is merely young, neglected and lonely. In most stories the victim must be important enough so their murder is worth solving and reading about the solution. Often this means the victim is rich (with many heirs who are then suspects), or important in some way, such as a CEO, politician, movie star, scientist, or religious leader.

Another technique to use if the victim is reprehensible is to make the prime suspect likable. In Christie's *Crooked House*, a ruthless businessman, Aristide Leonides, is murdered, yet the reader wants to unmask the killer because the likable main point of view character, Charles Haywood, is engaged to Aristide's beautiful, smart and likable granddaughter, Sophia. Leonides has left his entire estate to Sophia, giving her an excellent motive for murder. Since she is a prime suspect, Sophia refuses to marry Charles until the murderer is found, providing excellent motivation for Charles (and readers) to solve the mystery.

It would be difficult to devise believable motives for a cast of characters to want to murder a popular, saintly character. The most common way to create a sufficient list of suspects to murder a saintly character is to have their high morals lead to conflict with those around them. In the *Midsomer Murders* episode "Murder on St. Malley's Day," a student, Daniel Talbot, is murdered during a cross-country run at an elite English boarding school. He is well liked, popular and was a member of a prestigious dining club, which his grandfather founded. Why would anyone want to murder such a fine young man? As DCI Barnaby and Sergeant Troy investigate, they discover that Daniel's highly moral view of life clashed with the club's other members, many of whom drank at a local pub even though they are under age, while one of the ex-members sells food stolen from the school's kitchens to the local pub. Worse, the club has used ex-student members now in the British Foreign Service to steal and smuggle back to the school in diplomatic pouches priceless treasures from overseas, which fund the club and scholarships for its members. Characters abound with motives to murder the saintly Daniel.

Murdering a good character goes against the common belief that evil is punished while good is rewarded, although it does create a strong reason to solve the case. For a twist on this belief, you can slowly reveal that the saintly character was far from a saint, which also allows you to add suspects. In Scott Turow's *Presumed Innocent*, the victim, Carolyn Polhemus, at first appears to be a bright, hard-working assistant DA fighting corruption in the courts. As the story progresses, Turow reveals that she was far from a saint, appearing to sleep her way up the food chain in the DA's office as she went from lover to lover. As her background is slowly revealed, the number of suspects increase and so does the level of ambiguity.

Just as the victim is often unlikable, the murderer usually has negative traits; but be wary of camouflaging all of the suspects with negative traits. In the 2013 two-part television mystery, *Murder on the Home Front*, a pathologist and his ex-reporter female assistant investigate the brutal murder of a young woman during the London Blitz. The story is well told and the chemistry between the pair is entertaining, but all of the suspects appear equally unlikable: a Polish cryptographer who is creepy and clumsily hits on the assistant; a shy Anglo-German who collects risqué postcards of barely clad young women; and the gangster owner of a dance club. The ending lacks dramatic power since the audience dislikes all three suspects, which makes them care far less who did it, since they would prefer if all three suspects were guilty and punished.

Besides creating multiple suspects, many mystery authors today add ambiguity to their novels by portraying many different facets of the victim's life. Writers of Golden Age cozies usually focused the action in one setting, such as a country house (Christie's *The Secret of Chimneys*, 1925), a cruise ship (*Death on the Nile*, 1936), an island (*And Then There Were None*, 1939), a village (Ngaio Marsh's *Overture to Death*, 1939) or a theatre (Marsh's *Enter the Murderer,* 1935). This technique made for a clearly defined number of suspects, which increases certainty. Most modern mysteries have multiple settings and a victim who has a family life, career, circle of friends, and hobbies, any of which might contain the reason for their demise. Modern novels are also far more likely to be set in cities or towns with no clearly defined set of suspects, all of which increases ambiguity.

Elizabeth George expertly increases ambiguity by using multiple facets of characters' lives in her 1996 novel, *In the Presence of the Enemy,* in which a little girl is kidnapped. The girl is born as the result of a fling at a political convention between a prominent politician and the publisher of a newspaper that routinely attacks the politician's party. The couple has not spoken in years and the politician is now married. From the beginning, George presents several possible worlds that might contain the kidnapper:

- Personal: either parent, the politician's husband or the publisher's wife
- Political: someone involved in the battle between the publisher's newspaper and the politician's party

- Business: someone involved in the publisher's quest for higher circulation numbers
- Criminal: a piano teacher who was last seen with the girl might be a pedophile
- Historical: the crime may be related to the past life of the politician or the publisher
- International: the Irish Republican Army may be involved

The reader is left to determine which world contains the key clues to the identity of the villain and their motive for the kidnapping and later murder of the girl. By presenting a more complex story reflecting the many different facets of your characters' lives, you can, just like authors such as George, make your mystery not only more realistic, but also more deceptively ambiguous, difficult to solve and entertaining.

You also can make the crime itself ambiguous. In the Brother Cadfael mystery *One Corpse Too Many,* an extra body is found among 94 hanged rebels during an English civil war. Is the extra body just a bureaucratic error, a soldier killed in the war or is it murder? Only Brother Cadfael's dogged diligence uncovers the truth. In *The Hound of the Baskervilles,* Conan Doyle leaves the question open about whether it is a case of death by natural causes, murder or death by supernatural causes. In *Murder at the ABA,* Isaac Asimov starts his mystery with a death that could be an accident or murder.

In romances, you can increase ambiguity by adding suitors. Scarlett O'Hara has many suitors and even marries three of them. Jane Austen's plots are always full of multiple suitors to increase the chance readers will be surprised by which pairs end up at the altar. Thrillers increase ambiguity by keeping the characters behind the conspiracy shadowy and ambiguous. In some cases, such as *The Bourne Identity,* even the point-of-view character's identity is uncertain and filled with ambiguity: is Jason Bourne a cold-blooded hitman, an international spy á la James Bond or something else entirely? And who does he work for? Even he doesn't know.

In literature, ambiguity can increase suspense and drama. Ghosts and hallucinations are sometimes left ambiguous. Is the character hallucinating, is there something really there or is someone creating an illusion? Emily Bronte in *Wuthering Heights* and Henry James in *The Turn of the Screw* leave such questions wonderfully ambiguous.

Sometimes an entire story is left ambiguous. Many French films from the 1960s sought ambiguity. In 1968's *Belle de Jour,* a wife who has been moonlighting as a prostitute becomes involved with a gangster. The gangster shoots her husband, but is then shot and killed by the police. The husband is paralyzed and the wife cares for him and, in a final scene, he is healthy again and they are happy. Is it reality or just a dream? It is left ambiguous. More recently, *The Life of Pi* leaves it to the reader to decide which reality to believe: a story about a young boy adrift in a lifeboat with a Bengal tiger or a deranged human companion. The classic for raising ambiguity is Frank Stockton's "The Lady or the Tiger?", with an ambiguous ending that leaves open the title's question.

Increase Certainty

If you decide to increase ambiguity with multiple cover stories, you have several chances to deceive your audience, since you are using several cover stories. If you choose to increase certainty in relation to a cover story, you have one chance: your audience must believe that the single cover story is the real story. It may sound risky, but it isn't as risky as it sounds, and the dramatic payoff is often greater than when authors choose to increase ambiguity with multiple cover stories. Classics such as *Witness for the Prosecution, The Planet of the Apes* and *And Then There Were None* show the power of using one cover story to increase certainty.

Besides the fact that deception, whether by increasing ambiguity or certainty, is almost always effective, one reason increasing certainty to deceive an audience is easier than expected is because of the human tendency to look for evidence to support what we already believe. This confirmation bias is rooted in cognitive dissonance theory, which hypothesizes that to avoid emotional conflict humans tend to seek information that confirms our beliefs (which makes us happy) and avoid information that refutes our beliefs (which causes stress or dissonance). This bias is so strong that even scientists, trained to be objective, follow a scientific method that focuses on searching for information that refutes—not supports—their theories to diminish its influence and discover the truth. Even so, even scientists often see what they expect to see. There was once a planet called Vulcan that orbited the sun near Mercury.

From 1859 to 1915 many scientists believed that the elusive Vulcan and its gravitational pull caused Mercury to wobble. Astronomers and scientists repeatedly reported finding Vulcan; finding what they were certain they would find. Finally Albert Einstein proved that the wobble observed in Mercury's orbit was explained by his general theory of relativity and not by the non-existent Vulcan.

Spy masters, politicians and generals are as inclined to believe information that confirms their beliefs as scientists, if not more so. After ten long years of siege, the dawn's early light showed the Trojans that the Greeks had finally admitted what the Trojans had known for years: the Greeks would never conquer Troy. The Trojans were certain the Greeks had abandoned their siege because the Greeks had not only sailed away, but they had left an offering in the form of a symbol of Troy: a horse. The Trojans, of course, were certain, but wrong.

In the late 1920s, Western leaders were certain that Soviet despotism would spark a rebellion in the USSR. Sure enough, rebels in the USSR contacted anti-Soviet émigrés in the West. The rebels organized jail breaks, blew up police stations and fed vital information to the West. Western intelligence services became certain they had found a force to oppose Soviet rule, which they had always expected to arise. Unfortunately, the jail breaks, attacks and information leaks had all been carefully staged by Soviet spymasters to reinforce the Western belief that such anti-Soviet groups existed in order to gain the West's trust and gather information on real anti-Soviet groups in the Soviet Union. The deception operation lasted eight years and was a major success—for the Soviets. They captured and shot many domestic opponents, who became involved in what they believed was an anti-Soviet movement.

During the Gulf War (1990-91), Iraq's Saddam Hussein and his generals believed that, since the goal of the US-led Coalition was to liberate Kuwait, the Coalition would invade Kuwait across the Saudi border while US Marines stormed Kuwait's beaches. The Coalition increased the Iraqi's certainty by having US Marines practice amphibious landings nearby, which were extensively covered by the media, and by maneuvering armored units near the Kuwaiti border. The Iraqis became certain, but wrong. The Coalition shifted their armored units inland and attacked out of the desert far to the west, sweeping around and behind the Iraqi forces in Kuwait, catching them entirely by surprise.

Mystery readers fall victim just as easily to confirmation bias as scientists, political leaders, spymasters, and generals. Therefore, if you can increase reader's certainty about one suspect or one theory of a crime (a cover story), the reader will seek information that confirms that theory, even as you mask clues to a completely different explanation of the crime (the real story).

Harry Kemelman uses the confirmation bias to increase certainty about one suspect in *Thursday the Rabbi Walked Out.* An anti-Semitic millionaire, Ellsworth Jordan, is murdered in the small town of Barnard's Crossing, New England. Kemelman subtly provides evidence against Jordan's 18-year-old son, Billy, whom his mother raised in New York. Billy had an argument with Ellsworth the night of the murder over a gun Billy took from the bank where he worked. Ellsworth locked Billy in his room. Billy's alibi is thin. He admits climbing out the window and spending the evening in New York. Kemelman establishes Billy as the prime suspect, whom some readers will become certain is the murderer as they focus on clues that point to Billy. Readers will be certain, but wrong.

In Agatha Christie's *Five Little Pigs*, a famous painter and his wife are at odds over his newest mistress. Christie presents the love triangle as if the painter is on the verge of leaving his aging wife for his young lover; a trope many readers will be certain will occur. Christie uses facts to reinforce her readers' invalid conclusion. The painter has had a long string of mistresses, but the key fact is that he has never left his wife for any of his mistresses and the key conclusion is that he isn't going to leave his wife for his current mistress. Christie loads on clues that the artist will leave his wife, but each clue has a completely different interpretation. The mistress confronts the wife with the news that the painter is going to leave her. The scene upsets the painter, not because he was stalling telling his wife as most readers will conclude, but because he wanted the mistress just long enough to paint her. The wife appears to be upset and angry throughout the story, as if she is about to be deserted. She also makes statements about the situation being "too much to bear," suggesting a looming marital split. In reality, the situation she is talking about is not her own, but how her husband is treating the young mistress; keeping her just long enough to paint her portrait.

In the end, the solution to the murder hinges on the fact that the painter is *not* going to leave his wife.

In her mystery *Towards Zero*, Christie first increases certainty about one suspect, reveals that certainty to be wrong and then increases certainty about a second suspect, which also proves to be wrong. Lady Tressilian is murdered and all evidence points to Neville Strange as the murderer. Readers become certain Neville is the murderer until Superintendent Battle sees through the evidence pointing toward Neville and begins to gather evidence against Audrey Strange, Neville's ex-wife. The evidence includes the murder weapon, a heavy golf club, hidden in a fire place in her room; a speck of blood on one of her gloves; and her cosmetic powder and hairs on a coat that links her to the murder. Christie makes Battle and, therefore, the reader work for these clues, so readers become certain that Audrey is guilty. It is only at the end of the novel that Battle reveals the truth: Audrey is innocent. Neville committed the murder. He framed himself with weak evidence so he would be exonerated, and then framed his ex-wife with far more damning evidence.

You also can make readers certain which crime is the real crime before proving them wrong. In *Wolf to the Slaughter*, Ruth Rendell tells a story about the disappearance and probable murder of a wealthy young woman. Rendell makes the missing girl's recently dumped boyfriend the prime suspect. Married, he was having an affair with the young woman and was attempting to win her back, even though she was dating someone new. He also suffered the indignity on the night of the woman's disappearance of having to show up to try to take her out in a gaudily painted little car that advertised the cosmetics he sold. She laughed at him and his little car. Besides motive, he admitted he waited for her outside a party she said she was going to, but which she never attended. Rendell creates a situation in which the reader becomes increasingly certain the ex-boyfriend is the murderer and that the girl's murder is the real mystery. The reader doesn't learn until more than three-quarters of the way through the novel that the boyfriend is not her murderer nor is her murder the real crime. The young woman is alive and well. She wanted to get away for a time and took a trip to the Continent. The real murder victim is someone else entirely.

Stories with a twist ending tend to increase certainty about one interpretation of the story before in the final scene revealing the real story. *Witness for the Prosecution* is the story of a man who seduces and then murders an older, wealthy woman. The man's wife appears to be furious with him and agrees to appear for the prosecution. The audience is certain about the wife's motives but on the stand, in the twist that reveals the real story, she shows that she is still in love with him, has forgiven him, and her testimony destroys the crown's case against him for murder. In the original *Planet of the Apes*, the audience is certain the hero has landed on an alien world ruled by apes, but it is not. In the final scene, the hero learns that the nightmarish world ruled by apes is not some alien world, but is the future Earth.

You can increase certainty to deceive your audience in any genre. In romances, authors increase certainty by making it appear the heroine will end up with one man, only to reveal the real Mr. Right in the final scenes. In *Emma*, Jane Austen has Emma attempt matchmaking between Harriet Smith and Mr. Elton, the local vicar. Since Emma is the heroine, most readers will be sure that her matchmaking will succeed. They are wrong. In *Bridget Jones's Diary*, Helen Fielding makes the audience believe that Bridget will end up with reformed lady's man, Daniel Cleaver, while avoiding staid, boring and apparently morally challenged Mark Darcy. Such a conclusion seems certain, but it never comes to pass. In part *Gone with the Wind* is a classic because Margaret Mitchell at first seeks to make her audience certain that Scarlett and Rhett will end up together and live happily ever after. Mitchell eventually does have the couple get together, marry and even have a daughter, making the audience more and more certain of the outcome. Then Mitchell tears Scarlett and Rhett apart, destroying her audience's certainty in the final scene.

Richard Matheson's 1954 horror novel *I am Legend* features a scientist who survives a pandemic that turns people into vampire-like creatures. Readers believe the creatures are monsters, yet the monsters begin to adapt and build a new society. The later movies touch on this aspect of the novel to varying degrees, but Matheson's novel confirmed readers' certainty by making the vampire-like infected creatures unthinking monsters, before slowly revealing that they are far from such.

In science fiction stories you can increase certainty to deceive your audience. In Arthur C. Clarke's *Childhood's End*, an alien race comes to Earth and brings health, peace and prosperity to all mankind. As the novel progresses, it appears that all is well and good and the Overlords, as they are called, are mankind's saviors. Late in the novel that certainty vanishes as the Overlords' real mission is slowly revealed: overseeing the evolution of human children into a higher life form.

In thrillers, you can increase certainty to create powerful plot twists. In 1987's *No Way Out*, Kevin Costner plays US Navy Lieutenant Tom Farrell, who becomes involved in a love affair with a woman who is also seeing the Secretary of Defense. Her death leads to a manhunt and the man being hunted is Farrell. A cover story the Secretary cooks up to explain the hunt—that they are seeking a Soviet sleeper agent—makes the audience confident that Farrell is just an innocent man in the wrong place at the wrong time. If so, the audience is certain, but wrong. In the story of the girlfriend's death, Farrell is in the wrong place at the wrong time, but the real story reveals that Tom is far from innocent: he *is* a Soviet sleeper agent.

Stories aimed at a younger audience often increase certainty to deceive. The 2014 animated comedy/adventure movie *Big Hero 6*, which was based on a comic book series, focuses on the story of a young inventor, Hiro Hamada, who creates micro-robots called nanobots. He shows off his invention at a convention and draws the attention of industrialist Alistair Krei, who offers to buy the nanobots. Before Hiro can respond, Professor Callaghan, who runs the robotics program at the university Hiro wants to attend, accuses Krei of being an unscrupulous businessman. Hiro turns down Krei's offer and accepts a position in the university robotics program. Then a fire engulfs the convention hall. Hiro's brother rushes in to save Professor Callaghan. The building explodes, killing Hiro's brother and Callaghan. Hiro later learns that his nanobots, which he believed had been lost in the fire, are still operating, controlled by a villain in a kabuki mask. Hiro and the audience become certain the man in the mask is Krei. It is only much later that the villain's real identity is revealed: Professor Callaghan. The real story involves Krei conducting a teleportation experiment that cost the life of Callaghan's daughter, thereby explaining Callaghan's hatred of Krei and why Callaghan deceived everyone about his own death to use the nanobots as a weapon to destroy Krei.

Increase Certainty or Ambiguity?

Although techniques to increase certainty and ambiguity often can be used together, it is crucial to decide when to increase certainty or ambiguity, and which approach to apply to which aspects of your story. A mystery writer can increase ambiguity or certainty about the following in the real story:

- The murderer's identity
- The murderer's motive
- How the murder or crime was committed (means)
- Which crime is the real crime

You can increase certainty or ambiguity about all four variables or mix and match in a multitude of possibilities, increasing certainty about some variables, while increasing ambiguity about others. You also can increase certainty or ambiguity in relation to all of or parts of each of your cover stories.

Increasing ambiguity usually involves the use of disguises (who is who?), dazzle (which clues are important?), and certain types of red herrings (multiple cover stories, suspects, motives, crimes, or clues to make the real story harder to discern). Increasing certainty usually relies on the use of camouflage (I didn't even consider her as a suspect), framing (the murderer must be at the country house or work for the DA), conditioning (the pattern will repeat), changing the rules (the old rules of the murder mystery will apply to this mystery), and some types of red herrings (making readers certain a cover story is the real story or an innocent suspect is the killer).

Michael Connelly's *The Lincoln Lawyer* shows the techniques of increasing ambiguity and certainty well. The story involves the murder of a P.I. who works for Mickey Haller, the lawyer of the title. Connelly increases the certainty that one of Haller's clients, Louis Roulet, is the murderer. The motive is certain: the P.I. was investigating a murder Roulet appears to have committed, which occurred before the one Roulet is currently charged with. The means is also certain: the P.I. is shot with Haller's gun. The opportunity, however, is full of ambiguity, since Roulet was wearing a tracking ankle bracelet. It is unclear how he could have murdered the P.I. when the tracking system showed that Roulet never went near the P.I.'s home where the murder occurred. The reader is correct that the method was to use Haller's gun and that the murder was committed to protect Roulet, but any readers who became certain that Roulet committed the murder have been deceived. His mother committed the murder to protect her son. This shattering of the certainty about the identity of the murderer clears up the ambiguity regarding opportunity, since Roulet's mother, unlike Roulet, could easily have been at the P.I.'s house to murder the P.I. with Haller's gun.

Questions for Authors:

Do you plan to increase certainty or ambiguity about the identity of the murderer?

Do you plan to increase certainty about one suspect being guilty, then another and another in succession, thereby increasing ambiguity in the story overall?

Do you plan to slowly increase certainty about one suspect's guilt over the entire novel until that certainty is destroyed in the final scenes in a twist ending that reveals the real murderer?

Do you increase ambiguity or certainty about the motive for the crime? About the time, location and means by which the murder was committed?

What do you want the reader to think about the guilt or innocence of each character after each scene? After each chapter?

What do you want the reader to think about the nature of the real crime as the story progresses? Have you included other crimes readers may think are the real crime to increase ambiguity or do you use one cover crime to increase certainty and to mask the real crime until the end of the novel?

Common Mistakes and How to Fix Them:

The two most common mistakes related to increasing certainty or ambiguity are to increase certainty so much that the character you are attempting to make the reader believe is guilty is too obvious, or to increase ambiguity so much that readers are buried in cover stories and deceptive techniques so much they have difficulty following any story at all.

Whatever the genre, to make a cover story designed to increase certainty less obvious, use deceptive techniques to hide the "clues" related to the false suspect. Don't just offer readers a suspect with a clear motive, means and opportunity as a way of increasing certainty. The harder your hero has to work to track down the suspect, the more readers will become certain the suspect is guilty, only to be surprised when the real story is finally revealed.

If you have too many cover stories and too much ambiguity to the point of confusion, cut back on the details and events in the cover stories, possibly even cutting an entire cover story. Go back through your novel or screenplay and mark with different colored pens clues and scenes that relate to the real story and those that relate to each cover story. Use the color coding to determine whether the real story disappears from several scenes in a row. If it does, you should either reorder the scenes, so your real story doesn't disappear for longer than a scene or two, or add clues about the real story to more of your scenes that relate to your cover stories.

Chapter 19

Nesting: Putting it All Together

While the use of a single deceptive technique is effective, the use of several together greatly increases a novel or screenplay's deceptiveness and entertainment value. Arthur Conan Doyle's classic *The Hound of the Baskervilles* shows how to combine or nest deceptive techniques based on the principles of deception to create a wonderfully deceptive novel. *The Hound of the Baskervilles* opens with a mini mystery and a red herring: Sherlock Holmes and Dr. Watson speculate on the identity of the owner of a cane that an unknown visitor has left in their office. Wowing Watson with his exceptional powers of observation and deduction, Holmes predicts the appearance of James Mortimer, the cane's owner. The reader probably assumes Mortimer will be an integral part of the story, but in the real story he is tangential at best, merely serving as an entrée into the baffling curse of the Baskervilles. As Raymond Chandler advised, Conan Doyle has started his story by setting readers to solving the wrong mystery.

Mortimer recounts the story of the lecherous Hugo Baskerville. Hugo captured and imprisoned a young, country lass at his Devonshire estate, only to fall victim to a hellhound as he pursued her along the lonesome moors late one night. Ever since, the Baskerville line has been plagued by a mysterious, supernatural black hound. The recent death of Sir Charles Baskerville has rekindled fears, although Conan Doyle keeps readers guessing whether the mystery is a case of murder, death by natural causes or a supernatural incident. The next of kin, Sir Henry Baskerville, has arrived in London to take up his post at Baskerville Hall, but he has already been intimidated by an anonymous warning note and the strange theft of one of his shoes.

Holmes and Watson discover that Sir Henry is being trailed in London by a mysterious bearded stranger. Holmes, however, announces that he is too busy to accompany Mortimer and Sir Henry to Devonshire, and he sends Watson, insisting the doctor report back regularly. Once in Devonshire, Conan Doyle introduces a cover story: an escaped convict is roaming the moors. The convict is a suspect in the murder of Sir Charles and a potential threat to Sir Henry. Conan Doyle dazzles readers by adding even more suspects, including:

- The domestic help, Mr. and Mrs. Barrymore; Mr. Barrymore is caught skulking around the mansion at night
- Baskerville's neighbors, Mr. Jack Stapleton and his sister Beryl, who warns Watson to leave.
- Watson spies a lonely figure keeping watch over the moors: is it the escaped convict or another suspect?
- Watson hears a dog howling; is Conan Doyle going to change the rules and have a canine murderer?
- Watson learns of a secret meeting on the night of his death between Sir Charles and Laura Lyons, a local woman. She was going to ask him to help finance her divorce, but she claims she didn't keep the appointment.

Doing his best to uncover the real story beneath all the cover stories, Watson discovers that Mr. Barrymore's nightly jaunts are his attempt to aid the escaped convict, who turns out to be his brother-in-law. The doctor also discovers that the lonely figure wandering the moors is none other than Holmes, which removes one possible suspect, but still leaves the convict, the neighbors, the servants, and the supernatural as possibilities.

It is only at this point that Conan Doyle provides a key clue to the real story. Holmes discovers that the Baskerville's neighbor, Jack Stapleton, is in line to inherit the Baskerville fortune, and as such becomes the prime suspect. Holmes discovers that Jack convinced Laura Lyons to make and then miss the appointment with Sir Charles the night he was murdered. Having deceptively lured Sir Charles onto the moors, Stapleton released his ferocious pet hound, which terrified the superstitious nobleman and triggered a heart attack.

In a dramatic final scene, Holmes and Watson use the younger Baskerville as bait to catch Stapleton red-handed. After a late supper at the Stapleton's, Sir Henry heads home across the moors, only to be waylaid by the enormous Stapleton hound. Despite a dense fog, Holmes and Watson are able to subdue the beast and Stapleton, in his panicked flight, drowns in a marshland. Beryl Stapleton, who turns out to be Jack's wife and not his sister, is discovered tied up in his house, having refused to participate any longer in his dastardly scheme. Jack forced Beryl to assume the disguise of brother and sister so he could seduce and persuade Laura Lyons to set up the meeting with Sir Charles the night he was murdered. Holmes explains that the stolen shoe was used to give the hound Sir Henry's scent, making it a crucial clue and not a red herring.

In *The Hound of the Baskervilles,* Conan Doyle shows himself to be a master of the principles of deception. He made the cover stories as realistic and believable as the real story (an escaped convict, a spouse helping a convict brother-in-law, a woman seeking assistance from an influential and wealthy man to gain a divorce).

Conan Doyle uses facts to deceive. The story of a curse on the Baskervilles is a real myth that has been passed down through the family. Someone did steal Sir Henry's shoe. Laura Lyon did have an appointment with Sir Charles the night he died. A convict did escape from prison. Mr. Barrymore is trying to hide his movements as he sneaks out onto the moor. A hound, albeit not supernatural, did cause the death of Sir Charles.

Conan Doyle gave readers a range of choices about suspects, motives and the type of story. He also doled out information slowly (about the relationship between the Barrymores and the convict, the Stapletons' relationship, the ownership of the dog, why Sir Henry's shoe was stolen, and Jack Stapleton's relationship to the Baskervilles). He also let readers discover information to confirm their suspicions (Laura is a suspect and conveniently claims not to have kept her appointment with Sir Charles; the suspicious Mr. Barrymore sneaks out onto the moor to help his brother-in-law; and a convict escapes before a figure is seen skulking about on the moors). He also has the cover stories last until nearly the end of the novel. Throughout the novel, Conan Doyle increases uncertainty about the nature of the death and the suspects, as well as the possible motivations, means and opportunities to commit the real crime.

Conan Doyle also showed himself a master of the techniques of deception. He frames the mystery around the Baskervilles, but adds the escaped convict, neighbors and a mysterious figure on the moors to make the frame appear porous. Any reader who focuses on the Baskerville family as being crucial to the solution is correct, although the key clue—Jack Stapleton is a Baskerville heir—doesn't appear until late in the novel. Therefore, the villain is outside the Baskerville frame until that crucial late clue.

To deceive readers, Conan Doyle uses plenty of dazzle, with multiple suspects (the convict, the servants Mr. and Mrs. Barrymore, the Stapletons, the figure on the moors, Laura Lyons, the howling dog), motives (an ancient curse, inheritance, love [Laura Lyons], and madness [the convict]), as well as uncertainty about whether there was even a murder.

Conan Doyle has his villain use conditioning. Jack Stapleton uses the myth of Hugo Baskerville's demise at the paws of a supernatural hound to scare Sir Charles Baskerville to death. In the final scenes the myth once again appears on the verge of being repeated as the hound chases Sir Henry across the moors. Conditioning suggests that Sir Henry will share the same fate as Sir Charles, but Conan Doyle breaks the pattern and surprises the audience when Holmes and Watson save the day and Sir Henry.

Mystery readers expect the murderer to be human and to murder directly, but Conan Doyle breaks the rules by having the murderer use an enormous dog and a myth to frighten the victim into suffering a heart attack.

Conan Doyle does not manipulate time, but he includes red herrings galore: the escaped convict, the mysterious figure on the moors, Beryl Stapleton's warning to Watson, Sir Charles' possible love interest (Laura Lyons), the suspiciously acting servants, and the possibility of a deadly supernatural curse.

Holmes uses a disguise to stalk the moors and gather information without telling Watson, adding a layer of uncertainty to the story and another possible suspect. Jack Stapleton's hound is disguised as a supernatural source of retribution for the Baskervilles, while Jack and Beryl Stapleton are disguised as siblings when, in fact, they are married.

Conan Doyle uses many of his characters as his agents of deception. Jack Stapleton lies about his relationship to the Baskervilles, conceals his pet dog, and lies about his relationship to Beryl. Beryl also lies about their relationship, at least at first. Jack also conceals his relationship with Laura Lyons. The servants, the Barrymores, lie about the fact that the convict is Mrs. Barrymore's brother. Even Holmes lies, telling Watson that he is not going to come down to Baskerville Hall.

In terms of deceptive storytelling, Conan Doyle increases ambiguity by leaving the question about the type of death open until the end of the novel. Is it a murder mystery, a supernatural thriller or a case of death by natural causes? He also increases ambiguity with all his suspects: the Barrymores, the Stapletons, Laura Lyons, and the convict. By relying on the principles of deception and using a range of deceptive techniques to hide the real story beneath layers of cover stories, Conan Doyle created a masterful classic mystery in *The Hound of the Baskervilles.*

Agatha Christie was a master of deception and one of her masterpieces was *And Then There Were None*, which showed how to integrate a broad range of techniques into a wonderfully deceptive novel. Eight strangers are invited to Indian Island off the English coast. Vera Claythorne, a former governess, thinks she has been hired as a secretary. Philip Lombard, an adventurer, and William Blore, an ex-detective, think they have been hired to look out for trouble over the weekend. Dr. Armstrong is hired to look after the wife of the island's owner. Emily Brent, General Macarthur (No, not that General MacArthur), Tony Marston, and Judge Wargrave are coming to meet old friends.

When they arrive, the guests are greeted by Mr. and Mrs. Rogers, the butler and housekeeper, who report that their host, Mr. U. N. Owen, won't arrive until the next day. As the guests gather in the drawing room they hear a voice on a record player accuse each of them in turn of a murder committed in the past and never uncovered. They realize that none of them, including the servants, knows Mr. Owen.

As they discuss what to do, Tony Marston chokes on poisoned whiskey and dies. Vera Claythorne notices the similarity between the death of Marston and the first verse of a nursery rhyme, "Ten Little Indians," that hangs in each bedroom: "One choked his little self, and then there were nine." The next morning, the guests find that Mrs. Rogers died in her sleep. The guests hope to leave that morning, but due to a storm the boat that regularly delivers supplies doesn't appear. The frame Christie has created is now closed. Blore, Lombard and Armstrong search the island for the mysterious Mr. Owen, but find no one. The oldest guest, General Macarthur, feels sure he is going to die and goes to look out at the ocean. Before lunch, Dr. Armstrong finds the general dead of a blow to the head. The remaining guests decide that one of them must be the killer. The next morning, they find that Rogers has been murdered while chopping wood. The guests feel sure the murders are being carried out according to the dictates of the nursery rhyme. Ten Indian figures were on the dining-room table but with each death one of the figures disappears.

After breakfast, Emily Brent feels ill. She is soon found dead, having been injected with poison in the neck. Judge Wargrave organizes a search of everyone's belongings and they lock away anything that could be used as a weapon. Vera goes to take a bath, but is startled by a piece of seaweed hanging from the ceiling and cries out. Blore, Lombard and Armstrong run to help her, only to return downstairs to find Judge Wargrave draped in a curtain that resembles courtroom robes and with a red mark on his forehead. Dr. Armstrong examines the body and declares that Wargrave has been shot in the head.

That night Blore hears footsteps in the hall. He finds that Dr. Armstrong is not in his room. Blore and Lombard search for Armstrong, but they can't find the doctor. When they return from their search, they discover another Indian figure missing from the table.

Vera, Lombard and Blore go outside, resolving to stay in the safety of the open. Blore decides to return to the house for food. The other two hear a crash and they find someone has pushed a statue out of a second-story window, killing Blore as he approached the house. Was it Armstrong? Vera and Lombard retreat to the shore, where they find Armstrong drowned on the beach. Vera and Lombard are the only two characters left alive. Convinced that Lombard is the killer, Vera grabs Lombard's gun and shoots him. She finds a noose in her room, feels a compulsion to enact the last line of the nursery rhyme, and hangs herself.

The mystery baffles the police until a manuscript written by Judge Wargrave and sealed in a bottle is found washed ashore on a nearby beach. When a doctor told Wargrave he was dying, the judge decided to die in a blaze of glory. He planned the murders because he wanted to punish those whose crimes are not punishable by law. Wargrave describes how he tricked Dr. Armstrong into helping him fake his own death, promising to meet the doctor by the cliffs to plan how to unmask the murderer. When Dr. Armstrong arrived, Wargrave pushed him over the edge, then returned to the house and pretended to be dead. His ruse enabled him to dispose of the remaining guests. Once Vera hanged herself, Wargrave shot himself in such a way that his body would fall onto the bed as if it had been laid there. The police would find ten dead bodies on an empty island and an unsolvable mystery.

Just as Conan Doyle showed in *The Hound of the Baskervilles*, Christie displays her mastery of the principles of deception in *And Then There Were None*. Christie expertly cloaks the real story of Judge Wargrave's plan beneath a bodyguard of cover stories with 10 suspects and motives, each relating to a different murder in their past for which they escaped justice. All the cover stories appear realistic, dramatic and believable, including:

- A character who kills two children by driving recklessly
- A companion whose husband with her knowledge withholds life-saving medicine from her employer leaving the wife a large inheritance
- An army officer who sends his wife's lover on a mission he was certain not to survive
- A woman who dismisses her maid for being pregnant out of wedlock, who then drowns herself

Each cover story is also partially hidden, since it is unclear which stories are true and which are not. Each cover story could also hide a suspect intent on revenge. Over all of the other cover stories is the main cover story about Mr. U. N. Owen, who invited everyone to the island. He, of course, does not exist, so the "unknown" Owen cover story is a red herring.

A detective novel must have a plausible, even if highly unlikely solution. *And Then There Were None* is remarkable in that Christie's sense of detail and careful revelations make it believable. Still, there are moments when the novel seems contrived, such as when everyone believes the judge is dead just because the doctor announces his demise and Vera Claythorne's decision to hang herself. For millions of readers, the puzzle makes up for the highly unlikely albeit plausible aspects of the plot.

Christie follows the 4th Principle of deception by basing the cover stories on the truth, since as the story unfolds first two and then more and more of the accusatory stories about past murders turn out to be true. Each of the characters, save one, is also truthful in trying with increasing desperation to figure out the identity of the murderer. Even the villain, once they are all on the island, does not lie by commission, except maybe about their host.

With ten suspects, readers have a plethora of choice in deciding who will be the next victim, why someone is murdering all the guests, and who is behind it all. All but two of the characters deny the initial accusations, leaving the reader with a range of choices about which characters are lying. Christie even uses ten different methods to murder the characters, adding to the deception by decreasing the chance that one method might give away the identity of the murderer due to the need to be strong, familiar with poisons or some reason related to a certain type of murder. The flip side of creating a closed setting that limits the number of suspects is that everyone present could be the murderer, thereby increasing readers' choices.

In a masterful display of doling out information slowly and carefully, the murders are spaced out throughout the novel, ensuring that clues are also spaced out throughout the novel. By having the main cover story—that the murderer must be the last character alive—remain viable until the final pages, Christie increases the surprise when the real story is finally revealed in the postscript. By delaying the revelation of the real story until after the novel seems to be over with all of the characters dead, Christie significantly increases the dramatic impact of the revelation of the real story.

The novel also shows that Christie is a master of the techniques of deception. She frames the mystery as being on an island that no one can get to or leave after the first day. The murderer is in the frame, at least until he fakes his own death, which, in a masterfully deceptive stroke, removes him from the tightly constructed frame, increasing the surprise when his identity is finally revealed.

Christie employs dazzle with ten suspects (or nine after the first murder). As a motive, each character has a crime in their past to keep secret. Every character has the opportunity and means to commit each of the murders, since none require much, if any, special skill, knowledge or weaponry. Having ten murders is also dazzle, since readers try to figure out which murders are the most important in terms of solving the mystery. The murders of Judge Wargrave and Dr. Armstrong are the key ones to figure out the identity of the killer, but they are well masked by all the other murders.

Christie conditions the reader to accept that when a character is murdered they are, indeed, dead. Then, unbeknownst to the reader, Christie has Judge Wargrave and Dr. Armstrong conspire to fake Wargrave's death, breaking that conditioning.

Christie breaks the rules in several ways, including having:
- One of the victims fakes his own death
- Not one or two, but nine apparent murders in the story (and one suicide)
- Every character a detective character, leaving the reader baffled as to which character they are supposed to identify with; who is the hero or heroine?
- The final character commits suicide, so it appears that there is no solution to the mystery, a key requirement of a murder mystery
- The murderer explains what happens, fulfilling the role of the detective character

Christie doesn't manipulate time directly, although Wargrave's note at the end of the novel goes back in time to explain how he arranged the entire deadly plot, as well as his own faked murder. The phonograph also allows Wargrave, in a sense, to be in two places (or times) at once: he is in the room when his accusations against the others are heard.

Christie uses red herrings, including:

- All of the guests, save Wargrave, are lured to the island by red herrings, such as the offer of a job or to meet friends
- Wargrave is not dead when he appears to have been murdered
- The accusation against Wargrave—that he sentenced a criminal to hang who might have been innocent—is the weakest of the accusations, but places him among the accused
- Mr. Owen does not exist; he is Judge Wargrave
- With two characters left alive, the reader assumes one is the murderer
- Vera commits suicide, appearing to confirm that she is the murderer

Christie camouflages Judge Wargrave as one of the guests and then as one of the victims. The trip is disguised as a pleasure or business trip, when murder is the host's goal. Lombard is disguised as the murderer, since he is one of the last two characters alive and he has a gun. Then Vera is disguised as the murderer when she is the sole survivor and hangs herself.

Christie uses several of her characters as her agents of deception. She has Wargrave lie to the others about why they are on the island, who brought them there, and his role in the entire affair. Wargrave and Dr. Armstrong lie to the others about Wargrave's "death." Given that all of the characters have also been accused of crimes worthy of hanging, readers conclude that all of them are quite capable of lying, making it difficult to believe anything they say. Some confess to their past "crimes," while others do not. Are they lying?

In terms of deceptive storytelling, Christie increases certainty. As characters die, readers become increasingly certain that the final character alive, Vera Claythorne, is the murderer. Christie then confirms that suspicion when she has Vera hang herself; an insane murderer driven by guilt or psychosis to commit suicide. The audience becomes certain, but wrong. It is only in the postscript that Wargrave's nefarious plot and the real story are revealed.

Christie nests all of the techniques of deception firmly based on the principles of deception in a story that has sold millions of copies, been made into several successful movies and is world famous for its deceptive and devilishly entertaining plot. One final deception is the title. In some versions the title is *Ten Little Indians*, but 11, not 10 "little Indians" are murdered. Wargrave murders Isaac Morris, an unethical lawyer who buys Indian Island for Wargrave. Morris sold drugs to the daughter of one of Wargrave's friends, who becomes addicted and then committed suicide. But *Eleven Little Indians* isn't nearly as good a title as *Ten Little Indians* and, besides, Wargrave wasn't really murdered, he committed suicide, so there really were just ten murders.

P.D. James was a master of the mystery and her 1989 novel *Devices and Desires* is an example of a longer, modern mystery relying on the principles of deception and using the full range of deceptive techniques. James bases *Devices and Desires* on a relatively simple real story. Alex Mair, director of a nuclear power plant in Norfolk, is about to be offered a high government post in London. Alex is delaying the release of a negative report until the new position is offered to him, but his assistant, Hilary Robarts, threatens to make it public unless Alex marries her. Alex lives with his sister, Alice Mair. Alice fears losing Alex and that if Robarts publishes the report, Alex's career will be ruined. Alice murders Robarts. James then adds deceptive cover stories involving a mass murderer, an anti-nuclear group, affairs, an engineer's suicide, a threatened eviction, a vagrant's new shoes, and the theft and vandalism of a portrait to mask the real story and create an entertaining and deceptive murder mystery.

James uses deception from the start. A mass murderer, the Whistler, is disguised as a woman so he can get close to and murder a 15-year-old girl on a lonely road in Norfolk. The Whistler is not the only one to employ deception. James uses the first chapter, in which the girl is murdered, to frame the story so the reader focuses on solving the mystery of the identity of the Whistler. Just as Raymond Chandler suggested, James sets the reader to solving the wrong crime.

A detective, Commander Adam Dalgliesh, is visiting Norfolk, taking care of his aunt's estate after her death. Based on the unwritten rules of a murder mystery readers expect a reluctant detective and James establishes Dalgleish as the reluctant adversary of the Whistler. Dalgleish is on holiday and has no interest in searching for the mass murderer. When Robarts is murdered she appears to be the Whistler's fifth victim. Since Dalgliesh is the first on the scene of the murder, it appears to be another step along the path that will lead to Dalgleish matching wits with the Whistler. It is not until page 191 of the 503-page novel that the reader learns the Whistler committed suicide in an Easthaven hotel just before Robarts' murder. For almost 40 percent of the novel the reader has in all likelihood been focused on the deceptive cover story of identifying the mass murderer. All of the reader's time spent looking for clues that might suggest psychopathology, sexual deviance or an a-social personality in one of the suspects is voided and the frame of the novel shifts to who killed Hilary Robarts for a far more rational motive.

Even after the Whistler is found dead, the effect of framing the novel in terms of a psychopathic killer remains. Given the brutality of the crime, which copied the Whistler's methods, the reader is left with the deceptive impression that the murder will be motivated by an overriding passion or a great hatred. Deceptively, James makes the motive for the murder altruistic. The killer murders Robarts to save her brother from blackmail. There is no passion and little, if any, hatred involved.

Hilary Robarts' body was found just above a beach where she swam each evening. When Dalgleish and the local police search Robarts' home, they find two glasses on the counter in her kitchen. The local police conclude the pair of glasses means she had a guest before her swim, but Dalgleish notices that one of the glasses has a crack on the rim. Playing the part of Watson to misdirect the audience, a local policeman concludes, "Two glasses, two drinkers. That's the common sense explanation." Dalgleish disagrees; "Only when the obvious proved untenable was it necessary to explore less likely explanations. But it could also be the first fatally easy step into a labyrinth of misconceptions. He wondered why his instinct insisted that she had been drinking alone" (p.194). Unlike many mysteries, James has already shown the reader that Robarts took a glass down to have a drink alone, noticed the chip and used another glass. She didn't throw away the chipped glass because the set was a gift from her lover. Therefore, the clue is meant to deceive the police, allow Dalgleish to appear brilliant, and focus the reader's attention on the glasses. But the glasses are a red herring, although they support the police's later theory that another woman from the power station met the victim for a drink and then murdered her.

Two local police ponder the meaning of size-10 footprints left by a distinctive type of sneaker near Robarts' body. A detective says, "It's odd, though. Too plain, too distinctive, too opportune. You could almost believe it's been deliberately made to deceive us" (p.210). He is correct, but deceptively so, since the rules of mysteries dictate that lesser detectives don't discover key clues. The murderer, a tall woman, wore the sneakers as a disguise to appear to be a large man. She stole the shoes from stocks collected for a church bazaar and after the murder threw them into an abandoned World War II pillbox. A vagrant sleeping in the pillbox adds another layer of dazzle and another suspect when the police find him with the sneakers. Yet the vagrant had nothing to do with the murder, save asking a hopefully benevolent God for a better pair of shoes and suddenly having them flung through the doorway of the pillbox in which he was sleeping.

James takes a moment during a discussion of the meaning of the footprints to comment on the complexity of arriving at the truth and the essence of dazzle. Confused about the shoes, detective Rickards tells a suspect, "It's helpful to get different people's views of an incident. You get a more accurate picture that way." The suspect, Jago, replies, "More accurate? Different maybe. It'd only be more accurate if they were all telling the truth" (p.282).

James uses linguistic conventions to deceive readers in a type of red herring. She has the coroner use the pronoun "he" to describe the murderer. Although it is a convention to call an unknown person "he," it is a red herring in that the murderer is a woman. Of course, if the coroner had said "she," it would have given away far too much. The use of "he" also reinforces the initial frame of the novel with the male Whistler murdering a woman, conditioning the reader to believe that when another woman is murdered, it's his work. Even when the reader learns the Whistler committed suicide before the last murder, the reader has been conditioned to think the murderer is a man. Furthermore, the last murder mimicked the murders of the other women, with an "L" carved into the victim's foreheads and their pubic hair cut off and stuffed into their mouths. This brutal form of murder reinforces the invalid conclusion that the murderer is a violent man. James has detective Rickards reinforce this red herring when he states that the murder is a "male" crime, unlikely to be committed by a woman.

To mask the real story, James adds a cover story about an anti-nuclear group plotting to attack the nuclear power station where Robarts worked. The anti-nuclear angle added to the Whistler character leave the reader wondering about the type of novel they are reading: a serial killer tale, a cozy murder mystery or an international thriller. As another red herring, the "L" carved into the forehead of the Whistler's victims might stand for Larksoken, the name of the power station. James makes Robarts' murder and the anti-nuclear cover story overlap by having three of the suspects in Robarts' murder—an unemployed man who lives in a trailer above the beach, Neil Pascoe, and his girlfriend, Amy Camm, and the station director's assistant, Carolyn Amphlett—active in the anti-nuclear group.

James uses Carolyn to add multiple layers of deception to the novel. Carolyn has seduced an engineer at the station, Jonathan Reeves. When the director, Alex Mair, wonders why Carolyn is dating such an uninspiring individual, it appears he is just jealously complaining. The conclusion masks the fact that Carolyn seduced Reeves to obtain information about the power station for a planned terrorist attack. James also has Carolyn lie when she tells Amy that she is a member of an animal rights group and doesn't tell her about a plan to seize nuclear power stations in three countries.

James uses the anti-nuclear angle to include a red-herring cover story involving postcards that someone has been leaving in the ruins of an abbey. Carolyn and Amy have been using the postcards to communicate secretly. Alice Mair, the sister of the power station director, says she saw Carolyn in disguise meeting a man who is not her engineer boyfriend at a cathedral. Hearing the story, Reeves investigates. Carolyn hears that a man is asking about her and incorrectly concludes that the police are closing in on her. She flees, making her appear guilty of Robarts' murder—a convincing red herring.

James frames the mystery in terms of the power station. Two women who worked at the station have been murdered, one by the

Whistler and one by Alice Mair. Crucially, Alice doesn't work at the station; she is the director's sister. James also initially frames the novel as related to a serial killer to deceive readers.

Using the concept of having the reader focus on solving the wrong crime, James includes multiple cover story crimes, including stories related to the identity of the serial murderer, the mystery of the suicide of a power station engineer, and, on the night of the murder, the theft of a portrait of Robarts from an artist's shed, which was slashed and thrown through the window of Robarts' cottage, as well as minor mysteries, such as the theft of shoes from the church bazaar stocks. Each crime offers readers a choice and a chance for James to deceive her audience.

James uses characters to lie for her. A key witness and suspect, Meg Dennison, doesn't tell the police when another suspect, Alice Mair, lies to them. Alice tells the police that the night of the murder she was alone in her cottage all evening. The area is remote and, when Alice went to commit the murder, she locked her cottage. If anyone came by she planned to claim to have been asleep. She forgot that she gave her best friend and neighbor, Meg, a key and when Meg's plans change because her car won't start, she stops by Alice's cottage to find no one home at the time of the murder. The reader doesn't know this until very late in the novel, unless they can piece together the mention of the loan of the key, Meg's often un-announced visits, and her odd reaction when the police interview Alice. Meg's nervousness over Alice's (inaccurate) answers to the police is masked by misattribution because Meg arrives at Alice's home upset about the recent murder. James plays fair by having Alice tell the police she was home all evening. Then Meg arrives and Alice repeats her crucial answer, which Meg knows is a lie. Alice then mentions that she did go out at 9:30 p.m., well after the murder, to pick up a painting from the artist Ryan Blaney, which was not in a shed where it was supposed to be. It was the painting that was later thrown through the window of Robarts' cottage. In a classic misattribution red herring, it would take an adept reader to realize that Meg's agitation is caused by Alice lying rather than by the recent murder.

Since Meg's evidence is crucial to solving the mystery, James seeks to make readers certain that Meg is the murderer, thereby casting doubt on her evidence. A police detective asks Meg if she was in all evening. Meg says no, she did not leave her house. It is a lie, since she went to see Alice and found no one home. In a cliché of bad mysteries when the criminal hastily changes their story, Meg corrects herself and adds that she was in the garden for a time. Later, another character says that he called Meg at 9:15 p.m. and got no answer, but did get an answer 30 minutes later, all of which casts suspicion on Meg. If readers become certain Meg is the murderer, they are certain, but wrong.

James also casts doubt on Meg's reliability. Readers learn early in the novel that Meg had a mental breakdown while teaching at a school in London. Just as James does with Meg, authors often mislead readers by using apparently unreliable witnesses to provide crucial clues. In the *Midsomer Murders* episode "Murder on St. Malley's Day," the writers make Dudley Carew, a conspiracy crackpot, provide key evidence about a murder at a local boarding school. Most viewers will discount his advice to DCI Barnaby and Sergeant Troy that the murder is related to the school. In the end, Carew's correct, even if it costs him his life. Agatha Christie took this technique to an extreme in *Dumb Witness* when she had a wire-haired fox terrier provide a key clue that is required to solve a murder. Dogs may be man's best friend, but how reliable can they be in a witness box?

James uses infinite clues; clues that appear to limit the number of suspects yet actually rule out almost no one. One such clue is that the murderer needed to know that Robarts swam each night at 9 p.m. At first this appears to limit the suspects to those close to the victim, yet it becomes clear that almost everyone at the power station knew about her nightly dips. Another such clue relates to the portrait of Robarts, which was stolen and thrown through her cottage's window the night of the murder. At first it appears few knew about the portrait, thereby casting suspicion on the local artist of the portrait and his family. The painting, however, hung in a local pub and almost everyone saw it. The large sneakers also rule out almost no one, except the painter's young daughter, Theresa.

James uses multiple suspects as dazzle to deceive readers. Her suspects include: the director's assistant, Carolyn Amphlett; the anti-nuclear activist Neil Pascoe and his girlfriend Amy; the director, Alex Mair, and his sister, Alice Mair; the vagrant; the neighbor Meg; and the painter, Ryan Blaney, and his eldest daughter, Theresa Blaney. Even Commander Dalgleish is a suspect, if an unlikely one. He knew the victim, knew the Whistler's modus operandi, and found the body, all of which suggests that he had the means and opportunity to commit the murder. Motive appears to be lacking and, given he is a recurring character, it is unlikely he is the murderer. The suggestion, however, raises a small, but nagging possibility in the reader's mind, adding a sliver more deception to the already deception-filled novel.

A prime suspect is the power station director, Alex Mair. James uses facts to make him appear guilty. James presents him as a cold fish, who had an affair with Robarts and with Amy, even though she lives with Neil Pascoe. After the murder, Alex lies, claiming his relationship with Robarts was over, even though Robarts had just rewritten her will in expectation of marrying him, leaving everything to him. The amount in the will is small, so the police dismiss money as a motive, although the reader soon learns Robarts was attempting to blackmail Alex into marrying her. Casting further negative light on Alex, early in the novel the reader learns that when he was a boy, Alex dragged his sister away after their father accidentally sliced his thigh open with a billhook. Unable to get help and abandoned by his children, the father bled to death. The father had been molesting the daughter, Alice Mair, and the now grown brother and sister share a house. Told from Alice Mair's perspective, the story is deceptive in that the focus of the story is on Alex. Most readers will draw the logical, yet incorrect conclusion that Alex is capable of murder. The true meaning of the story is that, just as Alex committed murder by omission to protect his sister, Alice will commit murder by commission to protect her brother from Robarts, who is blackmailing Alex into marriage.

Murderers are supposed to be evil, but James breaks the rules by making Alice Mair cultured, nice and altruistic. When the reader first meets her, Dalgleish, who is also a poet, is delivering cookbook proofs to her. Alice is framed as a cook and an author; not exactly the most murderous of occupations. She is presented as a refined woman who was a victim of incest, is devoted to her brother and, in one of her early scenes, helps a neighbor's children get back home, even while sharing with the daughter a dinner party's secret menu. Even on the night of the murder, she exhibits altruism. She sees the artist's daughter (Theresa Blaney) out alone. Alice realizes

that the artist, Ryan Blaney, will have no alibi since Theresa is not
home to provide one. Going against the convention that murderers
do no good deeds, James has Alice provide Ryan Blaney with an
alibi. Alice is supposed to pick up a painting from his cottage. He
told her to just pick it up from a shed and not to bother to knock
at the cottage. If she follows his instructions, she will not see him
and won't be able to provide him with an alibi. Conversely, if she
knocks at the cottage to say she picked up the portrait, it will raise
suspicions about why she knocked when he told her not to. Therefore, in a one-ahead trick straight out of magic that James uses
to manipulate time, Alice arrives at the Blaney's cottage, takes the
portrait from the shed and puts it in the trunk of her car. She then
knocks at the cottage to tell a severely drunk Ryan the painting is
missing. James then adds another deceptive layer to the story by
having Alice slash the painting and throw it through the front window of Robarts' house to accomplish three goals: dispose of the
supposedly stolen painting; remove any chance the police will think
Blaney, who hated the victim, killed her, since the destruction of
the painting appears to link someone who loathes the artist to the
crime; and, finally, use the smashed front window to gain entrance
to Robarts' house to hide the leather belt she used to strangle Robarts in the victim's cottage among her own belts (dazzle). One
of Alice's goals may be foiled since Dalgleish points out that the
slashes are clean, so the painting can be repaired fairly easily. The
reader may wonder whether Blaney slashed his own painting to
divert suspicion from himself, but that just adds another choice for
readers and another red herring.

The key to solving a mystery is to determine the character who
has the motive, means and opportunity to commit the crime. In
mysteries, authors often give many characters a motive. A common
way to accomplish this is to make the victim disliked by most, if not
all, of the other characters, allowing the reader to dislike them and
conclude they deserved to be murdered. This maintains our belief
in a just world; only evil or unlikable people are murdered. James
ensures that in *Devices and Desires* all of the main characters have a
motive to murder the victim. Robarts was planning to buy the cottage Blaney rented and evict the artist and his brood of children.
Blaney had painted a portrait of Robarts, which was described as
being "full of hatred," providing Blaney and his children, especially

his eldest daughter, Theresa, with ample motive. Robarts was also suing the anti-nuclear activist, Neil Pascoe, for libel. If he lost, he would be ruined, which would also cost Amy her home, since she lived with him. Robarts was also trying to blackmail Alex Mair into marrying her, possibly threatening his relationship with Alice and his sexual relationship with Amy. The plant's operations manager, Lessingham, disliked the overly officious Robarts. The director's assistant, Carolyn, had a favorite motive of some mystery writers: an old wrong done to her family. Robarts' father owned a plastics company that obliterated the life savings of Carolyn's mother.

James ensures that many of the characters also had the opportunity to commit the murder, increasing the choices readers face. Lessingham was alone out on his boat near the scene of the crime on the night of the murder. He also found the Whistler's previous victim, providing him with the mass murderer's modus operandi to copy if he murdered Robarts. Alice Mair was home alone and therefore lacked an alibi, while her neighbor Meg was also alone after having seen an elderly couple she lived with off in a taxi to the train station. Theresa Blaney was seen in the area at the time of the murder and her father, Ryan, only had a weak alibi provided by his daughter and Alice Mair, who came to pick up the portrait. Alice saw him soon after the time of the murder and found him too drunk to have driven a car or ridden a bike to the distant scene of the crime. Theresa's provision of an alibi for her father only makes Ryan Blaney appear guiltier since the reader knows Theresa was out the evening of the murder. The director's assistant, Carolyn, who also lacks an alibi, reinforces perceptions of her own guilt by asking her boyfriend, Reeves, to lie and tell the police they spent the evening together. Increasing the level of deception even more, Carolyn is guilty, but not of murder. She is planning a terrorist attack on the power station. Guilt, however, looks the same regardless of its cause.

To have the means to commit the murder, the murderer had to know how the Whistler killed his victims. This information is only known to the police, the characters who found the victims, and those who attended a dinner party at Alice Mair's home. One of the guests is late, having found one of the victims, and he tells the dinner party guests what he saw in detail. James shows patience with this information and only provides it after page 250, relatively late in the story. The dinner party includes: Alex Mair (who was checked in at the power station at the time of the murder, but as the director he might know a way to fake his presence); his sister, Alice; their neighbor, Meg; the artist's daughter, Theresa; Lessingham; and Dalgleish. All have motive and lack alibis that would satisfy a suspicious reader, except for Dalgleish. The key to dismissing Carolyn and her engineer lover Reeves as suspects are the fact that neither attended the dinner party nor found a Whistler victim.

The murderer also needed to know Robarts would be swimming shortly after 9 p.m. (which was common knowledge), where to find the sneakers at the church that left tracks at the murder scene, be tall enough to wear the sneakers (which rules out Theresa Blaney), and have the opportunity to dispose of the sneakers in the bunker. Of the five remaining suspects, these criteria fit Alex Mair, Alice Mair, Lessingham, and possibly Meg (if she is large enough to wear the sneakers). Most importantly, the murderer could not yet know that the Whistler had committed suicide or they wouldn't have attempted to make Robarts' murder appear to have been his work. Whoever fit all of the requirements is the murderer. James uses dazzle to make it a challenge for readers to identify the seven requirements, which are difficult to keep in mind without jotting them down. It is even more difficult to keep track of the crucial variables for all of the suspects, centering on the four dinner party guests (three if the reader rules out Dalgleish) and the two hosts (Alice and Alex Mair). This assumes the reader realizes the dinner party is crucial to winnowing down the suspects. Unlike Christie's novels and many other Golden Age mysteries, there is no handy list of characters at the front of the novel to aid in keeping all of the characters straight. Worse for the reader attempting to solve the mystery, many of the suspects in *Devices and Desires* fit one, two or even more of the requirements, and only one fits them all: Alice Mair.

The length of the novel, 503 pages in paperback, is a form of dazzle and makes it difficult to remember all of the key events, characters and clues. The fact that the novel would usually be read over several weeks makes it more difficult to penetrate James's deceptions and identify the murderer. The length also increases the depth of characterization in the novel making for far more complex characters than for the most part existed in the shorter novels of the Golden Age. This very depth, however, adds dazzling information that makes it far more difficult to winnow out the clues from the characterization chaff. Furthermore, some of the links between the murderer and the key clues are slight. It is mentioned in a general description when the reader first meets Alice Mair that she is "tall." This single clue will prove crucial in allowing her to wear the size-10 sneakers at the murder site. If a reader forgets this one fact, they may rule her out as a suspect because she is a woman and erroneously focus on the male suspects.

James uses the truth to mask her real story. There is a mass murderer called the Whistler who murders women. There is an antinuclear group targeting the power plant. Alex Mair is having an affair with Amy and had an affair with Carolyn. Carolyn and Amy are passing notes secretly via their hiding place in the abandoned abbey. The vagrant does find the size-10 sneakers. Carolyn is having an affair with the engineer, Reeves. Robarts was threatening to evict Blaney and his family. Robarts was blackmailing Alex Mair into marriage.

Showing her patience, James uses one cover story as the ending of the novel before revealing the true story at the very end for maximum dramatic effect. Near the end of the novel, Detective Rickards and his assistant Oliphant conclude that Carolyn and Amy committed the murder. In terms of motive, Amy wanted to stop Robarts' libel case against the man she lives with, which might cost her their home, and Robarts recently shoved Amy's child. In terms of opportunity, Reeves changes his story and tells the police that Carolyn was alone the night of the crime. The pair of women, who are suspected lovers, have motive and opportunity, but even Rickards wonders how they could have known the Whistler's modus operandi; neither found a victim nor where they at the dinner party. He can't question them because the terrorists Carolyn fled in a boat to meet murder her and Amy, since they believe Carolyn's cover has been blown. With the pair lost at sea, the means issue is left unresolved and the story appears to be over. Dalgleish, however, continues to wonder.

Displaying the utmost patience, James uses a chain of suspects to slowly reveal the real story. In a scene just before her death, Carolyn mentions she saw Theresa Blaney near the site of the murder on the night of the crime, casting suspicion on the artist's daughter.

As Theresa rushes to the hospital for an emergency appendectomy, she tells her father that she saw Meg near the murder site the night of the crime. Meg claimed she didn't leave her cottage that night, so the reader then suspects her. James then shows that Meg did leave her cottage that night, but stopped at Alex and Alice Mair's cottage and found no one home, although Alice said she was home all evening. The truth finally comes out. Alice was not at home when the murder occurred (opportunity), had the means (a knife in her kitchen to mimic the "L" the Whistler cut in his victims' foreheads), and knew how the Whistler killed because she hosted the dinner party at which the guest described finding one of his victims. James gives Alice two motives. Counter-intuitively, by providing multiple motives, James provides a choice, which increases uncertainty and thereby makes the crime harder to solve. The murdered woman, Robarts, had been Alex Mair's lover, with the suggestion that they might marry. If they did, Alice would "lose" her brother. The story of how Alex defended her as a child by letting their father, who had been molesting Alice, accidentally die, shows the siblings' closeness to each other. Alice appears to be guilty. She is the murderer and did kill for her brother, but for a different motive. She murdered to avoid letting Robarts ruin Alex's future by blackmailing him into marriage. Alice believes that Robarts, a secretary, would never do as the wife of a high government official. Meg elicits the key clues in a conversation with Alice and then gives her a night to consider turning herself in. James shrouds the case in deception until the end when Alice burns down her cottage to commit suicide, so no one is ever charged for the murder of Hilary Robarts.

Elizabeth George's 1996 novel *In the Presence of the Enemy* begins when a young girl, Charlotte Bowen, the daughter of right-wing politician Eve Bowen, is kidnapped. Ransom notes sent to the politician and a left-wing tabloid publisher, Dennis Luxford, state that for the girl to be released unharmed, the publisher must "Use page one to acknowledge your firstborn child." The note is a red herring at the core of the real story.

Charlotte was the result of a fling at a political convention a decade before. Even though she is now married, Eve Bowen has built her reputation on being a single mother abandoned by her child's father, who rose to the highest level of government without help from anyone. Throughout her career, Bowen has kept the identity of her daughter's biological father secret. If Luxford prints that he is the father, it will destroy Bowen's career. How could a right-wing politician ever have a child with the scandal-mongering, muckraking editor of a left-wing tabloid? The revelation of their tryst would also damage the government, which has been suffering through a series of morals scandals after it campaigned on a platform of reaffirming family values.

George increases certainty by using a realistic and believable cover story to focus on one suspect: Luxford. Bowen believes Luxford kidnapped his daughter and sent the ransom note to justify publishing news of their fling, which will harm the right-wing government and boost his tabloid's circulation. Is George using Luxford as an agent of deception? Believing the girl's biological father will not harm his own child, Bowen refuses to respond to the ransom note or even call the police.

Although he agrees not to involve the police, Luxford refuses to do nothing, so he enlists the help of a forensic scientist, Simon St. James. Many mysteries start with the police investigating the crime and failing before the detective hero appears. George breaks the rules by having an independent detective and not the police investigate. St. James is capable, intelligent and appealing, making it likely many readers will conclude he will solve the case. Even so, St. James fails and the main detectives in the story take over: Detective Inspector Thomas Lynley and Detective Sergeant Barbara Havers. St. James's failure makes Lynley appear more brilliant when he gets much further toward solving the crime, since a scientist who is far from stupid failed to solve the case. George is not done with St. James, however. In a deceptive twist that also breaks the rules, she has St. James and not her lead detective, Lynley, discover the crucial clue that unravels the case like a ball of yarn. (The word "clue" used to have one meaning: a ball of yarn. Therefore, when it acquired the second meaning related to a mystery, people "unraveled" clues, just as yarn is unraveled.)

George layers on another cover story by using one of her youngest characters to deceive readers; in fiction there are no age restrictions for agents of deception. Lynley and Havers discover that Charlotte had a best friend, Breta. The politician's housekeeper and music teacher mention Breta and St. James even finds a

girl with a similar name, Brigitta Walters, which could be a longer
version of Breta. St. James learns that Breta had lured Charlotte
into trouble before and may have convinced her to run away. Eve
Bowen confirms that her daughter has disappeared before. George
reinforces the cover story by writing scenes in which the kidnapped
Charlotte talks to Breta. George has created another choice for
readers: was Charlotte kidnapped or did she just run away? George
ensures her cover story lasts by having Lynley and Havers spend a
great deal of time and effort tracking down Breta before they learn
from Charlotte's stepfather (another possible suspect) that Breta is
Charlotte's imaginary friend—and a red herring.

In part by delaying the discovery of Breta's true nature, George
delays the moment when her readers realize the true nature of the
real crime. Charlotte may have run away or one of her parents may
be holding her, in which case it is assumed she is safe. Reinforcing the later possibility is the fact that Eve Bowen seems far from
alarmed, and both parents oppose involving the police. St. James
even suggests that one of the parents might know where Charlotte
is being held. Employing dazzle, George adds even more deceptive
cover stories by having Lynley and Havers pursue a range of possible explanations for Charlotte's disappearance: kidnapping by a
stranger; a family custody matter (Bowen denied Luxford contact
with Charlotte); a runaway; a politician (Eve Bowen) out for political advantage by playing the suffering mother of a kidnapped little
girl; or a political angle (Bowen is in the Home Office and has taken
a hard line on Northern Ireland). The IRA red herring is strengthened when a music teacher, Damien Chambers, who was the last
person known to have seen Charlotte, is found to have connections
to the IRA. George doesn't stop there; Bowen's housekeeper, who
looked after Charlotte, is Irish. Choices abound about the type of
crime and the motive, and with each choice the reader may choose
the wrong option and be deceived.

George even includes choice in the interpretation of the ransom
note. The kidnapper makes no demand for money, only asking that
Luxford acknowledge his "firstborn." Therefore the motive appears to be personal. The kidnapper seems to bear a grudge against
either Luxford or Bowen, which suggests the kidnapper knows one
or both of them, especially since the kidnapper knew Charlotte

was Luxford's daughter. Most readers will conclude the kidnapper personally knew the publisher, yet it is another red herring.

Then Charlotte is found drowned in a canal. Havers is sent to the Wiltshires to investigate where the body was discovered. She works with a local detective, Robin Payne, who just returned from the capital after attending a detective's course. The new location enlarges the geographic frame of the crime, greatly increasing the number of suspects (dazzle).

George continues to add red herrings. Back in the capital, Lynley investigates a report about a police constable who was seen rousting a vagrant near where Charlotte was last seen. The police find an apartment in an abandoned building where someone kept watch on Charlotte as she walked from school to her music lesson, after which she was kidnapped. The abandoned room suggests that the vagrant is the kidnapper, but after a long investigation, he is found to be innocent. Even so, George is not done with the vagrant. It is a case of a red herring that swallowed a clue. Once the reader learns the vagrant is not the kidnapper, they are likely to dismiss his importance, yet his story is crucial to solving the mystery. George displays her patience doling out information when much later the reader learns that the vital person to find in the vagrant-being-rousted scene is not the vagrant, but the police officer. After checking with every police officer in the area, Lynley concludes that the murderer used a disguise to kidnap Charlotte: who notices a police constable talking to a little girl? Lynley believes it was either a civilian wearing a police uniform or a police officer from somewhere else. In either case, it is an infinite clue in that it does little, if anything, to narrow down the suspects. Anyone can rent a police uniform from a costume shop and there are multiple police officers in the novel.

Then Luxford's son, Leo, is kidnapped. Until the second kidnapping the reader may still be uncertain about the target of the crimes because George keeps the choices open. When Charlotte is taken, the target could be Bowen, Luxford or both. Leo's kidnapping means Luxford is the target, thereby narrowing the number of suspects to only those with a motive against the publisher. Since George doesn't want to greatly decrease her dazzling number of suspects, she immediately raises the possibility that Luxford's wife kidnapped their son.

Another note demanding that Luxford acknowledge his first-born arrives, setting a time deadline that increases suspense. To save his son, Luxford prints the story about his tryst with Bowen. Readers and everyone else in the story except the murderer assumes the kidnapper will now increase his demands, as is the rule in such stories. George breaks the rules. In a surprise, the kidnapper calls and laconically says Luxford "got it wrong." Luxford and Bowen have no idea what could be wrong in the published account. George again provides readers with a choice and readers are deceived into concluding that Luxford and/or Bowen are lying. George then reinforces the possibility that Luxford is lying by focusing on the fact that he talked to the kidnapper alone and no one else heard the call. Is George using Luxford to lie for her to deceive readers? She isn't. It's another red herring.

George adds yet another possibility when Lynley concludes that Luxford must have another child. The reader will assume the hero is right. It is, in fact, yet another red herring hiding a clue, since Luxford doesn't have another child, the kidnapper just thinks he does.

After George makes Lynley and Havers work hard to discover more clues, the reader finally learns that the kidnapper, the rural constable Havers works with, Robin Payne, believes he is Luxford's firstborn. Even the politician Bowen is just a red herring. Years before, Luxford went to a school in the Wiltshires when the kidnapper's mother was doing "favors" for boys from the school for money until she got pregnant. She denies she ever told her son Luxford was his father, but Robin remembers she told him and believes it. Worse, Payne remembers his mother telling him Luxford raped her. Payne has kidnapped and murdered to force the man whom he believes to be his father to acknowledge him and what Luxford did to his mother years before.

Payne and Luxford are linked in several ways, but some are facts and some are lies that only Payne believes, making the novel doubly deceptive. A crime with a motive based on a lie is a deceptive crime indeed. Years before, Luxford opened a savings account for Charlotte in case she ever needed money. Payne's girlfriend, Celia Matheson, works at a bank, which is how Payne gained access to the bank's computer and found Luxford's account for Charlotte. Payne jumped to the erroneous conclusion that Luxford had raped

someone else. Payne originally wanted to see Luxford's bank accounts to know how much to ransom Luxford's son for, but then
learned about Luxford's daughter with Bowen and decided to kidnap Charlotte first. The reader learns that Celia works in a bank
and that she is Payne's girlfriend, but George provides the clues in
different scenes. The key to solving the crime is to link the chain of
clues from Luxford through the account for Charlotte to the bank
teller/girlfriend, and finally to Payne. George has ensured that each
link in the chain involves choice and at each link readers have a
chance to make the wrong choice.

George hides her kidnapper/murderer with a disguise. He is a
police constable. To increase the deception, George has Havers fall
in love with Payne. Mystery readers have been conditioned to expect a love affair as a subplot that is often only tangentially related
to the real crime. The romantic subplot between Havers and Payne
mirrors the romance between the lead detective, Lynley, and his
girlfriend, St. James's assistant, Lady Helen. The reader may assume
that George has given Lynley's assistant a love interest to mirror
his own, especially since Havers rarely, if ever, has a love interest in
George's novels.

George hides Payne with a disguise as a constable and as a love
interest, but she also hides him in a third way: he helps the investigation, especially by discovering the mill where Charlotte was held.
Unlike some mysteries in which readers may conclude that the suspect who "discovers" crucial clues is the murderer, George lets the
reader come along as Payne doggedly searches the area and, finally,
after a long and arduous search, finds the mill. It is easy for readers to be deceived into believing the search was genuine, since it is
told first-hand, instead of just having Payne announce what he has
found. Information that is shown is more powerful and is assumed
to be true more often than information that is told to the reader.
Furthermore, when Payne arrives at the scene where Charlotte's
body is discovered, the scene is told from his point of view. He
is nervous, arriving at the scene of his first murder as a detective,
and the reader follows him as he appears to piece together what
happened before his domineering superior officer. Most readers
will feel sorry for him. Payne feels ill when he sees the body, even
though the entire scene is a deceptive red herring since Payne murdered Charlotte and dumped her in the canal.

George places Payne outside the frame of the crimes, both chronologically and geographically. In terms of time, Payne does not appear as a character until page 223. Therefore, it is impossible for the reader to solve the mystery until at least page 223. The appearance of the villain is much later than in many Golden Age mysteries, when the murderer appears early in the novel, if not in the first few pages. This delay also separates the crime from the villain in the reader's mind, given the time (and page) difference between the kidnapping in the first few pages and Payne's first appearance as a character. Geographically, Payne appears in the Wiltshires where Charlotte's body was found, not in the capital, where almost all of the action up to that point has occurred, including the kidnapping of Charlotte and later of Leo. Payne appears to be geographically out of the frame and is never shown in the capital.

Just as Agatha Christie did in *The Murder of Roger Ackroyd*, George relies on a casually mentioned time discrepancy to mask her murderer. She does not lie through her villain by commission, merely by omission. The crucial clue is included in a dazzling wealth of information about Payne when the reader first meets him, an excellent time to provide crucial clues since at that point readers don't even know if the character is going to be a major, minor or even just a bit character in the novel, let alone the murderer. The reader learns that it has been three weeks since Payne finished his training course and two weeks since he made detective. The week discrepancy and the later information that the detective course was in London are the only clues tying Payne to the location and timing of Charlotte's kidnapping. Given that Payne is introduced late and in a section that is told from his point of view, it would be a sharp-eyed reader indeed who saw such clues as crucial to solving the crime. Furthermore, the clue is told to the reader, not shown, thus lessening the chance readers will attune to it, much less remember it. George also develops a twist on the narrator or point-of-view character being the murderer by having one of her many point-of-view characters (and a detective at that) turn out to be the murderer.

In 623 pages (paperback), George creates a relatively open mystery without a single clear setting. She uses the various settings (geographic, professional, political, and social) to provide a dazzling array of suspects to mask her real story. At first the prime suspect is Luxford. She provides ample evidence based on the truth to tie him to the kidnappings and the murder. Luxford mimics some of the traits usually attributed to a fictional criminal and is portrayed in a negative light. He runs a scandal-mongering tabloid. He is pushing his young, artistic son to go to a school his son hates and to act more like a man. Luxford appears brusque, uncouth and willing to do anything for a story. He sends photographers to get pictures of a wife leaving her politician husband who was seen in a car behind a station with a boy prostitute. Luxford had the fling at the political conference with Bowen when he was engaged to his current wife, Fiona. Beyond the negative traits, George uses facts as clues to tie Luxford to the crimes. Charlotte's glasses and hair are found in his car, even though Luxford claims he never had contact with her. (Payne planted the evidence.) Luxford recently visited his old school, Baverstock, in the Wiltshires near where Charlotte's body was found. When he was a boy at the school, Luxford was in a club that explored the area, including the abandoned mill where Charlotte was held before she was murdered. The cover story is a masterful example of deception based on the truth. The reader is wrong if they conclude Luxford is guilty, but they are also wrong if they reject him as being crucial to solving the crime. In the kidnapper's mind, Luxford is crucial to the motive.

George also makes the politician, Eve Bowen, a suspect. Bowen may have kidnapped her daughter to gain public sympathy as her government suffers through a storm of scandals. Like Luxford, George makes her a dislikable character. She is a distant, uninvolved mother who has used her daughter's illegitimacy to further her political career. She even refers to her daughter as a "mistake" for which she is still paying. When Charlotte is kidnapped, Bowen is so out of touch with her daughter that she isn't even aware Charlotte has been kidnapped until Luxford calls her hours after the fact. To add to the suspicion that Bowen may have kidnapped her own daughter, Bowen's reaction to the kidnapping is described as "unnatural" (p.45). She shows no fear or concern for her daughter's safety and doesn't even stop working, let alone call the police. Her reaction is shown in sharp contrast to the girl's stepfather who reacts with frantic alarm and demands they call the police. George uses this contrast to further cast suspicion on Bowen, with even the stepfather wondering if his wife is guilty.

George also casts Charlotte's music teacher as a suspect. He is nervous, acts oddly and seems to be hiding something. The music teacher is the last person known to have seen Charlotte. George once again offers readers a choice: the teacher may be nervous because he fears losing his other young clients if news gets out that he is linked to the disappearance of a young girl or he may be guilty of kidnapping or as von Moltke warned, maybe there is another possibility. The teacher is nervous when the police interview him at his flat. He excuses himself, rushes upstairs to the bathroom and quickly returns, flustered. In a classic use of misattribution, readers may attribute the teacher's nervousness and odd behavior to guilt over the kidnapping. The music teacher does have something to hide, but it is unrelated to the kidnapping. He is homosexual and is having an affair with the macho star of a police television series, whose image and career will be ruined if the public finds out he is gay. When the police arrived, the star hid in the bathroom upstairs.

George also includes as a suspect one of Eve Bowen's political rivals, Alistair Harvey, who attended Baverstock, the same school as Luxford. Harvey represents the area and owns the land where Charlotte's body was found. His land houses heavy machinery that uses the same kind of grease as was found under Charlotte's fingernails. Even more incriminating, he was at the political conference where Luxford and Bowen had their tryst that produced Charlotte. It all makes for a compelling case against Harvey, but it is a red herring based on facts created by George to mask the real story.

George creates yet another possible suspect when the police arrest a mechanic after part of Charlotte's uniform is found in his garage. The police find the same type of grease as was found under Charlotte's nails at the garage, but the mechanic is innocent. He bought the uniform as rags at a church sale and by coincidence he uses the same grease as was found on the body. Even so, he serves as one more red herring to distract readers.

George uses subplots as cover stories to mask the real story. Bowen's husband, Alexander Stone, slowly realizes that his wife values her political career over everything else, including him and Charlotte. In the end, he leaves her. This subplot, developed far more than in detective novels of the Golden Age when characterizations were often thin, let alone with any character arcs, is a deceptive distraction as readers attempt to figure out what the husband will do, even though it has nothing to do with solving the murder mystery. Other subplots involve the love story between Lynley and Lady Helen, and between Havers and Payne. The romance between the latter couple is complicated by Payne's engagement to a local woman, Celia Mathewson. Celia says Payne has been "different" since he returned from his detective course, which most readers will attribute to the strain on their relationship caused by the sexual tension between Havers and Payne. In truth the change is caused by Payne having kidnapped and murdered Charlotte, whom he believes is his half-sister. These romantic sub-plots are far more developed than when Poirot fell for Countess Vera Rossakoff or Holmes for Irene Adler. This change in depth of subplots reflects the evolution of mysteries from the Golden Age when they were mystery puzzles to today when they are often literary novels about a crime. The subplots, however literary, serve as cover stories to mask the real mystery.

The setting of *In the Presence of the Enemy*, at least for non-English readers, adds a mildly deceptive layer to the story. Set in England, the mention of mews, MG cars, constables, the Wiltshires, public schools, mills, and Marmite add texture to the story that might distract foreign readers as they focus on the setting more than the crime. (The authenticity of the setting is also impressive because George is an American.)

George plays fair with readers by providing clues to the kidnapper's identity. The kidnapper tells Charlotte he is taking her to a safe house because of a danger related to her mother's work for the government. This suggests the kidnapper was posing as a government agent or policemen to make Charlotte accompany him. In another scene, the kidnapper telephones Luxford and, when Luxford explains that he didn't publish the acknowledgement of his firstborn out of deference to Bowen's wishes, the kidnapper asks why Luxford should care for a mother now, since he "never cared for Mum." It is a significant clue that the kidnapper believes Luxford had a relationship with his mother. The twist is that the mother may have only had a relationship with Luxford in the kidnapper's mind, since his mother can't remember which boys she had sex for money with years before.

George makes it appear that the kidnapper must have seen Luxford and Bowen together at the political convention years before to know that Luxford is Charlotte's father. Luxford and Bowen deny telling anyone the father's identity. Apart from doubting them, given that both have strong reasons not to divulge their secret, the convention appears to be the only possible source for the information to reach the kidnapper. George makes readers certain, but wrong. The brief mention that Luxford opened a savings account for Charlotte is the only clue that suggests how the kidnapper gained the information: using his girlfriend who worked at a bank, Payne discovered that Luxford opened an account for Charlotte.

George establishes multiple cover stories to mask the real story, each with a mystery, including how the kidnapper discovered the relationship between Charlotte and Luxford, where Charlotte was held, what the music teacher is hiding, the identity of the policeman who rousted the vagrant, the vagrant's involvement, the role of the IRA, politician Alistair Harvey's role, Charlotte's stepfather Alexander Stone's plans in relation to Eve Bowen, Haver's romantic future, and several minor mysteries. The mystery of where Charlotte is being held lures readers in as Charlotte provides clues about her prison. It has a "Maypole," brick walls and thick doors, like a church, as well as a giant wheel with teeth, like a giant clock. She is in an old mill, but knowing where she is held actually does little to help solve the mystery of who kidnapped her, let alone why. Another mystery is how Charlotte's body ended up in a canal. One method the police pursue is that the kidnapper rented a boat, so they investigate all those who recently rented canal boats. It is a red herring. Payne lives nearby and just dropped the body in the canal. All of the cover stories and their related mysteries give readers the opportunity to focus on the wrong mystery. Worse, only some of the solutions contribute to solving the real mystery, while most do not.

George doles out clues slowly and late in the novel. It is not until page 469 that the hair in Luxford's car is matched to Charlotte, which further deceptively implicates him. It is not until page 470 that the vagrant is found and explains that a constable rousted him from the street where Charlotte was kidnapped. It is a crucial clue, but it is deceptive. Payne is a police officer, but he has just made detective and no longer wears a uniform. Even more deceptive for readers, George relies on the differing dramatic impact of telling versus showing because Payne never appears in uniform in the novel.

In relation to the most important clue, George also relies on the human tendency to value images over words. A photograph of Charlotte's corpse appears to be important, but the critical clue is not the image. The key is how her name is written on the back. The printing matches the printing in the ransom notes. As early as page 25, St. James compares the printing on the notes to samples of writing from Luxford and Bowen and rules them out as the note's author. The reader is left to conclude that the ransom note will play little, if any role in solving the crime. It would take an attentive reader to realize that both the note and the printing on the photograph are the same: both are in block letters. Payne printed them both. Breaking the rule of having the detective hero discover the crucial clue that unmasks the villain, George has St. James match the writing on the back of the photograph to the ransom note printing. Even after he realizes the importance of the printing on page 483, as every good deceiver should, George delays and just tells the reader that St. James has spotted something he "should have seen on the picture" long before. St. James doesn't tell Inspector Lynley (or the reader) until page 565, more than 80 pages later that the printing on the photograph and in the ransom notes are the same. The interim is taken up by various detectives pursuing clues related to several cover stories. George's use of multiple detectives delays the pursuit of vital clues, increases suspense and ratchets up the level of deception.

Deception in the form of misreading the ransom note is at the core of the real story. All of the characters, and therefore most readers, jump to the conclusion that Charlotte is Luxford's "firstborn." As Raymond Chandler suggested, George sets the reader to solving the wrong mystery. The real mystery is who believes they are Luxford's firstborn, not who really is his firstborn, but this problem is not even presented as a possibility until almost the end of the novel. It would take an alert reader to conclude that only Luxford's firstborn (or maybe his mother) would want him to acknowledge his firstborn, yet Charlotte, who is Luxford's firstborn, is only a child and her mother is desperate to keep the information secret. Therefore, someone else must erroneously believe they are Luxford's firstborn.

Besides the double interpretation of firstborn, George uses double meanings to deceive her readers. At one point, Payne discusses elite public schools with Havers and says there is "no one at all in my (family) tree" (p.475). Most readers probably conclude that he means his family lacks anyone of stature to have the connections to get him admitted to an elite school. He really means that his father, or at least the man he has been told is his father, has not acknowledged his existence. Therefore, he has no acknowledged family tree on his father's side, which is key to his motivation to kidnap and murder two children.

In terms of means, motive and opportunity, Luxford, Bowen, the IRA, the piano teacher, the vagrant, and the unidentified constable who rousted the vagrant all had the means to kidnap Charlotte, the opportunity, especially since they could have been working with others, and motives ranging from the political to the sexual. Unlike many mystery novels that increase uncertainty by providing five or six relatively strong suspects and leave it until the end for the detective to unravel all of the clues to unmask the villain, George increases ambiguity in another way by making every suspect appear to have significant weaknesses as a suspect. Would Luxford, even as circulation-hungry as he might be, murder his daughter? Would Bowen, even as power hungry as she is portrayed, murder her daughter? Would the IRA change their standard operating procedure and kidnap a politician's daughter and murder her? Why would the vagrant kidnap Charlotte since no money was demanded? Why would the vagrant, the IRA, the music teacher, or Bowen want Luxford to acknowledge his firstborn? All are weak, leaving the reader to wonder who did it and why. The key is to realize that the real mystery centers on who believes they are Luxford's first born, and then to expand the frame of the puzzle and realize that someone outside the list of suspects did it: the rural detective, Robin Payne.

The novel is effective as a deception in large part because the murderer is motivated by a lie. Payne believes that his mother told him Luxford is his father, but she later denies telling him such a thing. Therefore, only Payne knows the motive for the crimes. Having the motive only in the criminal's mind makes it extremely difficult for the detectives or readers to discover the motive for the kidnappings and murder, and makes for an entertainingly deceptive mystery.

Chapter 20

Solving the Mystery:
Detecting the Real Story

After devising the real crime and the deceptive cover stories, you must devise the third part of your story: how your detective hero works through all the cover stories and discovers the truth of what really happened—the real story of the murder. As G. K. Chesterton wrote in his short story "The Blue Cross," "The criminal is the creative artist; the detective only the critic." As critic, the detective character points out what the criminal did wrong, since a clue is just another name for a mistake. When you devise your cover stories, keep in mind that your detective hero must notice a flaw in the cover story to reveal it as false or notice a clue that reveals the real story, such as the fire lit in the height of summer (*The Mysterious Affair at Styles*), the alibi based on an accomplice (*Evil Under the Sun*), or a suspect knowing something only the murderer could know (often used in the TV series *Murder, She Wrote*. In Ellery Queen's *The*

Egyptian Cross Mystery, the murderer knows that an unlabeled blue bottle contains iodine to treat his wound, something only the man who lives in the cabin where the murder occurs could have known).

Your detective hero can solve the mystery using four approaches to problem solving. In rare cases detective heroes proceed through trial and error. They focus on one suspect, find she is innocent and move on to the next suspect and the next until they discover the real culprit. This form of investigation leaves little room for the detective to show their brilliance, so it is more common in the hard-boiled school of mystery.

Some detectives develop a hypothesis and then test it before either refining it or discarding it for an entirely new hypothesis. A detective might assume that a murder was for financial gain. The hypothesis leads the detective to focus on who gained financially the most from the untimely death of the victim. Did that suspect have the means and opportunity to commit the murder? If so, the case is solved. If not, the detective devises another hypothesis to test.

The most famous detective characters rely on algorithms to solve mysteries. Sherlock Holmes, Hercule Poirot, Miss. Marple, and Nero Wolfe use step-by-step methods. They gather information, develop hypotheses, and test those hypotheses against the facts, slowly refining the hypothesis until it fits the facts and identifies the murderer.

In some cases, a hero uses a heuristic, believing that the current case is similar to a previous case, which may assist in solving the current mystery. Lipstick on a glass in the room where a man was murdered suggests the murderer was a woman, as was the case in some previous case. Heuristics may lead the hero astray, especially if the author is breaking the rules. The lipstick on the glass may have been left by a man who recently kissed a woman.

In most cases, the detective hero uses a mix of the four approaches, thinking both inductively (gathering facts to develop a theory) and deductively (applying a hypothesis or heuristics to the facts to then refine the theory). In every case, the hero must suffer setbacks. As Hercule Poirot exclaims at just such a time in *Murder on the Links*, "My little idea was all wrong. *Eh bien*! I must start again."

You can make your story more deceptive and entertaining if your heroine has to combine clues to solve the mystery. In Agatha

Christie's short story "How Does Your Garden Grow?", Miss Barrowby is poisoned, although her housemaid ate the same meal as she did. The key clues are an unfinished unsymmetrical shell edging in Miss Barrowby's symmetrical garden; a poison, strychnine, that is bitter; and that Miss Barrowby loved oysters as a treat but was not supposed to eat them. Hercule Poirot combines the clues to realize that Miss Barrowby's niece and her husband fed Miss Barrowby a secret treat of poisoned oysters and then hid the shells in the garden so the housemaid would not see them in the trash. Only by combining the clues does Poirot discover the answer to the mystery of Miss Barrowby's murder.

Authors usually use a trigger, a small hint or clue, to cause their detective hero to realize the importance of a clue or to see the case in a new light. Triggers make a detective's sudden realization of the real story more plausible and believable. In Agatha Christie's *The A.B.C. Murders*, Hastings comments that a third letter from the serial murderer sent to Poirot that was misaddressed might have been addressed incorrectly on purpose. Poirot realizes this simple answer is the key, but not quite as Hastings meant. The letter was misaddressed on purpose and sent to Poirot, not to Scotland Yard, because the murderer wanted to make sure the third letter arrived too late to allow Poirot to warn the third victim, Sir Carmichael Clarke. If the letter had been sent to Scotland Yard, even if the address was slightly wrong, the letter would have been delivered on time. Hasting's comment is the trigger for Poirot to realize the truth and solve the case.

In *A Few Good Men*, Lieutenant Daniel Kaffee (Tom Cruise) of the Judge Advocate Generals' Office is defending two Marines charged with murdering a fellow Marine, Private William Santiago, in Guantanamo Bay, Cuba. Santiago's commanding officer (Jack Nicholson) said that he ordered Santiago to be on the first flight out of Guantanamo after it became known that he had bypassed the chain of command to accuse a fellow Marine of unlawfully discharging his weapon. Santiago is due to leave at 6 am, but is murdered the night before. Kaffee sees that Santiago's uniforms are all hanging neatly in his closet. Much later, one of Kaffee's colleagues has put the baseball bat Kaffee always holds when he is thinking through a case in his closet. Kaffee goes to get it and eyes his clothes hanging in the closet. The clothes are a trigger, highlighting that the uniforms in Santiago's closet are a crucial clue. If Santiago was due to fly out at 6 am as his commanding officer claims, why wasn't he packed? The commanding officer lied. That lie leads Kaffee to the solution of the mystery.

To solve a deception based on a frame, the detective hero usually mentally steps back and realizes that the murderer is outside the frame. The hero includes suspects outside the location or setting of the murder to include the murderer in the list of suspects, something no one else has done. In *4:50 From Paddington,* Mrs. Marple realizes the murderer is the doctor, Dr. Quimper, who visits the country house where most of the story is set, but does not live in the house that frames the mystery. Horace Rumpole, the barrister hero of "Rumpole and the Bright Seraphim," realizes that the murder of an unpopular officer at a British army base was not committed by one of his men, much as they loathed him, but by his wife. Rumpole realizes that although it must have been horrible to serve under the victim, being married to him must have been hell. The realization allows him to see outside the frame of the army base to consider the victim's wife as a suspect. In some cases the detective hero doesn't see outside the frame until new evidence appears to break the frame. In Ruth Rendell's *Wolf to the Slaughter,* the initial frame that focuses the novel on the disappearance and possible murder of a young woman is only broken when the young woman returns from a jaunt to Europe alive and well.

A detective sees through dazzle not by collecting more clues, but by realizing which clues are related to the real story instead of to cover stories. Often this involves the detective hero developing a theory of the case á la Sherlock Holmes. He uses deduction to move from the theory down: which facts support the theory? If correct, the facts will support the theory. If not, another theory is required. The failure of the first theory is usually the basis of the second act, in which the hero fails (Poirot asking himself how he could have been so stupid), before the hero revises the theory and finally discovers the real story. Holmes sees through dazzle in "The Adventure of the Reigate Squire," in which he realizes the crooks involved didn't actually find what they were seeking and took various random objects to dazzle the police. In *The List of Adrian Messenger,* Anthony Gethryn struggles to figure out why Messenger compiled a list of men almost all of whom have died.

They range in social position from high to low and are from all across Britain. It is only when he realizes that one place such a cross-section of British manhood would have met is in the military that he discovers that all of the men served in the same unit during World War II. The realization helps him discover the reason behind their deaths. In *One Corpse Too Many*, Brother Cadfael sees through the murderer's dazzle by sticking to the law. When the king orders the execution of 94 traitors during an English civil war, Cadfael finds 95 bodies and refuses to accept that the extra corpse may be a bureaucratic mistake or just an extra body from a recent battle. His diligence and perseverance leads to the unmasking of a murderer. Dazzle in the form of a setting or the length of a novel rarely confuses a detective character since such forms of dazzle are aimed more at the reader than the detective character.

If you use conditioning, your detective hero usually realizes that one incident is not the same as the other incidents. In *The A.B.C. Murders*, Poirot realizes that the letter foretelling the murder of Sir Carmichael Clarke, which went astray, marks that murder as different from the first two murders and the fourth, for which warning letters arrived on time. Then Poirot can focus on the third murder, which allows him to realize who would benefit from that particular death, and solve the case. In some cases the hero never sees through the conditioning until the truth is revealed by the villain or another character. In *Pascali's Island*, Pascali expects Bowles to double-cross him and only realizes that the betrayal he expects based on his past conditioning is not going to happen when he sees a note from Bowles explaining to be ready to leave early. Bowles was not going to leave early without him. Sometimes the villain's conditioning fails because of reasons beyond their control and having nothing to do with the detective hero. In *Devices and Desires*, Alice Mair attempts to make the murder of Robarts appear to be the work of the Whistler, but unbeknownst to Alice, he commits suicide before Robarts' murder. Often conditioning is a storytelling technique aimed at the audience that the hero doesn't have to solve or see through. In *Star Wars – A New Hope*, the audience is conditioned to believe that Han Solo is motivated solely by money, but he changes his ways and acts out of friendship to help attack the Death Star in the final scenes. In A Simple Plan, the audience is conditioned to believe that the goal of all of the characters is millions in cash, but in the end Hank burns the money himself, having realized he doesn't deserve it.

If an author breaks the rules, it usually requires the detective to realize that this crime is unlike all others they have faced. Poirot realizes that instead of just one or two murderers, *Murder on the Orient Express* involves 13 murderers. Usually a spark of inspiration based on the clues leads to this realization, often after the detective follows clues to a dead-end or two. In "The Adventure of Silver Blaze," Holmes rules out the other possible suspects, especially the gypsies, and, as he had stated before, "Once you eliminate the impossible, whatever remains, no matter how improbable, must be the truth." He is left with the conclusion that the horse murdered the thief trying to steal the equine. Some novels that break the rules are not solved by the detective hero, such as *And Then There Were None*, leaving it to the reader to learn the truth.

When an author manipulates time, the key clues usually relate to inconsistencies between different witness's statements about the timing of events. In *Evil Under the Sun,* Poirot realizes that two of the hotel guests have told tales that disagree with the timing of all the other guests. His realization starts him on the trail toward solving the mystery. Sometimes the detective learns a new key fact or clue to reveal how time has been manipulated. In "Until Death Do Us Part," one of the *Death in Paradise* series, Detective Inspector Humphrey Goodman learns that salt will slow the burning of candle, which then allows him to realize how the murderer tried to alter the apparent time of death. In *The Mysterious Affair at Styles*, Poirot's knowledge of poisons allows him to figure out how the murder was committed and how the murderers attempted to manipulate time. In "The Sign of the Broken Sword," Father Brown notices that a dead major's watch is on his desk, even though there is another watch shattered on his wrist. The murderer smashed a watch and put it on the major's wrist to suggest an erroneous time of death.

Red herrings are discovered by realizing that a certain clue is unrelated to the real crime. In *Devices and Desires*, Dalgleish realizes that the story that Carolyn and Amy were lesbian lovers who murdered Hilary has a hole: how did they know the Whistler's modus operandi? If they didn't, then someone else must have murdered Hilary Robarts. In *Wolf to the Slaughter*, the detective hero realizes that the report by one character that a woman's recently dumped boyfriend was hanging around outside a party also provides the witness with an alibi. If a murderer, such as in Christie's *Crooked House,* stages a murder attempt on themselves, the hero must realize the attempt was false, usually largely because it failed. Often new information or clues reveal the real story, which then shows the cover stories based on red herrings to be false. In *Murder at the A.B.A.*, Just does not believe the murderer's attempt to make the murder appear to be an accidental fall in the shower because the victim's hotel room, normally so neat, is messy. In *The Guilty*, the revelation about the neighbor's children playing a choking game casts the strangulation death of the boy in a new light as an accidental suicide, not murder.

The hero often notices some key trait that reveals a disguise was used. The motive for a disguise, such as using a disguise to look like another character to buy poison to frame the other character, can also lead the hero to see through a disguise. Poirot mentions in *Evil Under The Sun* that one young sun-tanned body looks very much like the next, which proves crucial to realizing the murderer used an accomplice disguised as the dead woman lying on a beach before the real murder even happened to manipulate time. In the *Midsomer Murders* episode "Judgment Day," an old acquaintance of the disguised murderer is the one who sees through the disguise, and is then murdered. The disguise is then crucial to the motive for the murder. In *For the Sake of Elena*, the detectives attempt to link the first murder victim to the second and find no relationship. It is only then that the lead detective realizes the second murder was based on the fact that the murderer mistook the second victim for another jogger, a witness she was trying to kill. Your hero may realize that if a character appears to have been in two places at once, such as in *Lord Edgware Dies*, when actress Jane Wilkinson is at a dinner party even as she is seen entering the house where Lord Edgware is murdered, then a disguise seems likely. In *Bridget Jones's Diary*, Bridget sees through Daniel's disguise as her true love when she finds another woman in his flat.

If one character lies, they are usually exposed when someone else reveals they are not telling the truth. In *Devices and Desires*, Meg realizes Alice Mair is lying when Alice said she was home the evening of the murder because Meg used her key to check Alice's house and no one was home. Sometimes the truth is only revealed as the villain's plans proceed. In *Kidnapped*, David Balfour only realizes his uncle is a lying scoundrel and had him press-ganged when he awakens onboard a ship leaving Britain for foreign shores.

Deceptive storytelling is aimed at the audience, so the detective hero gets a break in not having to unravel such a deceptive technique. Even so, usually solving the real crime clears up the ambiguity about a crime, such as in *The Hound of the Baskervilles*. Certainty about a cover story is also exposed to be wrong when the real crime is solved, such as in *Five Little Pigs*, when the truth that the painter is not going to leave his wife leads to the unraveling of the mystery of his murder.

If a detective can see through all the deceptive techniques used by the villain (and the author), then she can solve the mystery. The nesting of various deceptive techniques makes it more difficult, but tackling each deception one after the other can allow your hero to arrive at the truth, or one new theory may explain everything after several dead ends in one flash of brilliant deduction, especially if it is triggered by some word, thought or deed.

Questions for Authors:

Your story must have an ending, so your hero must identify the murderer or, if it is a thriller, must unravel the conspiracy. To do that, the villain must make a mistake, but not a big one, or it will be too easy for the hero.

Which aspects of the cover stories are flawed, allowing your detective hero (or hero in a conspiracy) to see through them?

Since your hero can't find just one clue that leads him directly to the solution, what clues will lead the way down blind alleys or a single step toward the solution? What subtle mistakes did the murderer make that your heroine can discover to unveil the truth? Which aspect of the conspiracy can the hero discover to lead her to the information required to expose the entire plot? List all of the clues that lead to the solution and then put them in order from the most to the least apparent, so you can have your detective hero work from the easiest clue to the hardest. Such a progression will help build your novel or script to a satisfying climax.

In a love story, what behavior or statement will trigger the heroine's realization that Mr. Wrong is really Mr. Wrong and Mr. Right is, in fact, her Mr. Right?

Common Mistakes and How to Fix Them:

Many new writers create a mystery that is airtight. They leave no clues for the detective to discover to solve the real mystery. In some novels, the heroine just jumps to the right answer without any crucial clue, let alone trigger, leading to the solution. Always make sure you seed some creative and challenging clues in your mystery that your detective heroine can then notice, realize the importance of, and thereby show her brilliance as she solves the mystery.

In some mysteries, the heroine has no trigger for their realization. Having the lead character suddenly figure out the mystery is far less believable than if a word, act or deed triggers the solution. Usually the sidekick supplies this trigger and only the hero notices its importance, thereby proving the hero's brilliance.

Chapter 21

Perfecting Deception: Feedback

Almost no one planning a deception operation in the real or a fictional world gets it right the first time. Feedback allows the fine tuning that deception requires for success. Magicians spend months polishing new acts, often performing a new illusion in front of family members or a mentor to ensure a real audience will be deceived when they perform the illusion on stage. Conmen practice the cons that support their illegal livelihood. Militaries conduct war games to perfect strategies and tactics, including deception operations. In the intelligence realm, espionage services ensure there is a mechanism to gather feedback from the adversary. During World War II, a crucial aspect of the Allied effort to deceive the Germans was that the British had a feedback mechanism. Decoded German military messages provided the Allies with information on how the Germans were reacting to the British deception operations. If an operation was failing, the British could tweak it to increase its effectiveness, while reinforcing operations that were succeeding. In the

1980s, the Iran-Contra scandal involved the shipment of US arms
to Iran in exchange for help freeing Western hostages in Lebanon.
The CIA initially rejected Iranian feelers to initiate the operation.
Using that feedback, the Iranians refined their story to appeal to
fears that Iran would tilt toward the Soviets unless moderates in
Iran gained control of the country. With the refined story, the Iranians found others in the Reagan administration, especially in the
National Security Council, who were more receptive than the CIA.
Feedback helped the Iranians develop a successful deception op-
eration which netted the Iranians tons of arms without helping to
free any hostages.

   When it comes to feedback, writing a deceptive mystery, thriller or any other type of story is no different from creating a new
magical illusion or running an intelligence operation or con game.
Authors ask friends, mentors or editors to provide feedback on
manuscripts. Mystery authors use feedback to refine and hopefully
perfect their deceptive story before their novel or script is seen by
agents or publishers, who provide even more feedback. The final
version the public sees is almost always far different from what
the author first drafted. The goal is a mystery with no logical flaws
and a puzzling, deceptive and entertaining story. Any story using
deception can benefit from feedback, as can any story, so be sure
to ask friends, fellow authors and acquaintances to read your novels
or scripts before you send them out into the world for (hopefully)
mass consumption. Without feedback, a successful deception operation is difficult, if not impossible, to achieve.

   Given that most writers work alone, feedback is even more important to authors than to militaries, spies and conmen, who usually work in groups, especially since writers are often poor judges
of the quality of their own work. Arthur Conan Doyle wrote several historical novels which he believed were his best works. He believed they were far better than his Sherlock Holmes stories. After
World War II, P. G. Wodehouse, who had enjoyed great success on
Broadway in the 1920s and 1930s, believed his future lay once again
on the Great White Way. Audiences had changed and his plays
flopped. His real future was in Jeeves, Bertie Wooster and what he
called "the butler line." In his seventies, having written a series of
comedic masterpieces, he wrote a close friend, "The awful part of
the writing game is you can never be sure the stuff is any good"

(McCrum, p.400). Feedback is key to learning if your "stuff is any good." When Neil Simon was writing *The Odd Couple*, he thought the play was good. After he heard the first reading, however, he thought the third act was terrible. He rushed back to his hotel and rewrote the third act until he loved it. The actors played the new third act and, again, it was terrible. The play did poorly in Delaware and it was only after seven weeks and 50 pages of rewrites that Simon eventually got it right, leading to a long run on Broadway and a successful television series. The anecdote should be a warning to authors to be open to feedback, because their beliefs about their own work are often wrong.

Difficulty evaluating their own work isn't restricted to playwrights. The acclaimed director Steven Spielberg made many great movies from *Jaws* and *E.T. The Extra-Terrestrial* to the *Indiana Jones* series, *Saving Private Ryan* and *Schindler's List*, but he also made *1941*, which was a critical and now almost completely forgotten failure. George Lucas of *Star Wars* fame also produced the horrendous *Howard the Duck*. As William Goldman pointed out, when they were making the flops, Spielberg and Lucas probably believed those movies were going to be just as good as their films that were critically acclaimed and financially successful.

One way to see the value of feedback is by reading and then seeing the movie versions of *Pascali's Island*, *Dances with Wolves* and *Gone to Texas* (filmed as *The Outlaw Josey Wales*). All three novels are well written, engaging stories with great plots that deserved to be made into movies. With the benefit of feedback in the form of comments and notes from the directors and others, the screenwriters turned these powerful novels into even better movies. Study the differences between the novels and the movie versions to learn how stories can be dramatically and deceptively improved in small and big ways.

Playwrights have an advantage over novelists and screenwriters in terms of feedback. Although all writers can ask for feedback when they are in the drafting stage, once their works are produced, the differences in the three art forms are profound. Once a novelist publishes a novel with a traditional publisher the author has little to no chance to ever revise it. If you self-publish your novel, you can edit the electronic files to produce a revised version, although such revision is rarely done. A novelist may have a slim chance of revising their work, but once a scriptwriter's work is filmed, it can never be revised. Even to alter a single line of dialogue, let alone an entire scene would cost hundreds of thousands of dollars, even if it could be done by recalling the cast and crew, who have probably all moved on to other films. As Academy-Award winning director Billy Wilder lamented in his conversations with writer/director Cameron Crowe, once the screenwriter is done, there is no going back, no revision. Not so the lucky playwright. The reason Shakespeare's plays are difficult to date and to establish a definitive version is that the Bard spent years revising them as they were played repeatedly before audience after audience. Like all playwrights, between performances Shakespeare could tweak a line, change a scene or even an entire act to perfect the play. In terms of deception, the playwright is like the British during World War II. Based on feedback from the Germans, the British could refine their deception operations to achieve their goals. The novelist and screenwriter have no such ability once their work is produced; they are one and done. Anything they learn from a work can only be used to make their next novel or movie that much better, or at least to avoid the previous work's mistakes. Luckily for them, artists are remembered for their finest, not their worst, works. In contrast, the playwright can incorporate feedback from the audience even as the play is running to improve the current play. Neil Simon even called one of his memoirs *Rewrites* to reflect his focus on continuing to rewrite a play as it was performed in New Haven, Boston or Philadelphia, well before it ever reached Broadway. Even so, whatever your form, try to take the opportunity whenever you can to gather feedback from others to improve your novel, play or script, and ensure a deceptive and entertaining story before you send it out into the real world to deceive, surprise and entertain your audience.

Conclusion

Of all the deceptions writers attempt, the greatest deception is on themselves. Every writer believes that one day they will be wealthy and famous. Given the number of individuals writing and, now with the Internet and ease of self-publishing, the numbers publishing, most novelists will be lucky to sell a few dozen copies of their novel, let alone ever make a living writing. Thousands of screenwriters never see even one of their works reach the little screen, let alone the silver screen. Even so writers keep writing. If they don't, then they aren't writers. If you can quit, quit. If you aren't driven to write, why suffer through the demoralizing process? As my wife once said, "Writing is one of the longest unreinforced behaviors known to man." If writing is flowing well, it is a joy, but if the story or words don't flow, writing can be your personal version of hell, let alone when you add the enormous uncertainty of publishing a novel, bringing a play to Broadway, or selling a script to the equation.

Given the lottery like odds, any objective observer would conclude writers are insane. They spend thousands of hours creating fictional characters doing fictional things in fictional worlds that matter only, at first, to the writer. Publishing is no less an insane activity, with only a child's handful of writers ever making enough money to write full-time. I am sure you know the numbers that sometimes but only temporarily dent most writers' self-deception.

Even so, I urge you, as my father always urged me, if you can, to keep writing. Like nature, which created millions of species over billions of years, letting the vast majority become extinct, art allows millions of artists to write, paint, film, sculpt, and create, while only a few, a very, very few, ever become recognized, let alone acknowledged as a genius. But don't let that deter you; take your shot, buy your lottery ticket, put your money down, because somewhere the next Christie, Doyle or Poe, the next Dickens, Tolstoy or Austen, De Vega or Cervantes, or maybe even Shakespeare is out there today, and it may be you. Ignore the odds, keep writing and keep deceiving your audience into believing in your fictional worlds and characters—and deceiving yourself that one day you may write a great novel, play or screenplay because one day, you may be right. Remember, the best deceptions are based on the truth and one day your writing deception may become not only partly true, but entirely true.

Selected Bibliography

Non-fiction Books / Articles

Annemann, Ted. 202 *Methods of Forcing*. New York: Max Holden, 1933.

Bogdanovich, Peter. *Who the Devil Made it*. New York: Knopf, 1997.

Bowyer, J. Barton. *Cheating*. New York: St. Martins, 1982.

Brown, Anthony Cave. *Bodyguard of Lies*. New York: Harper & Row, 1975.

Crowe, Cameron. *Conversations with Wilder*. New York: Knopf, 1999.

Epstein, Edward Jay. *Deception: The Invisible War Between the KGB and the CIA*. New York: Simon and Schuster, 1989.

Ghosh, Tannistho. *Renaissance Tragedy and Investigator Heroes, The role of the investigator in Renaissance tragedy, with special reference to Shakespeare's Hamlet and Thomas Kyd's The Spanish Tragedy*. www.english-literature.org, June 2002.

Lefcourt, Peter and Laura J. Shapiro. *The First Time I Got Paid for It*. New York: Public Affairs, 2000.

Macdonald, Scot. *Propaganda and Information Warfare in the Twenty-First Century: Altered Images and Deception Operations*. Abingdon, UK: Routledge, 2007.

Marks, Leo. Between *Silk and Cyanide*. New York: Harper Collins, 1998.

Maugham, W. Somerset. *A Writer's Notebook*. Garden City, New York: Doubleday, 1949.

McCrum, Robert. *Wodehouse: A Life*. New York: W. W. Norton, 2004.

Miller, George A. "The Magical Number Seven." *Psychological Review*, March 1956, vol.63, No.2.

Simon, Neil. *Rewrites A Memoir*. New York: Simon and Schuster, 1996.

Simon, Neil. *The Play Goes On*. New York: Simon and Schuster, 1999.

Whalen, Barton. *Stratagem: Deception and Surprise in War*. London: Artech House, 2007.

Wells, Carolyn. *The Technique of the Mystery Story*. Springfield, MA: Home Correspondence School, 1913.

Short Stories

Block, Lawrence. "Keller's Therapy," in Martin H. Greenberg, ed. *The Edgar Award Book*. New York: Barnes & Noble, 1996.

Conan Doyle, Arthur. "The Reigate Squires," in Conan Doyle, Arthur, *The Memoirs of Sherlock Holmes*. Harmondsworth, UK: Penguin, 1950.

Conan Doyle, Arthur. "The Naval Treaty," in Conan Doyle, Arthur, *The Sherlock Holmes Mysteries*. New York: Signet Classic, 1984.

Conan Doyle, Arthur. "A Scandal in Bohemia," in Conan Doyle, Arthur, *The Sherlock Holmes Mysteries*. New York: Signet Classic, 1984.

Conan Doyle, Arthur. "Silver Blaze," in Conan Doyle, Arthur, *The Sherlock Holmes Mysteries*. New York: Signet Classic, 1984.

Ellison, Harlan. "Mefisto in Onyx," in Martin H. Greenberg, ed. *The Edgar Award Book*. New York: Barnes & Noble, 1996.

Hoch, Edward D. "The Most Dangerous Man Alive," in Martin H. Greenberg, ed. *The Edgar Award Book*. New York: Barnes & Noble, 1996.

James, P.D. "Moment of Power," in Martin H. Greenberg, ed. *The Edgar Award Book*. New York: Barnes & Noble, 1996.

Kornbluth, C. M. "Little Black Bag," in C. M. Kornbluth, *The Best Science Fiction of C. M. Kornbluth*. London: Faber and Faber, 1949.

Kraft, Gabrielle. "One Hit Wonder," in Martin H. Greenberg, ed. *The Edgar Award Book*. New York: Barnes & Noble, 1996.

Lewin, Michael Z. "The Reluctant Detective," in Martin H. Greenberg, ed. *The Edgar Award Book*. New York: Barnes & Noble, 1996.

Marsh, Ngaio. "Death of a Fool," in *Off With His Head*. London: Collins Crime Club, 1956.

Mortimer, John. "Rumpole and the Bright Seraphim," in *Rumpole's Last Case*. London: Penguin, 1987.

Poe, Edgar Allan. "The Murders in the Rue Morgue," in Vincent Price and Chandler Brossard, eds. *18 Best Stories by Edgar Allan Poe*. New York: Dell, 1965.

Pronzini, Bill. "Incident in a Neighborhood Tavern," in Martin H. Greenberg, ed. *The Edgar Award Book*. New York: Barnes & Noble, 1996.

Schutz, Benjamin M. "Mary, Mary Shut the Door," in Greenberg, Martin H. ed. *The Edgar Award Book*. New York: Barnes & Noble, 1996.

About the Author

K. Scot Macdonald is the author of five novels and four non-fiction books. Educated at the University of British Columbia (BA), University of Nevada, Reno (MA), and the University of Southern California (MA, PhD), he lives in Los Angeles with his wife, daughter and spoiled wheaten Scottish Terrier, Skye. He has been a commodity broker at the largest independent brokerage firm west of the Mississippi, adjunct professor at USC, marketing associate at a major medical center, and held a range of temporary jobs from driver to copy room clerk.

About Kerrera House Press

Kerrera House Press is an independent press dedicated to producing the books you keep. For more information about our books, please visit KerreraHousePress.com.

Other Books by K. Scot Macdonald

Non-Fiction

Deadly Dance: The Chippendales Murders (with Patrick MontesDeOca): The arsons, attempted murders and murder behind the Chippendales male exotic dance troupe and their founder, Somen "Steve" Banerjee.

Fiction

A Plunge Into Evil: Join Jonathan Traveler and Scarlett Wynter as they lead a tour of Greece. Just try not to get murdered.

The Shakespeare Drug: Neurosurgeon Julie Stein has discovered a drug that lets her write like Shakespeare, but it just might kill her.

In Justice Found: Los Angeles mediator Arden "Never-Fail" Jeffries seeks justice for the CEO who cost him his retirement and for the burglars who ransacked his home and knocked him unconscious. Will he find justice or only injustice?

Mouse's Dream: Commodity broker Anthony "Mouse" Maas is stuck in the Baby Boomer crunch with free-spending daughters and financially strapped parents. A reunion with his high school sweetheart leads to a plan to bilk his bosses of enough money to settle all his problems and pursue a long-held dream.

The Grizzly Extinction Plot (writing as Liam Shay): Anti-technology revolutionaries are plotting to blow up the Vancouver Grizzlies basketball team, which is having the winningest season in NBA history, in their new state-of-the-art arena. Only a romance-novel addicted, Romantic-poet quoting, community college English professor, Sebastian Giannini, stands in the path of the ruthless New Luddites.

www.ingramcontent.com/pod-product-compliance
Lightning Source LLC
Chambersburg PA
CBHW061011280326

41935CB00009B/922

9780991665372